BARRON'S

Regents Exams and Answers

English 2020

CAROL CHAITKIN, M.S.
Former Director of American Studies, Lycée Français de New York
Former English Department Head, Great Neck North High School,
Great Neck, New York

Published by Kaplan, Inc., d/b/a Barron's Educational Series
750 Third Avenue
New York, NY 10017
www.barronseduc.com

ISBN: 978-1-5062-5378-7

Printed in Canada

10 9 8 7 6 5 4 3 2 1

Kaplan, Inc., d/b/a Barron's Educational Series print books are available at special quantity discounts to use for sales promotions, employee premiums, or educational purposes. For more information or to purchase books, please call the Simon & Schuster special sales department at 866-506-1949.

Contents

Strategy and Review for Part 3 of the Regents ELA Exam   37

CHAPTER 3 **Text-Analysis Response**

Reading and Writing About Literature   45

CHAPTER 4 **Reviewing Literary Elements and Techniques**

CHAPTER 5 **Glossaries of Terms**

A Guide to Proofreading for Common Errors   69

Appendices: **73**
The New York State Learning Standards for English Language Arts

Regents ELA Examinations and Answers   **83**

Introduction

THE NY STATE ELA STANDARDS AND THE READING AND WRITING WE DO IN HIGH SCHOOL ENGLISH COURSES

Most middle school and high school students in NY State should be familiar with the guidelines for curriculum and instruction in their English courses. These guidelines include the following:

- Students will read both informational texts and literary texts in their English courses. Alignment with the NY State learning standards requires a balancing of the two.
- In all academic subjects, students will be expected to build their knowledge primarily through engaging directly with text.
- Throughout secondary school, students will read texts of increasing complexity and will be expected to develop skills in close reading in all academic subjects.
- Students will be expected to engage in rich and rigorous **evidence-based** conversations/class discussions about text.
- Student writing will emphasize **use of evidence** from sources to express their understanding and to form and develop an argument.
- Students will acquire the academic vocabulary they need to comprehend and respond to grade-level complex texts. This vocabulary is often relevant to more than one subject.

HOW CAN THIS BOOK HELP YOU?

This book provides a detailed guide to the Regents ELA Exam, showing you exactly what each part of the exam looks like. Actual passages and multiple-choice questions, with analysis of the multiple-choice questions and guidelines for composing written responses, are included. The rubrics for the scoring of each section are fully explained. For your review, you will find a chapter on "Reviewing Literary Elements and Techniques" and detailed "Glossaries of Terms" that review structure and language in prose and poetry. There is also

"A Guide to Proofreading for Common Errors." In the Appendix, you will find the New York State Learning Standards for Reading, Writing, and Language. Actual ELA Regents Exams, all with sample essays and answers explained, are also included.

TERMS TO HELP YOU UNDERSTAND THE ENGLISH LANGUAGE ARTS LEARNING STANDARDS AND THE REGENTS ELA EXAM

These are the learning standards in ELA and math, developed and adopted by a consortium of over 40 states. New York State first adopted the CCLS in 2010 and implemented a revised set of standards in 2017. These revisions did not represent significant changes in the expectations for grades 11/12 expressed in the guidelines above.*

CCR—The phrase **"college and career ready"** is widely used in discussion of the curriculum and assessments. This refers to the fundamental principle of the learning standards: to reflect the knowledge and skills that all students need for success in college and careers.

ELA/Literacy—English Language Arts (ELA) refers to skills in reading, writing, speaking, and listening. Courses and exams once identified as "English" may also be identified as ELA. Literacy refers to the ability to read and write and to use language proficiently. The term also identifies the quality of being knowledgeable in a particular subject or field. For example, we often refer to "digital" or "computer literacy."

Assessment—You may hear teachers and other educators using the term **assessment** instead of test or examination. An **assessment** is more than a simple test (in vocabulary, say) because it seeks to measure a number of skills at one time. Although we continue to refer to the English Regents as an exam or a test, its goal is to be a valid **assessment** of a broad range of the reading, thinking, language, and writing skills outlined in the Standards.

Text—Broadly, the term text refers to any written material. The core curriculum uses the term to refer to the great variety of material students are expected to be able to read, understand, analyze, and write about. Texts may include **literary** works of fiction, drama, and poetry; and **informational**, or

---

*See the NY State Education Department's website *www.engageNY.org* for details on all the changes in Standards and Regents Examinations.

nonfiction, including essays, memoirs, speeches, and scientific and historical documents. The learning standards also emphasize the use of **authentic texts**; that is, students will read actual historical documents or scientific essays rather than articles about them.

Close Reading—Skill in close, analytic reading is fundamental to the CCLS and to the ELA Regents exam. The core curriculum focuses student attention on the text itself in order to understand not only what the text says and means, but also how that meaning is constructed and revealed. Close reading enables students to understand central ideas and key supporting details. It also enables students to reflect on the meanings of individual words and sentences, the order in which sentences unfold, and the development of ideas over the course of the text, which ultimately leads students to arrive at an understanding of the text as a whole.

Argument—What is an argument? In academic writing, an argument is usually a central idea, often called a **claim** or **thesis statement**, which is backed up with evidence that supports the idea. Much of the writing high school students do in their English courses constitutes essays of argument, in contrast to personal essays, descriptive pieces, or works of imagination.

Source-Based/Evidence-Based—The ability to compose sound arguments using relevant and specific evidence from a given text is central to the expectations of the learning standards.

Writing Strategy—This is the general term for a literary element, literary technique, or rhetorical device. Examples include: characterization, conflict, denotation/connotation, metaphor, simile, irony, language use, point-of-view, setting, structure, symbolism, theme, tone, etc. (See the Glossaries in this book for definitions and examples of the most widely used terms.)

THE REGENTS ELA EXAM—AN OVERVIEW

This 3-hour examination requires students to read, analyze, and write about both literary and informational texts.

PART 1—READING COMPREHENSION

This part of the exam requires close reading of three texts and will contain a literature passage (prose), a poem, and an informational text, followed by a total of 24 multiple-choice questions.

PART 2—WRITING FROM SOURCES: ARGUMENT

This part of the exam includes close reading of four or five informational texts. Students will compose an essay of argument with a claim based on the sources.

PART 3—TEXT ANALYSIS

Students will do a close reading of one informational or literature text and write a two to three paragraph response that identifies a central idea in the text and analyzes how the author's use of one writing strategy develops that central idea.

Strategy and Review for Part 1 of the Regents ELA Exam

CHAPTER 1
Reading Comprehension

WHAT DOES THIS PART OF THE EXAM REQUIRE?

This part of the exam requires close reading of three texts and will contain at least one prose literature passage, usually from a work of fiction; a poem; and one informational text, which may include a personal narrative, a speech, an account of historical significance, or a discussion of a scientific concept. The prose passages and the poems are sometimes works in translation. These passages are followed by a total of 24 multiple-choice questions. The questions require analysis of different aspects of a text, including: elements of character and plot development, comprehension of a central idea and how it is supported, elements of style, and understanding vocabulary in context. Most of the questions include more than one plausible answer; choosing the correct answer often requires comprehension of the text as a whole.

WHAT DOES THIS PART OF THE EXAM LOOK LIKE?

Sample Passage A and Multiple-Choice Questions

Passage A

Literary Text

     It was eleven o'clock that night when Mr. Pontellier returned from Klein's hotel. He was in an excellent humor, in high spirits, and very talkative. His entrance awoke his wife, who was in bed and fast asleep when he came in. He talked to her while he undressed, telling her anecdotes
(5) and bits of news and gossip that he had gathered during the day. From his

trousers pockets he took a fistful of crumpled bank notes and a good deal of silver coin, which he piled on the bureau indiscriminately with keys, knife, handkerchief, and whatever else happened to be in his pockets. She was overcome with sleep, and answered him with little half utterances.

(10)   He thought it very discouraging that his wife, who was the sole object of his existence, evinced[1] so little interest in things which concerned him, and valued so little his conversation.

      Mr. Pontellier had forgotten the bonbons and peanuts for the boys. Notwithstanding he loved them very much, and went into the adjoining
(15) room where they slept to take a look at them and make sure that they were resting comfortably. The result of his investigation was far from satisfactory. He turned and shifted the youngsters about in bed. One of them began to kick and talk about a basket full of crabs.

      Mr. Pontellier returned to his wife with information that Raoul had a
(20) high fever and needed looking after. Then he lit a cigar and went and sat near the open door to smoke it.

      Mrs. Pontellier was quite sure Raoul had no fever. He had gone to bed perfectly well, she said, and nothing had ailed him all day. Mr. Pontellier was too well acquainted with fever symptoms to be mistaken. He assured her the
(25) child was consuming[2] at that moment in the next room.

      He reproached his wife with her inattention, her habitual neglect of the children. If it was not a mother's place to look after children, whose on earth was it? He himself had his hands full with his brokerage business. He could not be in two places at once; making a living for his family on the street, and
(30) staying at home to see that no harm befell them. He talked in a monotonous, insistent way.

      Mrs. Pontellier sprang out of bed and went into the next room. She soon came back and sat on the edge of the bed, leaning her head down on the pillow. She said nothing, and refused to answer her husband when he
(35) questioned her. When his cigar was smoked out he went to bed, and in half a minute he was fast asleep.

      Mrs. Pontellier was by that time thoroughly awake. She began to cry a little, and wiped her eyes on the sleeve of her peignoir.[3] Blowing out the candle, which her husband had left burning, she slipped her bare feet into a
(40) pair of satin mules at the foot of the bed and went out on the porch, where she sat down in the wicker chair and began to rock gently to and fro.

      It was then past midnight. The cottages were all dark. A single faint light gleamed out from the hallway of the house. There was no sound

---

[1]evinced—clearly showed   [2]consuming—wasting away   [3]peignoir—dressing gown

abroad except the hooting of an old owl in the top of a water oak, and the
(45) everlasting voice of the sea, that was not uplifted at that soft hour. It broke
like a mournful lullaby upon the night.

The tears came so fast to Mrs. Pontellier's eyes that the damp sleeve of
her peignoir no longer served to dry them. She was holding the back of her
chair with one hand; her loose sleeve had slipped almost to the shoulder of
(50) her uplifted arm. Turning, she thrust her face, steaming and wet, into the
bend of her arm, and she went on crying there, not caring any longer to dry
her face, her eyes, her arms. She could not have told why she was crying.
Such experiences as the foregoing were not uncommon in her married life.
They seemed never before to have weighed much against the abundance of
(55) her husband's kindness and a uniform devotion which had come to be tacit[4]
and self-understood.

An indescribable oppression, which seemed to generate in some
unfamiliar part of her consciousness, filled her whole being with a vague
anguish. It was like a shadow, like a mist passing across her soul's summer
(60) day. It was strange and unfamiliar; it was a mood. She did not sit there
inwardly upbraiding[5] her husband, lamenting at Fate, which had directed
her footsteps to the path which they had taken. She was just having a good
cry all to herself. The mosquitoes made merry over her, biting her firm,
round arms and nipping at her bare insteps.
(65) The little stinging, buzzing imps succeeded in dispelling a mood which
might have held her there in the darkness half a night longer.

The following morning Mr. Pontellier was up in good time to take the
rockaway which was to convey him to the steamer at the wharf. He was
returning to the city to his business, and they would not see him again at
(70) the Island till the coming Saturday. He had regained his composure, which
seemed to have been somewhat impaired the night before. He was eager to
be gone, as he looked forward to a lively week in Carondelet Street.

Mr. Pontellier gave his wife half of the money which he had brought
away from Klein's hotel the evening before. She liked money as well as most
(75) women, and accepted it with no little satisfaction. . . .

A few days later a box arrived for Mrs. Pontellier from New Orleans.
It was from her husband. It was filled with friandises,[6] with luscious and
toothsome[7] bits—the finest of fruits, pates, a rare bottle or two, delicious
syrups, and bonbons in abundance.
(80) Mrs. Pontellier was always very generous with the contents of such
a box; she was quite used to receiving them when away from home. The

---

[4]tacit—not actually stated   [5]upbraiding—severely scolding   [6]friandises—dainty cakes   [7]toothsome—delicious

pates and fruit were brought to the dining-room; the bonbons were passed around. And the ladies, selecting with dainty and discriminating fingers and a little greedily, all declared that Mr. Pontellier was the best husband in the (85) world. Mrs. Pontellier was forced to admit that she knew of none better.

—Kate Chopin
excerpted from *The Awakening*, 1899

Multiple-Choice Questions

1 The primary purpose of the first paragraph is to

   (1) create a metaphor
   (2) foreshadow an event
   (3) establish a contrast
   (4) present a flashback   1 _____

2 Placed in the context of the rest of the text, Mr. and Mrs. Pontellier's disagreement about Raoul's fever (lines 19–31) reflects

   (1) Mrs. Pontellier's resentment of her husband's night out
   (2) Mr. Pontellier's belief in his authority over his wife
   (3) Mrs. Pontellier's need for her husband's approval
   (4) Mr. Pontellier's concern for his wife's well-being   2 _____

3 In lines 26–31, the author presents Mr. Pontellier as a man who feels

   (1) defeated
   (2) anxious
   (3) distracted
   (4) arrogant   3 _____

4 The author's choice of language in lines 38–46 serves to emphasize Mrs. Pontellier's sense of

   (1) isolation
   (2) boredom
   (3) disbelief
   (4) inferiority   4 _____

5 One major effect of the simile used in lines 45–46 is to emphasize Mrs. Pontellier's

   (1) anger
   (2) distress
   (3) defiance
   (4) exhaustion   5 ____

6 Lines 52–56 demonstrate Mrs. Pontellier's desire to

   (1) protect her reputation
   (2) question her situation
   (3) abandon her dreams
   (4) disguise her sorrow   6 ____

7 Lines 73–79 contradict a central idea in the text by describing Mr. Pontellier's

   (1) generosity
   (2) honesty
   (3) sympathy
   (4) humility   7 ____

8 Based on events in the text, which quotation best reveals the irony of the statement that Mr. Pontellier's wife "was the sole object of his existence" (lines 10–11)?

   (1) "From his trousers pockets he took a fistful of crumpled bank notes" (lines 5–6)
   (2) "Then he lit a cigar and went and sat near the open door to smoke it" (lines 20–21)
   (3) "He assured her the child was consuming at that moment in the next room" (lines 24–25)
   (4) "He was eager to be gone, as he looked forward to a lively week in Carondelet Street" (lines 71–72)   8 ____

Answers

(1) **3**   (2) **2**   (3) **4**   (4) **1**   (5) **2**   (6) **2**   (7) **1**   (8) **4**

Looking at the Questions

1. *The primary purpose of the first paragraph. . .*

   This question asks you to analyze the introduction of characters, their interaction and its significance to the development of plot and theme.

2. *Placed in the context, lines 19–31 reflect. . .*

   This question asks you to understand how the interaction of the two characters develops over the course of the text.

3. *The author presents Mr. Pontellier as a man. . .*

   This question requires further analysis of how characters are introduced and developed.

4. *The author's choice of language. . . serves to emphasize*

   Here you must determine the meaning of words and phrases in context and the role of word choice in the passage.

5. *One major effect of the simile. . .*

   Here you should sense in the metaphor the feelings of both calm and sorrow in the character.

6. *Lines 52–56 demonstrate. . .*

   This question asks for analysis of what the text says explicitly as well as what can be inferred about the character's feelings.

7. *Lines 73–79 contradict. . .*

   Here you are asked to determine a central idea and understand its development over the course of the text.

8. *Which quotation best reveals the irony. . .*

   Here you are expected to recognize the incongruity between what the character says he feels and what he is actually looking forward to.

Sample Passage B
Poem

View with a Grain of Sand

We call it a grain of sand
but it calls itself neither grain nor sand.
It does just fine without a name,
whether general, particular,
(5) permanent, passing,
incorrect or apt.

Our glance, our touch mean nothing to it.
It doesn't feel itself seen and touched.
And that it fell on the windowsill
(10) is only our experience, not its.
For it it's no different than falling on anything else
with no assurance that it's finished falling
or that it's falling still.

The window has a wonderful view of a lake
(15) but the view doesn't view itself.
It exists in this world
colorless, shapeless,
soundless, odorless, and painless.
The lake's floor exists floorlessly

(20) and its shore exists shorelessly.
Its water feels itself neither wet nor dry
and its waves to themselves are neither singular nor plural.
They splash deaf to their own noise
on pebbles neither large nor small.

(25) And all this beneath a sky by nature skyless
in which the sun sets without setting at all
and hides without hiding behind an unminding cloud.
The wind ruffles it, its only reason being
that it blows.

(30) A second passes.
　　 A second second.
　　 A third.
　　 But they're three seconds only for us.

　　 Time has passed like a courier with urgent news.
(35) But that's just our simile.
　　 The character's invented, his haste is make-believe,
　　 his news inhuman.

—Wislawa Szymborska from Polish Poetry of the
Last Two Decades of Communist Rule,
translated by Stanislaw Barańczak and Clare Cavanagh
Northwestern University Press, 1991

Multiple-Choice Questions

1 The statement "Our glance, our touch mean nothing to it" (line 7)
　 helps to establish the concept of

　 (1) human resentment of the natural order
　 (2) nature's superiority
　 (3) human control over the environment
　 (4) nature's indifference　　　　　　　　　　　　　　　　1 _____

2 The purpose of lines 14 through 18 is to present

　 (1) a contrast with human reliance on the senses
　 (2) a focus on the complexity of natural events
　 (3) an emphasis on human need for physical beauty
　 (4) an appreciation for the role of nature in everyday life　　2 _____

3 Lines 30 through 33 contribute to the poem's meaning by

　 (1) questioning the finality of death
　 (2) commenting on human perception
　 (3) revealing the power of anticipation
　 (4) describing an unusual phenomenon　　　　　　　　　　3 _____

4 The inclusion of the figurative language in the final stanza serves to

   (1) modify an argument
   (2) stress a value
   (3) reinforce a central idea
   (4) resolve a conflict   4 _____

5 The poem is developed primarily through the use of

   (1) examples
   (2) exaggerations
   (3) cause and effect
   (4) question and answer   5 _____

Answers

(1) **4**   (2) **1**   (3) **2**   (4) **3**   (5) **1**

Looking at the Questions

1. *The statement. . . helps to establish the concept of*

   Reading the entire poem before answering the question helps you to recognize the central theme of the poem in this statement.

2. *The purpose of lines 14 through 18 is to present. . .*

   Here you are expected to see how specific details and imagery contribute to the development of the central theme.

3. *Lines 30 through 33 contribute to the poem's meaning by. . .*

   This question asks you to identify the tone of the passage and to hear the last line of the stanza as a comment on how humans perceive time.

4. *The inclusion of figurative language in the final stanza serves to. . .*

   Here you are expected to see how figurative language contributes to the meaning of a poem. In this case, the poet concludes with images of human perception of time as only a simile.

5. *The poem is developed primarily through the use of. . .*

   This question asks you to recognize in the sequence of stanzas the overall structure of the poem as a series of examples.

Sample Passage C
Informational Text

In this excerpt, Andrew Carnegie presents his philosophy regarding how the excess wealth of the rich should be used. Carnegie himself had risen from being an impoverished immigrant to one of the most successful industrialists of the 19th century.

The growing disposition to tax more and more heavily large estates left at death is a cheering indication of the growth of a salutary[1] change in public opinion. The State of Pennsylvania now takes—subject to some exceptions—one-tenth of the property left by its citizens. The budget presented inthe

(5) British Parliament the other day proposes to increase the death-duties; and, most significant of all, the new tax is to be a graduated one. Of all forms of taxation, this seems the wisest. Men who continue hoarding great sums all their lives, the proper use of which for public ends would work goodto the community, should be made to feel that the community, in the form

(10) of the state, cannot thus be deprived of its proper share. By taxing estates heavily at death the state marks its condemnation of the selfish millionaire's unworthy life. . . .

This policy would work powerfully to induce the rich man to attend to the administration of wealth during his life, which is the end that society

(15) should always have in view, as being that by far most fruitful for the people. Nor need it be feared that this policy would sap the root of enterprise and render men less anxious to accumulate, for to the class whose ambition it is to leave great fortunes and be talked about after their death, it will attract even more attention, and, indeed, be a somewhat nobler ambition to have

(20) enormous sums paid over to the state from their fortunes.

There remains, then, only one mode of using great fortunes; but in this we have the true antidote for the temporary unequal distribution of wealth, the reconciliation of the rich and the poor—a reign of harmony—another ideal, differing, indeed, from that of the Communist in requiring

(25) only the further evolution of existing conditions, not the total overthrow of our civilization. It is founded upon the present most intense individualism, and the race is prepared to put it in practice by degrees whenever it pleases. Under its sway we shall have an ideal state, in which the surplus wealth of the few will become, in the best sense, the property of the many, because

(30) administered for the common good, and this wealth, passing through the hands of the few, can be made a much more potent force for the elevation

---

[1]salutary—beneficial

of our race than if it had been distributed in small sums to the people themselves. Even the poorest can be made to see this, and to agree that great sums gathered by some of their fellow-citizens and spent for public
(35) purposes, from which the masses reap the principal benefit, are more valuable to them than if scattered among them through the course of many years in trifling amounts. . . .

Poor and restricted are our opportunities in this life; narrow our horizon; our best work most imperfect; but rich men should be thankful
(40) for one inestimable boon.[2] They have it in their power during their lives to busy themselves in organizing benefactions from which the masses of their fellows will derive lasting advantage, and thus dignify their own lives. The highest life is probably to be reached, not by such imitation of the life of Christ as Count Tolstoi gives us, but, while animated by Christ's spirit,
(45) by recognizing the changed conditions of this age, and adopting modes of expressing this spirit suitable to the changed conditions under which we live; still laboring for the good of our fellows, which was the essence of his life and teaching, but laboring in a different manner.

This, then, is held to be the duty of the man of Wealth: First, to set an
(50) example of modest, unostentatious[3] living, shunning display or extravagance; to provide moderately for the legitimate wants of those dependent upon him; and after doing so to consider all surplus revenues which come to him simply as trust funds, which he is called upon to administer, and strictly bound as a matter of duty to administer in the manner which, in his judgment, is best
(55) calculated to produce the most beneficial results for the community—the man of wealth thus becoming the mere agent and trustee for his poorer brethren, bringing to their service his superior wisdom, experience and ability to administer, doing for them better than they would or could do for themselves. . . .

(60)   Thus is the problem of Rich and Poor to be solved. The laws of accumulation will be left free; the laws of distribution free. Individualism will continue, but the millionaire will be but a trustee for the poor; intrusted for a season with a great part of the increased wealth of the community, but administering it for the community far better than it could or would
(65) have done for itself. The best minds will thus have reached a stage in the development of the race in which it is clearly seen that there is no mode of disposing of surplus wealth creditable to thoughtful and earnest men into whose hands it flows save by using it year by year for the general good. This day already dawns. But a little while, and although, without incurring the

---

[2]boon—benefit   [3]unostentatious—not showy

(70) pity of their fellows, men may die sharers in great business enterprises from
which their capital cannot be or has not been withdrawn, and is left chiefly
at death for public uses, yet the man who dies leaving behind many millions
of available wealth, which was his to administer during life, will pass away
"unwept, unhonored, and unsung," no matter to what uses he leaves the
(75) dross[4] which he cannot take with him. Of such as these the public verdict
will then be: "The man who dies thus rich dies disgraced."

Such, in my opinion, is the true Gospel concerning Wealth, obedience
to which is destined some day to solve the problem of the Rich and the Poor,
and to bring "Peace on earth, among men Good-Will."

—Andrew Carnegie
excerpted from "Wealth," 1889

---

[4]dross—waste

Multiple-Choice Questions

1 The first paragraph (lines 1–12) serves the author's purpose by

  (1) providing examples of alternative tax policies
  (2) contrasting the current taxation system with his proposal
  (3) comparing equal taxation with graduated taxation
  (4) distinguishing estate taxes from income taxes   1 _____

2 The expression "sap the root of enterprise" (line 16) refers to the

  (1) decline in consumer confidence
  (2) reduction in government funding
  (3) discouragement of private business
  (4) harm to international trade   2 _____

3 What evidence from the text best clarifies the author's claim in
lines 33–37 ("Even the poorest . . . amounts")?

  (1) lines 38–40 ("Poor and restricted . . . inestimable boon")
  (2) lines 49–50 ("This, then, . . . or extravagance")
  (3) lines 60–61 ("The laws . . . distribution free")
  (4) lines 61–65 ("Individualism . . . for itself")   3 _____

4 The author's tone in lines 49–59 can best be described as

   (1) confident
   (2) indifferent
   (3) humble
   (4) sarcastic   4 ____

5 A central idea in the text advocates that the wealthy should

   (1) be rewarded for their generosity to the public
   (2) contribute to the public during their lifetime
   (3) entrust their estates to charitable institutions
   (4) be focused on increasing their institutional worth   5 ____

6 Which statement best reflects a central argument used by the author?

   (1) There is no way to insure fair distribution of earnings.
   (2) People should only be paid what they actually earn.
   (3) Sharing wealth among all would limit large gifts from benefactors.
   (4) Equaling wealth among all would restrict the national tax base.   6 ____

Answers

(1) **1**   (2) **3**   (3) **4**   (4) **1**   (5) **2**   (6) **3**

Looking at the Questions

1. *The first paragraph (lines 1–12) serves the author's purpose by. . .*

   This question asks you to analyze how an author's ideas are developed in a particular paragraph and to recognize how an author effectively structures an argument.

2. *The expression "sap the root of enterprise" (line 16) refers to the. . .*

   Here you must recognize the use of figurative language and how it expresses a central claim of the argument.

3. *What evidence from the text best clarifies the author's claim in lines 33–37. . . ?*

   This question requires analysis of a complex set of ideas and how they develop over the course of the text.

4. *The author's tone in lines 49–59 can best be described as. . .*

   Here you must recognize tone as it is determined in the connotation of words and phrases.

5. *A central idea in the text advocates that the wealthy should. . .*

   Determining the central idea of a text is a fundamental skill in the learning standards.

6. *Which statement best reflects a central argument used by the author?*

   This question complements the one above because it asks you to identify the author's central argument of the passage as it is developed over the course of the text.

You can see that the questions in this part of the exam are primarily about:

identifying themes and central ideas and **analyzing** their development

recognizing the significance of tone and point of view

describing the author's use of structure, rhetorical and literary elements

determining the meaning of words and phrases as they are used in the text

understanding figurative language, connotation, and nuances in word meanings

STRATEGIES AND REVIEW

- Remember, close reading means reading to understand <u>what</u> the text says and means as well as to recognize <u>how</u> the meaning is constructed and revealed.
- Be sure to first read through to the end of the passage before trying to answer any of the questions.
- Make your choice of the <u>best</u> answer based on the meaning of the entire passage; there may be more than one plausible choice.
- Recognize the key terms commonly used in the multiple-choice questions.
- Review the Glossaries to support your knowledge and use of literary terms and writing strategies.
- Be confident that the reading, discussion, and writing in your high school courses have prepared you for the exam.
- Review the actual Regents ELA/Exams and the Answers Explained.
- Review the tasks based on a poem in the Regents ELA/exams in the Answers Explained.

Strategy and Review for Part 2 of the Regents ELA Exam

CHAPTER 2
Argument

WHAT DOES THIS PART OF THE EXAM REQUIRE?

First, you must read and comprehend four informational texts. Depending on the topic, these may be examples of literary non-fiction, journalism, scientific publications meant for the general reader, or historical documents. There are no multiple-choice questions in this part of the exam. As in Part 1 of the exam, you must:

- Determine the central ideas of texts, including how ideas within and across texts interact and build on one another.
- Analyze a complex set of ideas and events.
- Determine the meanings of words and phrases as they are used in texts, including figurative, connotative, and technical meanings.

Then, you must take a position on the question and compose an evidence-based argument supported by your analysis of the texts, using valid reasoning and relevant and sufficient evidence from at least three of the texts. An effective essay of argument must clearly establish a claim that can be sufficiently supported with reliable evidence. The organization must be clear and coherent, and the writing is expected to demonstrate command of standard written English. These are reading, research, thinking, and writing skills that high school students are expected to demonstrate across the curriculum.

WHAT DOES THIS PART OF THE EXAM LOOK LIKE?

The topic is often based on a controversial issue of recent or current interest. Here is an example from the January 2016 Regents ELA exam.

SAMPLE TASK – EVIDENCE-BASED WRITING

Directions: Closely read each of the *four* texts provided on pages 23 through 31 and write a source-based argument on the topic below. You may use the margins to take notes as you read and scrap paper to plan your response.

Topic: Should food be genetically modified?

Your Task: Carefully read each of the *four* texts provided. Then, using evidence from at least *three* of the texts, write a well-developed argument regarding the genetic modification of food. Clearly establish your claim, distinguish your claim from alternate or opposing claims, and use specific, relevant, and sufficient evidence from at least *three* of the texts to develop your argument. Do *not* simply summarize each text.

Guidelines:

Be sure to:

- Establish your claim regarding the genetic modification of food.
- Distinguish your claim from alternate or opposing claims.
- Use specific, relevant, and sufficient evidence from at least three of the texts to develop your argument.
- Identify each source that you reference by text number and line number(s) or graphic (for example: Text 1, line 4 or Text 2, graphic).
- Organize your ideas in a cohesive and coherent manner.
- Maintain a formal style of writing.
- Follow the conventions of standard written English.

Texts:

Text 1—GMOs 101

Text 2—GMO Reality Check

Text 3—GMO Foods: Key Points in the Genetically Modified Debate

Text 4—The Truth about Genetically Modified Food

Text 1

GMOs 101

The six questions on every shopper's mind about the new biotech foods. . . .

1 What are GMOs [Genetically Modified Organism], and what are they used for?

A GMO is created by injecting genetic material from plants, animals, or bacteria into a crop in hopes of creating a new and beneficial trait. For example, one of the most popular genetically modified (GM) crops is a corn plant that's capable of producing its own pesticide, called Bt, which is also
(5) used in spray form by some organic farmers. The idea is to make the plant resistant to insect damage and to limit the amount of harmful pesticides farmers have to spray. Other GM plants, such as Roundup Ready corn, were created to survive the spraying of the herbicide Roundup, which kills weeds and would normally kill the plant, too, says Stephen H. Howell, Ph.D.,
(10) director of the Plant Sciences Institute at Iowa State University.

Researchers are also using the technology experimentally as a way to nutritionally enhance fruits and vegetables.

Some GMO supporters say that both applications are necessary to help feed a growing world population, especially in poor countries where drought
(15) and famine are common. But there is very little agreement on whether biotechnology offers a uniform way to address world hunger. "We have plenty of food for the world right now. It's not the deficiency of technology that's a problem for developing countries," says Jane Rissler, Ph.D., a senior staff scientist with the Union of Concerned Scientists, a nonprofit watchdog
(20) group that partners with 80,000 researchers. The international hunger problem, she says, stems from "poverty, corruption, and poor distribution."

2 What kinds of foods contain GMOs?

About 80 percent of the food on grocery-store shelves already contains at least some ingredients made from altered genes. This means that almost any processed food, from salad dressing to snack crackers, could contain
(25) GMOs, unless it has been certified organic (federal regulations explicitly restrict food manufacturers from using the organic seal on products made with GMOs). That's because corn, soy, and canola are the top three GM food crops in the United States, so anything that is produced with corn syrup, high-fructose corn syrup, or soybean or corn oil might include GMOs.
(30)   Very little fresh produce on the market, though, is genetically engineered, with the exceptions of most papaya, some squash, and a few strains of

sweet corn. Meanwhile, we're not the only ones consuming GMOs—animals do, too. GM corn and soybeans are often used in livestock feed, though there's no evidence that GMOs show up in your steak or chops.

3 Should I be concerned about the safety of GM foods?

(35)   Federal agencies like the U.S. Food and Drug Administration (FDA) and the U.S. Department of Agriculture (USDA) say that they are safe, and there have been no documented cases of illness due to consumption of GMOs. The American Medical Association agrees at this point and has encouraged ongoing research in the field. . . .

4 What do GM crops mean for the environment?

(40)   "I think a lot of scientists agree that there are no known environmental problems with the crops that are out there now," says Allison Snow, Ph.D., who studies environmental risk and genetically modified crops as a professor of ecology at Ohio State University. But organic farmers are becoming increasingly concerned about maintaining the integrity of their crops. For
(45) example, if Bt corn is planted too close to a neighboring organic-corn crop, crosspollination could occur and contaminate the latter.

Scientists on both sides of the debate also widely agree that insects will eventually become resistant to the Bt crops, Snow says. "It could happen any year now. Then we would be back where we started, and we would have
(50) lost a valuable tool for managing insects," Snow says. . . .

5 Is it possible to live completely GMO-free?

Probably not. A study commissioned by the Union of Concerned Scientists and released in February already suggests that seeds that are supposedly non-GMO may be unintentionally tainted. Genetically engineered DNA was found in at least half of the small sample of tested
(55) corn and soybean seeds, and about 83 percent of the canola seeds. Even if you buy only certified-organic products, you probably can't avoid GMOs completely. That's because it is also possible for organic food crops to become inadvertently contaminated. . . .

6 What will we see next from the biotech-food market?

Here are some GM foods that might end up on store shelves:
(60)   • The FDA and USDA are currently reviewing safety data on a variety of genetically engineered wheat that would tolerate the herbicide Roundup.

(65)
- Researchers are also working on wheat varieties that would resist drought, be less allergenic to those with gluten intolerance, and be more nutritious.

Consumers may also start seeing major nutritional benefits in the future:

(70)
- Scientists at the University of California, Riverside, announced last year [2003] that they genetically engineered a corn plant to produce up to four times the normal amount of vitamin C by inserting a gene from wheat plants. The researchers have filed a patent application and are soliciting companies that might be interested in commercializing the product. . . .

(75)
- Other biotech foods that are currently in development include a vitamin A–enhanced rice and a tomato with increased amounts of the cancer-fighting antioxidant lycopene.
- Monsanto Co., which is the largest producer of GM seeds, is continuing to tinker with soybeans in hopes of developing a variety that could produce an oil containing few or no saturated and trans fats.

—Alisa Blackwood excerpted and adapted from
"GMOs 101" *Health*, May 2004

Text 2

GMO Reality Check

. . . GMO Basics

So what are GMOs? To put it simply, they're plants and seeds created in laboratories. Genetic engineers insert genes from bacteria, viruses, animals, or humans into the DNA of a food crop or animal to create an organism that would never occur in nature. Biotech companies do this for two main
(5) reasons: to make crops that are tolerant to herbicides such as RoundUp that kill other plants, and to make crops that produce their own insecticides.

The FDA's own scientists actually warned that these never-before-seen foods could create new toxins and new allergens and needed to be more thoroughly tested, but their concerns were largely ignored. Instead, the US
(10) government took the official position that GM foods were "substantially equivalent" to conventional foods and didn't require safety testing or labeling—in sharp contrast to 40 other countries that require such foods be clearly labeled. Commercial planting of genetically modified seeds in the United States began in 1996, and soon after, food products containing
(15) GMOs began appearing on store shelves, mostly without our knowledge.

By 2011, 94 percent of all soybeans and 88 percent of all corn grown in the United States was genetically modified. Soy and corn, along with other common GM foods (including canola oil. [sic] cottonseed oil, and sugar from sugar beets), are used as ingredients in countless other products, so
(20) many Americans—including health food shoppers—likely have been eating GM foods without realizing it.

No Benefits, Just Risks

What we didn't know about what we were eating may already be harming us. Based on animal research with GM foods, the American Academy of Environmental Medicine (AAEM) says that there are serious
(25) health risks associated with eating GM foods, including infertility, immune system problems, accelerated aging, disruption of insulin and cholesterol regulation, gastrointestinal issues, and changes in organs. In 2009, the AAEM urged doctors to prescribe non-GMO diets for all Americans, saying that doctors are probably seeing negative health effects in their patients
(30) right now without realizing that GM foods are major contributing factors.

Genetically modified crops pose risks to the environment, too, including the serious threat of GM seeds spreading to and contaminating both organic and conventional crop fields. Plus, the biotech industry claims that genetic engineering reduces the use of pesticides, but research shows otherwise.
(35) According to a 2009 report by the Organic Center, overall pesticide use dramatically increased—about 318 million pounds—in the first thirteen years after GM crops were introduced.

Herbicides sprayed in high amounts on GM herbicide-resistant crops have led to the development and spread of so-called "superweeds"—weeds
(40) that are able to adapt to and withstand typical herbicides. And the biotech companies' proposed solution to this problem? Create new GM crops that are resistant to ever more toxic chemicals, including 2, 4-D—a major component of Agent Orange.[1] It's a "crazy" idea because weeds would eventually adapt to that herbicide and any others, says Andrew Kimbrell,
(45) executive director of the Center for Food Safety and author of *Your Right to Know: Genetic Engineering and the Secret Changes in Your Food.*

The most important thing to know about GM foods is that they benefit only the chemical companies that produce them, says Kimbrell. "[The biotech companies] have yet to produce anything that benefits the consumer.
(50) There's no better taste, no better nutrition, no lower price. That's the dirty

---

[1]Agent Orange—chemical used as part of herbicidal warfare programs

little secret that's hardly ever reported. That's why those companies don't want GM foods labeled. They don't want the consumer to be able to have the choice to say, 'I want the same price, less risky version.'" . . .

—Melissa Diane Smith excerpted from "GMO Reality Check"
Better Nutrition, August 2012

Text 3
GMO Foods: Key Points in
the Genetically Modified Debate

. . . Safe or Unsafe?

Most studies show genetically modified foods are safe for human consumption, though it is widely acknowledged that the long-term health effects are unknown. The Food and Drug Administration generally recognized these foods as safe, and the World Health Organization has said
(5) no ill health effects have resulted on the international market.

Opponents on both sides of the Atlantic say there has been inadequate testing and regulation. They worry that people who eat genetically modified foods may be more prone to allergies or diseases resistant to antibiotics. But they have been hard pressed to show scientific studies to back up those fears.
(10) GM foods have been a mainstay in the U.S. for more than a decade. Most of the crops are used for animal feed or in common processed foods such as cookies, cereal, potato chips and salad dressing.

Europe largely bans genetically engineered foods and has strict requirements on labeling them. They do allow the import of a number of GM
(15) crops such as soy, mostly for animal feed, and individual European countries have opted to plant these types of crops. Genetically engineered corn is grown in Spain, though it amounts to only a fraction of European farmland. . . .

Can GM Food Help Combat World Hunger?

By 2050, the world's population is projected to rise to 9 billion from just over 7 billion currently. Proponents of genetically modified foods say they
(20) are safe and can boost harvests even in bad conditions by protecting against pests, weeds and drought. This, they argue, will be essential to meeting the needs of a booming population in decades to come and avoiding starvation.

However Doug Gurian-Sherman, senior scientist for the food and environment program at the Union of Concerned Scientists, an advocacy
(25) group, said genetic engineering for insect resistance has provided only a modest increase in yields since the 1990s and drought-resistant strains have only modestly reduced losses from drought.

Moreover, he said conventional crossbreeding or cross-pollinating of different varieties for desirable traits, along with improved farming, are
(30) getting better results boosting yields at a lower cost. In fact, much of the food Americans eat has been genetically modified by those conventional methods over thousands of years, before genetic engineering came into practice. . . .

Andrea Roberto Sonnino, chief of research at the U.N. food agency, said total food production at present is enough to feed the entire global
(35) population. The problem is uneven distribution, leaving 870 million suffering from hunger. He said world food production will need to increase by 60 percent to meet the demands of 9 billion by 2050. This must be achieved by increasing yields, he added, because there is little room to expand cultivated land used for agriculture.

(40)   Genetically modified foods, in some instances, can help if the individual product has been assessed as safe, he said. "It's an opportunity that we cannot just miss."

To Label or Not to Label?

Europe requires all GM food to be labeled unless GM ingredients amount to 0.9 percent or less of the total. The U.S. does not require labels
(45) on the view that genetically modified food is not materially different than nonmodified food. Opponents of labeling say it would scare consumers away from safe foods, giving the appearance that there is something wrong with them.

U.S. activists insist consumers should have the right to choose whether
(50) to eat genetically modified foods and that labeling would offer them that choice, whether the foods are safe or not. They are pushing for labeling at the state and federal level. California voters last year rejected a ballot initiative that would have required GM food labeling. The legislatures of Connecticut and Maine have passed laws to label genetically modified foods,
(55) and more than 20 other states are contemplating labeling. . . .

—Marjorie Olster excerpted from "GMO Foods:
Key Points in the Genetically Modified Debate"
http://www.huffingtonpost.com, August 2, 2013

Text 4
The Truth about Genetically Modified Food

... Benefits and Worries

The bulk of the science on GM safety points in one direction. Take it from David Zilberman, a U.C. Berkeley agricultural and environmental economist and one of the few researchers considered credible by both agricultural chemical companies and their critics. He argues that the
(5) benefits of GM crops greatly outweigh the health risks, which so far remain theoretical. The use of GM crops "has lowered the price of food," Zilberman says. "It has increased farmer safety by allowing them to use less pesticide. It has raised the output of corn, cotton and soy by 20 to 30 percent, allowing some people to survive who would not have without it. If it were more
(10) widely adopted around the world, the price [of food] would go lower, and fewer people would die of hunger." ...

Despite such promise, much of the world has been busy banning, restricting and otherwise shunning GM foods. Nearly all the corn and soybeans grown in the U.S. are genetically modified, but only two GM
(15) crops, Monsanto's $MON8_{10}$ maize and BASF's Amflora potato, are accepted in the European Union. Eight E.U. nations have banned GM crops outright. Throughout Asia, including in India and China, governments have yet to approve most GM crops, including an insect-resistant rice that produces higher yields with less pesticide. In Africa, where millions go hungry, several
(20) nations have refused to import GM foods in spite of their lower costs (the result of higher yields and a reduced need for water and pesticides). Kenya has banned them altogether amid widespread malnutrition. No country has definite plans to grow Golden Rice, a crop engineered to deliver more vitamin A than spinach (rice normally has no vitamin A), even though vitamin
(25) A deficiency causes more than one million deaths annually and half a million cases of irreversible blindness in the developing world. ...

A Clean Record

... Could eating plants with altered genes allow new DNA to work its way into our own? It is theoretically possible but hugely improbable. Scientists have never found genetic material that could survive a trip through the
(30) human gut and make it into cells. Besides, we are routinely exposed to—we even consume—the viruses and bacteria whose genes end up in GM foods. The bacterium *B. thuringiensis*, for example, which produces proteins fatal to insects, is sometimes enlisted as a natural pesticide in organic farming. "We've been eating this stuff for thousands of years," [Robert] Goldberg [a
(35) plant molecular biologist] says.

In any case, proponents say, people have consumed as many as trillions of meals containing genetically modified ingredients over the past few decades. Not a single verified case of illness has ever been attributed to the genetic alterations. Mark Lynas, a prominent anti-GM activist who last year
(40) publicly switched to strongly supporting the technology, has pointed out that every single news-making food disaster on record has been attributed to non-GM crops, such as the *Escherichia coli*—infected organic bean sprouts that killed 53 people in Europe in 2011. . . .

Plenty of other credible groups have arrived at the same conclusion.
(45) Gregory Jaffe, director of biotechnology at the Center for Science in the Public Interest, a science-based consumer-watchdog group in Washington, D.C., takes pains to note that the center has no official stance, pro or con, with regard to genetically modifying food plants. Yet Jaffe insists the scientific record is clear. "Current GM crops are safe to eat and can be grown safely in
(50) the environment," he says. The American Association for the Advancement of Science, the American Medical Association and the National Academy of Sciences have all unreservedly backed GM crops. The U.S. Food and Drug Administration, along with its counterparts in several other countries, has repeatedly reviewed large bodies of research and concluded that GM
(55) crops pose no unique health threats. Dozens of review studies carried out by academic researchers have backed that view. . . .

—David H. Freedman excerpted and adapted
from "The Truth about Genetically Modified Food"
http://www.scientificamerican.com, August 20, 2013

LOOKING AT THE TEXTS

Text 1—GMOs 101: The Six Questions on Every Shoppers Mind About the Bew Biotech Foods. . .

—Alisa Blackwood, excerpted and adapted from "GMOs 101," *Health*, May 2004

This is an article from a popular, generally well-regarded magazine. The question and answer format serves as a good introduction to the topic. The article is rich in information, and details and opinions are documented, which suggests that the sources are reliable. The tone and purpose seem to be objective.

Text 2—GMO Reality Check

—Melissa Diane Smith, excerpted from "GMO Reality Check," *Better Nutrition*, August 2012

This is a good example of a document in which one side of the issue is forcefully expressed. The writer cites sources for much of the information used to support her opposition to the use of GMO foods. This would be an excellent source for the student writer who establishes a claim opposed to the use of GMO foods.

Text 3—GMO Foods: Key Points in the Genetically Modified Debate

—Marjorie Olster, excerpted from "GMO Foods: Key Points in the Genetically Modified Debate," *http://www.huffingtonpost.com*, August 2, 2013

Here is an example of a document that outlines the key points in the debate and offers detailed information both on the development of GMO foods and on how governments in the United States and Europe regulate them. This article acknowledges competing points of view and offers information that could be used to support a variety of arguments.

Text 4—The Truth About Genetically Modified Food

—David H. Freedman, excerpted and adapted from "The Truth about Genetically Modified Food," *http://www.scientificamerican.com*, August 20, 2013

This article presents a very clear opinion on one side of the argument. It is well documented and offers strong evidence for the student writer who establishes a claim for the use of GMO foods.

Note that two of the texts are rich in background information and acknowledge opposing points of view. They can be helpful to the student writer when determining which argument to make. The other two texts offer forceful arguments for one side or the other. All texts include useful information and are documented with reliable sources.

KNOW THE RUBRIC

Here is the information from the chart on pages 79 and 80. The key terms for this part of the exam have been highlighted.

SCORING RUBRIC FOR PART 2

Content and Analysis: The extent to which the essay conveys complex ideas and information clearly and accurately in order to support claims in an analysis of the texts.

High Scores

6 Essays introduce **a precise and insightful claim**, as directed by the task and demonstrate **in-depth and insightful analysis** of the texts, as necessary to support the claim and to distinguish the claim from alternate or opposing claims.

5 Essays introduce **a precise and thoughtful** claim, as directed by the task and demonstrate **thorough analysis** of the texts, as necessary to support the claim and to distinguish the claim from alternate or opposing claims.

Middle Scores

4 Essays introduce **a precise claim**, as directed by the task and demonstrate **appropriate and accurate analysis** of the texts, as necessary to support the claim and to distinguish the claim from alternate or opposing claims.

3 Essays introduce a **reasonable claim**, as directed by the task and demonstrate **some analysis** of the texts, but **insufficiently distinguish** the claim from alternate or opposing claims.

Low Scores

2 Essays introduce a claim and demonstrate **confused or unclear analysis** of the texts, **failing to distinguish the claim** from alternate or opposing claims.

1 Essays **do not introduce a claim**; do not demonstrate analysis of the texts.

Command of Evidence: The extent to which the essay presents evidence from the provided texts to support analysis.

High Scores

6 Essays **present ideas fully and thoughtfully**, making highly effective use of a **wide range of specific and relevant evidence** to support analysis and demonstrate **proper citation of sources** to avoid plagiarism when dealing with direct quotes and paraphrased material.

5 Essays **present ideas clearly and accurately**, making **effective use of specific and relevant evidence** to support analysis and **demonstrate proper citation** of sources to avoid plagiarism when dealing with direct quotes and paraphrased material.

Middle Scores

4   Essays **present ideas sufficiently**, making **adequate use of specific and relevant evidence** to support analysis and **demonstrate proper citation** of sources to avoid plagiarism when dealing with direct quotes and paraphrased material.

3   Essays **present ideas briefly**, making use of **some specific and relevant evidence** to support analysis and demonstrate **inconsistent citation of sources** to avoid plagiarism when dealing with direct quotes and paraphrased material.

Low Scores

2   Essays **present ideas inconsistently and/or inaccurately**, in an attempt to support analysis, making use of **some evidence that may be irrelevant** and demonstrate **little use of citations** to avoid plagiarism when dealing with direct quotes and paraphrased material.

1   Essays present **little or no evidence** from the texts; do not make use of citations.

Coherence, Organization, and Style: The extent to which the essay logically organizes complex ideas, concepts, and information using formal style and precise language.

High Scores

6   Essays exhibit **skillful organization** of ideas and information to create a **cohesive and coherent essay** and establish and maintain a **formal style**, using **sophisticated language and structure**.

5   Essays exhibit **logical organization** of ideas and information to create a **cohesive and coherent** essay and establish and maintain **a formal style**, using **fluent and precise language and sound structure**.

Middle Scores

4   Essays exhibit **acceptable organization** of ideas and information to create a **coherent essay** and establish and maintain a **formal style**, using **precise and appropriate language and structure**.

3   Essays exhibit **some organization** of ideas and information to create a **mostly coherent essay** and establish but **fail to maintain a formal style**, using primarily **basic language and structure**.

Low Scores

2   Essays exhibit **inconsistent organization** of ideas and information, **failing to create a coherent essay and lack a formal style**, using some **language that is inappropriate or imprecise**.

1   Essays exhibit **little organization** of ideas and information, making assessment unreliable; use language that is **predominantly incoherent, inappropriate, or copied directly** from the task or texts.

> **Control of Conventions:** The extent to which the essay demonstrates command of conventions of standard English grammar, usage, capitalization, punctuation, and spelling.

High Scores

6   Essays demonstrate control of conventions with **essentially no errors, even with sophisticated language**.

5   Essays demonstrate control of the conventions, exhibiting **occasional errors only when using sophisticated language**.

Middle Scores

4   Essays demonstrate **partial control**, exhibiting **occasional errors** that do not hinder comprehension.

3   Essays demonstrate **emerging control**, exhibiting **occasional errors that hinder comprehension**.

Low Scores

2   Essays demonstrate a **lack of control**, exhibiting **frequent errors** that make comprehension difficult.

1   Essays are **minimal**, making assessment of conventions unreliable.

STRATEGIES AND REVIEW

- The reading, writing, and discussion you do in English, social studies, and science classes form the basis of your preparation for this part of the exam.
- There is no "right answer." The topic and the texts provide for a variety of legitimate claims. Your task is to compose a relevant and defensible argument.
- Plan your response. This need not be a formal outline, but take time to articulate clearly what your claim (argument) will be. Then number and underline in the texts three or four passages that you can cite to support your argument. Decide on the most effective order for the examples.
- Review the Glossaries in the chapters that follow in order to recognize literary and rhetorical elements.
- Review the actual ELA/Exams and the Answers Explained for additional examples with essays for Part 2 of the exam.

Strategy and Review for Part 3 of the Regents ELA Exam

CHAPTER 3
Text-Analysis Response

WHAT DOES THIS PART OF THE EXAM REQUIRE?

The Part 3 question is designed to assess reading, writing, and language standards. You will be required to do a close reading of a text (approximately 1,000 words). You will then write a two to three paragraph response that identifies a central idea in the text and analyzes how the author's use of one writing strategy (literary element, literary technique, or rhetorical device) develops this central idea.

There are no multiple-choice questions in this part of the exam.

WHAT DOES THIS PART OF THE EXAM LOOK LIKE?

Your Task: Closely read the text provided and write a well-developed, text-based response of two to three paragraphs. In your response, identify a central idea in the text and analyze how the author's use of one writing strategy (literary element, literary technique, or rhetorical device) develops this central idea. Use strong and thorough evidence from the text to support your analysis. Do *not* simply summarize the text. You may use the margins and scrap paper to take notes as you read and plan your response.

LOOKING AT THE TEXT

The following excerpt is from a speech delivered by suffragette Anna Howard Shaw in 1915.

. . .Now one of two things is true: either a Republic is a desirable form of government, or else it is not. If it is, then we should have it, if it is not then we ought not to pretend that we have it. We ought at least be true to our ideals, and the men of New York have for the first time in their lives, the rare
(5) opportunity on the second day of next November, of making the state truly a part of the Republic. It is the greatest opportunity which has ever come to the men of the state. They have never had so serious a problem to solve before, they will never have a more serious problem to solve in any future of our nation's life, and the thing that disturbs me more than anything else
(10) in connection with it is that so few people realize what a profound problem they have to solve on November 2. It is not merely a trifling matter; it is not a little thing that does not concern the state, it is the most vital problem we could have, and any man who goes to the polls on the second day of next November without thoroughly informing himself in regard to this subject is
(15) unworthy to be a citizen of this state, and unfit to cast a ballot.

If woman's suffrage[1] is wrong, it is a great wrong; if it is right, it is a profound and fundamental principle, and we all know, if we know what a Republic is, that it is the fundamental principle upon which a Republic must rise. Let us see where we are as a people; how we act here and what
(20) we think we are. The difficulty with the men of this country is that they are so consistent in their inconsistency that they are not aware of having been inconsistent; because their consistency has been so continuous and their inconsistency so consecutive that it has never been broken, from the beginning of our Nation's life to the present time. If we trace our history
(25) back we will find that from the very dawn of our existence as a people, men have been imbued[2] with a spirit and a vision more lofty than they have been able to live; they have been led by visions of the sublimest[3] truth, both in regard to religion and in regard to government that ever inspired the souls of men from the time the Puritans left the old world to come to this country,
(30) led by the Divine ideal which is the sublimest and the supremest ideal in religious freedom which men have ever known, the theory that a man has a right to worship God according to the dictates of his own conscience, without the intervention[4] of any other man or any other group of men. And it was this theory, this vision of the right of the human soul which led men
(35) first to the shores of this country. . . .

---

[1]suffrage—right to vote [2]imbued—inspired [3]sublimest—noblest [4]intervention—interference

Now what is a Republic? Take your dictionary, encyclopedia lexicon or anything else you like and look up the definition and you will find that a Republic is a form of government in which the laws are enacted by representatives elected by the people. Now when did the people of New (40) York ever elect their own representatives? Never in the world. The men of New York have, and I grant you that men are people, admirable people, as far as they go, but they only go half way. There is still another half of the people who have not elected representatives, and you never read a definition of a Republic in which half of the people elect representatives to govern the (45) whole of the people. That is an aristocracy and that is just what we are. We have been many kinds of aristocracies. We have been a hierarchy[5] of church members, than an oligarchy[6] of sex. . . .

Now I want to make this proposition, and I believe every man will accept it. Of course he will if he is intelligent. Whenever a Republic prescribes the (50) qualifications as applying equally to all the citizens of the Republic, when the Republic says in order to vote, a citizen must be twenty-one years of age, it applies to all alike, there is no discrimination against any race or sex. When the government says that a citizen must be a native-born citizen or a naturalized citizen that applies to all; we are either born or naturalized, (55) somehow or other we are here. Whenever the government says that a citizen, in order to vote, must be a resident of a community a certain length of time, and of the state a certain length of time and of the nation a certain length of time, that applies to all equally. There is no discrimination. We might go further and we might say that in order to vote the citizen must be (60) able to read his ballot. We have not gone that far yet. We have been very careful of male ignorance in these United States. I was much interested, as perhaps many of you, in reading the Congressional Record this last winter over the debate over the immigration bill, and when that illiteracy clause was introduced into the immigration bill, what fear there was in the souls of (65) men for fear we would do injustice to some of the people who might want to come to our shores, and I was much interested in the language in which the President vetoed the bill, when he declared that by inserting the clause we would keep out of our shores a large body of very excellent people. I could not help wondering then how it happens that male ignorance is so much less (70) ignorant than female ignorance. When I hear people say that if women were permitted to vote a large body of ignorant people would vote, and therefore

---

[5]hierarchy—order of authority   [6]oligarchy—rule by a few

because an ignorant woman would vote, no intelligent women should be allowed to vote, I wonder why we have made it so easy for male ignorance and so hard for female ignorance. . . .

—Anna Howard Shaw
excerpted from "The Fundamental Principle of a Republic"
delivered at Ogdensburg, New York, June 21, 1915
http://www.emersonkent.com

In this excerpted speech, suffragette Anna Howard Shaw uses several techniques to argue for the case of women's right to vote. She employs **repetition** and **rhetorical questioning** while discussing the **definition** of a Republic throughout her speech and a **sarcastic [ironic] tone** when referring to the consistent inconsistencies of men (paragraph 2) and the various requirements to vote in the U.S. (paragraph 3). Shaw's speech is also an excellent example of the use of **logical structure**, leading to her thinking "how it happens that male ignorance is so much less ignorant than female ignorance" (lines 69 and 70).

—*Analysis from "Questions with Annotations," NYSED, June 2014*

KNOW THE RUBRIC

Here is the information from the chart on pages 81 and 82. The key terms for this part of the exam have been highlighted.

SCORING RUBRIC FOR PART 3

> **Content and Analysis:** The extent to which the response conveys complex ideas and information clearly and accurately in order to respond to the task and support an analysis of the text.

4   Essays introduce a **well-reasoned central idea and a writing strategy** that clearly establish the criteria for analysis and demonstrate a **thoughtful analysis** of the author's use of the writing strategy to develop the central idea.

3   Essays introduce a **clear central idea and a writing strategy** that establish the criteria for analysis and demonstrate an **appropriate analysis** of the author's use of the writing strategy to develop the central idea.

2   Essays introduce a **central idea and/or a writing strategy** and demonstrate a **superficial analysis** of the author's use of the writing strategy to develop the central idea.

1   Essays introduce a **confused or incomplete central idea or writing strategy** and/or demonstrate a **minimal analysis** of the author's use of the writing strategy to develop the central idea.

> **Command of Evidence:** The extent to which the response presents evidence from the provided text to support analysis.

4   Essays present ideas **clearly and consistently**, making effective use of **specific and relevant evidence** to support analysis.

3   Essays present ideas **sufficiently**, making **adequate use of relevant evidence** to support analysis.

2   Essays present ideas **inconsistently**, **inadequately**, **and/or inaccurately** in an attempt to support analysis, making use of **some evidence that may be irrelevant**.

1   Essays present **little or no evidence** from the text.

> **Coherence, Organization, and Style:** The extent to which the response logically organizes complex ideas, concepts, and information using formal style and precise language.

4   Essays exhibit **logical organization** of ideas and information to create a **cohesive and coherent** response and establish and maintain a **formal style**, using **precise language and sound structure**.

3   Essays exhibit **acceptable organization** of ideas and information to create a **coherent response** and establish and maintain a **formal style**, using **appropriate language and structure**.

2   Essays exhibit **inconsistent organization** of ideas and information, failing to create a coherent response; lack a formal style, using language that is **basic, inappropriate, or imprecise**.

1   Essays exhibit **little organization** of ideas and information; use language that is predominantly **incoherent**, inappropriate, or copied directly from the task or text; or are **minimal**, making assessment unreliable.

> **Control of Conventions:** The extent to which the response demonstrates command of conventions of standard English grammar, usage, capitalization, punctuation, and spelling.

4   Essays demonstrate **control** of the conventions with **infrequent errors**.

3   Essays demonstrate **partial control** of conventions with **occasional errors** that do not hinder comprehension.

2   Essays demonstrate **emerging control** of conventions with **some errors** that **hinder comprehension**.

1   Essays demonstrate a **lack of control** of conventions with **frequent errors** that make comprehension difficult; are **minimal**, making assessment of conventions unreliable.

Note:
  • A response that is a personal response and makes little or no reference to the task or text can be scored no higher than a 1.
  • A response that is totally copied from the text with no original writing must be given a 0.
  • A response that is totally unrelated to the task, illegible, incoherent, blank, or unrecognizable as English must be scored as a 0.

STRATEGIES AND REVIEW

- Plan your response. This need not be a formal outline, but be sure to articulate clearly which literary element or rhetorical device you choose. List on the blank page provided, and underline in the text itself, three or four passages that convincingly support your topic. Decide on the most effective order for the examples.
- Recognize that the texts for this part are primary sources, often narratives or speeches. They will have distinctive voices and may be of a particular historical context.
- There is no "right answer." The texts will be rich in information and are likely to employ several rhetorical strategies for effect. Choose the one you can discuss most confidently.
- Review the chapter in this book on literary elements and the Glossaries to help you recognize and write about writing strategies.
- Review this part of the exam in the Answers Explained for actual ELA/exams.

Reading and Writing About Literature

CHAPTER 4
Reviewing Literary Elements and Techniques

ELEMENTS OF FICTION AND DRAMA

When we speak of fiction, we are generally speaking of narrative works—works in which events are recounted, are *told*, and which have been imagined and structured by the author. Although not narrative in form, drama shares many of the essential characteristics of fiction.

Plot and Story

The primary pleasure for most readers of narrative fiction is the story. If we become involved in a novel or short story, it is because we want to know how it turns out; we want to know what is going to happen to those characters. An author creates a plot when he or she gives order and structure to the action: in a plot, the **incidents** or **episodes** of the story have a meaningful relationship to one another. A story becomes a plot when we not only understand *what happened* but also *why*. In good fiction we are *convinced* of the causal relationship among incidents and we are convinced by the relationship of characters' motives and feelings to the action.

Plot and Conflict

At the end of any meaningful story, something has *happened*; something is significantly different in the world and lives of the characters from what it was at the beginning. **Conflict** in the most general sense refers to the **forces** that move the action in a plot. Conflict in plot may be generated from a search or pursuit, from a discovery, from a deception or misunderstanding, from opportunities to make significant choices, or from unexpected consequences of an action. Although the term conflict connotes an active struggle between opposing or hostile forces, conflict in fiction may refer to any progression, change, or discovery. The **resolution** of conflict in a plot may be subtle and confined to the inner life of a character or it may be dramatic and involve irreversible change, violent destruction, or death.

Conflict may identify an actual struggle between characters, for anything from dominance or revenge to simple recognition or understanding. A plot may also focus on conflict between characters and the forces of nature or society. These are essentially *external conflicts*. A work may center on *internal conflict*: characters' struggle to know or change themselves and their lives. Most works of fiction and drama contain more than one aspect of conflict.

In Shakespeare's *Romeo and Juliet*, the most dramatic conflicts are external, vivid, and literal: the street brawls between followers of the rival Capulets and Montagues and the fatal fight with Tybalt that leads to Romeo's banishment and the tragic deaths of the young lovers. In *Macbeth*, the primary interest is in the internal conflict between Macbeth's ambitious desires and his understanding of the moral consequences of the actions he takes to achieve those desires.

The action in Edith Wharton's most famous story, "Roman Fever," is ironically serene and pleasant: two middle-age women, long-time friends now both widowed, sit on a terrace overlooking the splendors of Rome and reflect on their common experiences and lifelong friendship. At the end of the conversation—and the story—their actual feelings of rivalry have come to the surface, and one of the two learns something that reveals how little she truly knew her husband or understood her marriage or the life of her friend. The conflict between the two women emerges almost imperceptibly and its meaning is only fully understood in the completely unexpected revelation of the last line.

Structure/Plot and Chronology

Narrative is not necessarily presented in chronological order, but it does have chronology. That is, incidents may be presented out of the order in which they actually occurred, but by the end of the work the reader does understand their order and relationship and appreciates why the story was structured as it was. Plots that are narrated in flashback or from different points of view are common examples.

The Great Gatsby by F. Scott Fitzgerald and *Ethan Frome* by Edith Wharton are novels in which the narrator first introduces himself and his interest in the story, then tells it in a narrative flashback whose full significance to the narrator (and reader) is revealed only at the end. Tennessee Williams's play *The Glass Menagerie* has a similar structure, in which the character of Tom serves both as a narrator in the present and as a principal character in the series of memory scenes that make up the drama. The memory scenes in Arthur Miller's play *Death of a Salesman*, however, are not flashbacks in the same way. Willy Loman relives incidents from the past while the other characters and action of the play continue in the present. As the play progresses, the shifts in time occur only within Willy's mind.

Shakespeare's tragedies are dramas in which normal chronology is preserved, as it is in such familiar novels as William Golding's *Lord of the Flies* and Mark Twain's *Huckleberry Finn*.

Narrative Point of View

The narrator of a work is the character or author's *persona* that tells a story. Point of view is the standpoint, perspective, and degree of understanding from which the narrator speaks. For many students and scholars, the question of how a story is told is one of the most interesting questions. What is the narrative point of view? Is the narration *omniscient,* essentially the point of view of the author? Or, who is the narrator? What is the narrator's relationship to the story? What is the narrator's understanding of the story? How much does the narrator really know? Appreciating how, or by whom, a story is told is often essential to understanding its meaning.

One of the most easily discerned narrative points of view is the **first person** (*I*) in which either the central character or another directly involved in the action tells the story. J. D. Salinger's novel *Catcher in the Rye* is a vivid and popular example of such narration. Fitzgerald's *The Great Gatsby* is also told in the first person. In each of these works, the fundamental meaning of the novel becomes apparent only when the reader understands the character of the narrator. In each of these works, what the narrator experiences and what he learns about himself and the world are the novel's most important themes.

In **first-person narration**, the incidents of the plot are limited to those that the narrator himself experiences. First-person narrators can, however, report what they learn from others. In Wharton's *Ethan Frome*, the engineer who narrates tells us that he has "pieced together the story" from the little he has been able to learn in the town of Starkfield, from his limited conversations with Frome himself, and from his brief visit to the Frome house. Wharton's method, of course, dramatizes Frome's inability to express or fulfill the desires of his heart and reveals the reluctance of the people of Starkfield to fully understand the lives of those around them.

Authors may also use first-person narration to achieve an ironic or satiric effect. In Ring Lardner's story "Haircut," a barber in a small midwestern town narrates a story about a local fellow who kept the town entertained with his practical jokes on people. As the story progresses, the reader understands how cruel and destructive the fellow's pranks were, but the barber does not. The narrative method in this story reveals, indirectly, a story of painful ignorance and insensitivity in the "decent" citizens of a small town. Mark Twain's masterpiece, *Huckleberry Finn*, is told by Huck himself. Through the morally naive observations of Huck, Twain satirizes the evils of slavery, fraud, hypocrisy, and nearly every other kind of corrupt human behavior. Edgar Allan Poe's story "The Tell-Tale Heart" is the confession of a cunning madman.

In **third-person** narration (*he, she, it, they*), a story is reported. The narrative voice may be *omniscient* and, therefore, able to report everything from everywhere in the story and also report on the innermost thoughts and feelings of the characters themselves. In many novels of the eighteenth and nineteenth centuries, the omniscient narrator even speaks directly to the reader, as if taking him or her into the storyteller's confidence. In Nathaniel Hawthorne's *The Scarlet Letter*, the narrator pauses from time to time to share personal feelings with the reader. Nick Carraway, the narrator of *The Great Gatsby* also does this, but the method is not common in contemporary fiction.

A widely used narrative method is the *limited omniscient* point of view. The narrative is in the third person but is focused on and even may represent the point of view of a central character. The actions and feelings of other characters are presented from the perspective of that character. Hawthorne's short story "Young Goodman Brown" is an excellent example.

Some third-person narration is dramatically **objective** and detached; it simply reports the incidents of the plot as they unfold. This narrative method, too, can be used for intensely **ironic** effect. Jackson's "The Lottery" is one of the best examples. The real horror of the story is achieved through the utterly detached, nonjudgmental telling of it.

In some plays, too, there is a character who serves a narrative role: the Chorus in Shakespeare's *Henry V*, the character of Tom in Williams's *The Glass Menagerie*, and the Stage Manager in Thornton Wilder's *Our Town* are familiar examples.

In each of the works discussed here, narrative method is not simply a literary device; it is an intrinsic part of the meaning of the work.

Setting

The setting of a work includes the time and places in which the action is played out; setting may also include significant historical context. In drama, setting may be presented directly in the set, costumes, and lighting. In narrative fiction, setting is usually presented directly through description. In some works, the physical setting is central to the plot and developed in great detail; in other works, only those details necessary to anchor the plot in a time or place will be developed. Regardless of detail, responsive readers re-create images of setting as they read.

In addition to the physical and natural details of the fictional world, setting also includes mood and **atmosphere**. In some works, social or political realities constitute part of the setting. *The Scarlet Letter* is not only set in Puritan Boston, it is also *about* that society; and *The Great Gatsby* presents a vivid picture of life in New York during Prohibition and the roaring twenties.

For some works, the author may create specific details of setting to highlight a theme. In Golding's novel *Lord of the Flies*, the island on which the story takes place has everything essential for basic survival: there is food and water, and the climate is temperate. In order to explore the moral questions of the boys' regression into savagery, Golding carefully establishes a setting in which survival itself is not a primary issue. In *Ethan Frome*, details of the harsh winter and of the isolation of a town "bypassed by the railroad" intensify the story of a man's desperately cold and isolated life.

Character and Characterization

We understand characters in fiction and drama as we do the people in our own lives, by what they say and do, and by what others say about them. Because characters are imagined and created by an author, we can even understand them more reliably and fully than we can many of the people around us. Many students find their greatest satisfaction in reading works about characters to whom they can relate, characters whose struggles are recognizable and whose feelings are familiar.

Understanding character in fiction means understanding a person's values and **motivation**, beliefs and principles, moral qualities, strengths and weaknesses, and degree of self-knowledge and understanding. To fully appreciate a work, the reader must understand what characters are searching for and devoting their lives to.

Literature also seeks to account for the forces outside individuals that influence the direction and outcome of their lives. These "forces" range from those of nature and history to the demands of family, community, and society. The response of characters to inner and outer forces is what literature depicts and makes comprehensible.

In literature courses and on examinations, discussions of character are the most common. That is because any meaningful or convincing plot stems from human thought, motive, and action. Depending on the narrative point of view (see page 47) a character's thoughts and feelings may be presented directly through **omniscient** narrative or first-person commentary. In "Young Goodman

Brown," the narrator tells us directly what the title character is thinking and feeling; in "Roman Fever," the most important revelations of character are discovered by the reader simultaneously with the two central characters. Character in drama is revealed directly in dialogue and action, but it may be expanded through soliloquies and asides. In Shakespeare's *Othello*, for example, the full extent of Iago's evil is revealed through the variety of methods he uses to manipulate different characters and through the soliloquies.

In some works, the author's primary purpose is to reveal character gradually through plot; in others, the author establishes understanding of character from the beginning in order to account for what happens. In the opening pages of *The Great Gatsby*, the narrator, Nick, who is also a character in the novel, introduces himself and declares his judgment of the moral quality of the people and events he is about to narrate. With Nick's own character and motives clearly established, the reader then shares his gradual discovery of the truth about Gatsby and his life.

Theme

The subjects of literature may come from any aspect of human experience: love, friendship, growing up, ambition, family relationships, conflicts with society, survival, war, evil, death, and so on. **Theme** in a work of literature is the understanding, insight, observation, and presentation of such subjects. Theme is what a work *says about* a subject. Themes are the central ideas of literary works.

One way to think about theme is to consider it roughly analogous to the topic or thesis of an expository essay. If the author of a novel, story, or play had chosen to examine the subjects of the work in an essay, what might be the topic assertions of such an essay? The student is cautioned, however, not to overinterpret the analogy. Themes in literature are rarely "morals," such as those found at the end of a fable, but neither are they "hidden meanings." Although scholars and critics often express thematic ideas in phrases, students are often required to express themes in full statements. In the next paragraph are some examples of statements about theme.

Macbeth is a play about the temptation to embrace evil forces and about the power of ambition to corrupt; Macbeth himself makes one of the most important statements of theme in the play when he says, "I do all that becomes a man/ who does more is none." *Ethan Frome* and Lardner's "Haircut" both illustrate that people in small towns do not truly understand the innermost needs and desires of people they think they know. William Golding's novel *Lord of the Flies* illustrates the bleak view that human beings' savage nature will prevail without external forces of authority, that human beings are not civilized in their fundamental natures. In contrast, in *Adventures of Huckleberry Finn*, Twain presents civilization as the source of corruption and finds truly moral behavior only in the runaway slave, Jim, and the ignorant boy, Huck.

ELEMENTS OF NONFICTION

Fiction and nonfiction share many common elements; they also make similar demands and offer comparable rewards to the thoughtful reader. In broad contrast to fiction, where characters and plot are imaginative creations of the author, nonfiction is about actual persons, experiences, and phenomena. Nonfiction also speculates on abstract and philosophical questions of history and politics, ethics and religion, culture and society, as well as the natural world. In biography and autobiography, the writer focuses on what is meaningful and interesting in the life of an individual.

On the Regents ELA exam you will read several examples of nonfiction. In Part 1 Reading Comprehension, you can expect to read one informational text, often on a historical or scientific topic. Part 2 requires reading at least four texts of informed argument and evidence to support a claim; and Part 3 Text Analysis often includes works of nonfiction, personal **narrative**. Authors of literary nonfiction often make imaginative use of **structure**, **chronology**, and **characterization**.

ELEMENTS OF POETRY

Part 1 of the Regents ELA exam will include one poem for close reading. The multiple-choice questions are designed to measure your skill at reading for the meaning. You are also expected to recognize and identify elements of poetry.

Poetry and Experience

In poetry, we are meant to sense a structure and to feel the rhythm (see **meter and rhythm**, page 64). The structure and rhythm of poetry may be formal, informal, even "free." Poetry is also characterized by its directness of effect and by its concentration—ideas and feelings are expressed in relatively few words. Karl Shapiro says, "Poems are what ideas feel like." Where the writer of prose may seek immediate clarity of meaning above all, the poet often seeks **ambiguity**, not to create "confusion," but to offer multiplicity of meaning: in single words, in images, in the meaning of the poem itself.

The experience of poetry is conveyed in vivid **imagery**, which appeals to the mind and to the senses. It is often expressed in **figurative language**; that is, through imaginative use of words and comparisons that are not literal but which create original, vivid, and often unexpected images and associations. (See **metaphor**, page 64, and **simile**, page 65.) Finally, in poetry there is particular significance in the way words and lines sound. The story or experience is enhanced through musical effects. A poem must be felt and heard!

Theme in Poetry

Some poems may assert a belief. Others may be a comment on the nature of human experience—love, death, loss or triumph, mystery and confusion, conflict and peace, on the humorous and the ironic, on the imagined and the unexpected in all its forms. Some poems reflect on the nature of time, of existence. Many poems are about poetry itself. These aspects of human experience are what we refer to as the **themes** of poetry.

Tone

Tone in poetry, as in prose and all forms of human communication, expresses the *attitude* of the speaker toward the reader or listener and toward the subject. Tone in literature is as varied as the range of human experience and feeling it reflects. When we speak of the *mood* of a piece of writing, we are also speaking of tone, of an overall feeling generated by the work.

Here are some terms to help you recognize and articulate **tone** or **mood** (see also Structure and Language in Poetry, beginning on page 61):

ambiguous	insistent	reconciled
amused	**ironic**	reflective
angry	melancholy	regretful
bitter	mournful	reminiscent
celebratory	mysterious	satiric
elegiac	nostalgic	sorrowful
grateful	optimistic	thoughtful
harsh	**paradoxical**	**understated**
humorous	questioning	

Note: Terms in bold are included in the glossary.

Reading and Writing About Literature

CHAPTER 5
Glossaries of Terms

STRUCTURE AND LANGUAGE IN PROSE

abstract In contrast to the *concrete*, abstract language expresses general ideas and concepts apart from specific examples or instances. Very formal writing is characterized by abstract expression. As a noun, *abstract* denotes a brief summary of the key ideas in a scientific, legal, or scholarly piece of writing.

analogy An expression of the similarities between things that are not wholly alike or related. (See *metaphor* in Structure and Language in Poetry, page 64.)

anecdote A very brief, usually vivid story or episode. Often humorous, anecdotes offer examples of typical behavior or illustrate the personality of a character. Writers of biography and autobiography make extensive use of anecdote to reveal the lives of their subjects.

antithesis In formal argument, a statement that opposes or contrasts a *thesis* statement. Informally, we use the term to refer to any expression or point of view completely opposed to another. In literature, even an experience or a feeling may be expressed as the *antithesis* of another. (See also *thesis*.)

argument In persuasive writing or speaking, the development of reasons to support the writer's position; it is the method of reasoning used to persuade. Informally, we may use the term to describe the development of a topic in any piece of expository writing. Historically, it has also denoted a summary of a literary work's plot or main ideas.

atmosphere Closely related to *tone* or mood, it refers to a pervasive feeling in a work. Atmosphere often stems from setting and from distinctive characters or actions. The atmosphere in many of Poe's stories is mysterious, troubling, even sinister. Hawthorne's "Young Goodman Brown" reflects the threatening and morally ambiguous world of its Puritan setting.

autobiography A formally composed account of a person's life, written by that person. Although we must trust, or be skeptical of, the reliability of the account, we often appreciate the firsthand narration of experience. Autobiography is also a rich source of information and insight into a historical period or into literary or artistic worlds. Autobiography, like the novel, has *narrative* and chronology. (See also *journal, memoir.*) We describe literary works that are closely based on the author's life as **autobiographical.** Eugene O'Neill's *Long Day's Journey into Night* and Tennessee Williams's *The Glass Menagerie* are plays that reflect many details of their authors' lives.

biography A narrative, historical account of the life, character, and significance of its subject. Contemporary biography is usually researched in detail and may not always be admiring of its subject. A critical biography of a literary figure includes discussion of the writer's works to show the writer's artistic development and career. Biographies of figures significant in history or public affairs also offer commentary on periods and events of historical importance.

character The imagined persons, created figures, who inhabit the worlds of fiction and drama. E. M. Forster distinguished between *flat* and *round* characters. Flat are those, like stereotypes, who represent a single and exaggerated human characteristic. Round are those whose aspects are complex and convincing, and who change or develop in the course of a work. In good fiction, plot must develop out of character. It is the desires, values, and motives of characters that account for the action and conflict in a plot.

characterization The method by which an author establishes character; the means by which personality, manner, and appearance are created. It is achieved directly through description and dialogue and indirectly through observations and reactions of other characters.

concrete The particular, the specific, in expression and imagery. That which is concrete can be perceived by the senses. Concrete also refers to that which is tangible, real, or actual, in contrast to *abstract*, which is intangible and conceptual.

conflict In the most general sense, it identifies the forces that give rise to a plot. This term may identify an actual struggle between characters, for anything from revenge to simple recognition or understanding. A plot may focus on conflict between characters and the forces of nature or society. These are essentially external conflicts. A work may also center on internal conflicts: characters' struggles to know or change themselves and their lives. Most works of fiction and drama contain more than one aspect of conflict. (See Plot and Conflict, page 45.)

denouement A French term meaning "untying a knot," it refers to the way the complications or conflict of a plot are finally resolved. It also refers to what is called the "falling action" in a drama: that part of the play that follows the dramatic climax and reveals the consequences of the main action for minor characters; it also accounts briefly for what happens in the world of the play after the principal drama is resolved. In Arthur Miller's *Death of a Salesman*, the "Requiem" may be considered a denouement: it accounts for the response to Willy's death of his wife, sons, and only friend. In Shakespeare's *Macbeth*, the climax is in the scene following the death of Lady Macbeth in which Macbeth understands that he has destroyed all capacity for feeling and has rendered his life meaningless; the denouement occurs in the battle scene in which Macbeth comprehends the treachery of the witches and is killed by Macduff, thus restoring the throne to the rightful heir, Malcolm.

determinism The philosophical view that human existence is determined by forces over which humans have little or no control. The concept that fate predestines the course of a character's life or a tragic figure's downfall is a form of determinism.

episode A series of actions or incidents that make up a self-contained part of a larger narrative. Some novels are structured so that each chapter is a significant episode. Fitzgerald's *The Great Gatsby* and Mark Twain's *Huckleberry Finn* are good examples. A *scene* in a play is often analogous to an episode in a narrative. Many television series are presented in weekly episodes.

essay Denotes an extended composition, usually expository, devoted to a single topic. Essays may be composed to persuade, to reflect on philosophical questions, to analyze a subject, to express an opinion, or to entertain. As a literary form, the essay dates from the sixteenth century and remains a popular and widely practiced form. The origin of the term is the French word *essai*, which means an attempt, a trying out of something. (See *formal/ informal essay*.)

exposition Writing whose purpose is to inform, illustrate, and explain. In literature, exposition refers to those passages or speeches in which setting, offstage or prior action, or a character's background is revealed.

In *The Great Gatsby*, Nick Carraway pauses in the narrative to give the reader additional information about Gatsby's background. The prologue to Shakespeare's *Romeo and Juliet* is an example of exposition.

flashback A presentation of incidents or episodes that occurred prior to the beginning of a narrative itself. When an author or filmmaker uses flashback, the "present" or forward motion of the plot is suspended. Flashback may be introduced through the device of a character's memory, or through the narrative voice itself. William Faulkner's "Barn Burning" and *Light in August* include vivid passages of memory and narrative flashback. Jack Burden's recounting of the Cass Mastern story in Robert Penn Warren's *All the King's Men* is also a form of flashback.

foreshadowing Establishing details or mood in a work that will become more significant as the plot progresses. Thoughtful readers usually sense such details and accumulate them in their memories. In one of the opening scenes of *Ethan Frome*, Ethan and Mattie talk about the dangers of sledding down Starkfield's steepest hill. In the second paragraph of Shirley Jackson's well-known story "The Lottery," the boys stuff their pockets with stones and make piles of them on the edge of the square.

form The organization, shape, and structure of a work. Concretely, form may refer to *genre* (see below); for example, the sonnet form, the tragic form. More abstractly, form also refers to the way we sense inherent structure and shape.

formal/informal essay In contrast to the formal essay, which emphasizes organization, logic, and explication of ideas, the informal essay emphasizes the voice and perspective of the writer. In the informal essay, also called a *personal essay*, the reader is aware of the author's *persona* and is asked to share the author's interest in the subject. Examples of a personal essay might be included in Part 1 Reading Comprehension, among the texts in Part 2 Argument, or in the Part 3 Text Analysis.

genre A type or form of literature. Examples include *novel, short story, epic poem, essay, sonnet,* and *tragedy.*

image Although suggesting something that is visualized, an image is an expression or recreation through language of *any* experience perceived directly through the senses. (See also Structure and Language in Poetry, page 64.)

irony In general, a tone or figure of speech in which there is a discrepancy—a striking difference or contradiction—between what is expressed and what is meant or expected. Irony achieves its powerful effect indirectly: in satire, for example, to ridicule or criticize. We also speak of dramatic irony when the narrator or reader understands more than the characters do.

journal A diary or notebook of personal observations. Many writers use journals to compose personal reflection and to collect ideas for their works. The journals of many writers have been published. Students are often urged to keep journals as a way to reflect on their reading, compose personal pieces, and practice writing free of concern for evaluation.

melodrama A plot in which incidents are sensational and designed to provoke immediate emotional responses. In melodrama, the "good" characters are pure and innocent and victims of the "bad" ones, who are thoroughly evil. The term refers to a particular kind of drama popular in the late nineteenth century and, later, in silent films and early Westerns. A work becomes melodramatic when it relies on improbable incidents and unconvincing characters for strong emotional effect.

memoir A form of autobiographical writing that reflects on the significant events the writer has observed and on the interesting and important personalities the writer has known. The Regents ELA Exam often includes examples of memoir among the texts for comprehension or analysis.

monologue In a play, an extended expression or speech by a single speaker that is uninterrupted by response from other characters. A monologue is addressed to a particular person or persons, who may or may not actually hear it. In Ring Lardner's short story "Haircut," a barber tells (narrates) the story to a customer (the reader) who is present but does not respond. (See also *dramatic monologue* in Structure and Language in Poetry, page 62.)

motivation The desires, values, needs, or impulses that move characters to act as they do. In good fiction, the reader understands, appreciates, and is convinced that a character's motivation accounts for the significant incidents and the outcome of a plot.

narrative point of view The standpoint, perspective, and degree of understanding from which a work of narrative fiction is told. (See *omniscient point of view, objective point of view.*)

narrator The character or author's *persona* that tells a story. It is through the perspective and understanding of the narrator that the reader experiences the work. In some works, the narrator may inhabit the world of the story or be a character in it. In other works, the narrator is a detached but knowledgeable observer.

naturalism Closely related to *determinism*, naturalism depicts characters who are driven not by personal will or moral principles but by natural forces that they do not fully understand or control. In contrast to other views of human experience, the naturalistic view makes no moral judgments on the lives of the characters. Their lives, often bleak or defeating, simply *are* as they are, determined by social, environmental, instinctive, and hereditary forces. Naturalism was in part a reaction by writers against the nineteenth-century Romantic view of man as master of his own fate. It is important to note, however, that none of the Naturalistic writers in America (Crane, Dreiser, London, Anderson, and Norris chief among them) presented a genuinely deterministic vision. Several of these authors began their careers in journalism and were drawn to the Naturalistic view of life as a result of their own experience and observation of life in America. (See also *realism.*)

objective point of view In fiction or nonfiction, this voice presents a story or information without expressed judgment or qualification. A fundamental principle of journalism is that news *reports* should be objective. Ernest Hemingway's short story "The Killers" is an example of fiction rendered in a completely detached, objective point of view.

omniscient point of view Spoken in third person (*she, he, they*), this is the broadest narrative perspective. The omniscient narrator speaks from outside the story and sees and knows everything about the characters and incidents. Omniscient narration is not limited by time or place. In *limited omniscient* point of view, the author may choose to reveal the story through full understanding of only one character and limit the action to those incidents in which this character is present.

persona A term from the Greek meaning "mask," it refers in literature to a narrative voice created by an author and through which the author speaks. A narrative persona usually has a perceptible, even distinctive, personality that contributes to our understanding of the story. In Nathaniel Hawthorne's *The Scarlet Letter,* the omniscient narrator has a distinctive persona whose attitudes toward Puritan society and the characters' lives are revealed throughout the novel.

plot The incidents and experiences of characters selected and arranged by the author to create a meaningful story. A good plot is convincing in terms of what happens and why.

poetic justice The concept that life's rewards and punishments should be perfectly appropriate and distributed in just proportions. In Ring Lardner's short story "Haircut," Jim Kendall's ironic fate is an example of poetic justice: he is a victim of one of his own crude and insensitive practical jokes. The short story "They Grind Exceeding Small," by Ben Ames Williams, is also a vivid example of what is meant by poetic justice.

point of view In nonfiction, this denotes the attitudes or opinions of the writer. In narrative fiction, it refers to how and by whom a story is told: the perspective of the narrator and the narrator's relationship to the story. Point of view may be *omniscient*, where the narrator knows everything about the characters and their lives; or, it may be *limited* to the understanding of a particular character or speaker. Point of view may also be described as *objective* or *subjective*. *Third-person* narrative refers to characters as "he, she, they;" *First-person* narrative is from the "I" point of view. J. D. Salinger's *Catcher in the Rye* and Mark Twain's *Huckleberry Finn* are told in the first person. *Second person*, the "you" form, is rare but is found in sermons addressed to a congregation or in essays of opinion addressed directly to a leader or public figure: "You, Mr. Mayor (Madame President), should do the following . . ." Political columnists occasionally write pieces in the second-person voice for the Op-Ed pages of newspapers.

prologue An introductory statement of the dramatic situation of a play. Shakespeare's *Romeo and Juliet* begins with a brief prologue. The first two pages of Fitzgerald's *The Great Gatsby* are a prologue to the story Nick Carraway will tell.

prose Most of what we write is prose, the expression in sentences and phrases that reflect the natural rhythms of speech. Prose is organized by paragraphs and is characterized by variety in sentence length and rhythm.

protagonist A term from ancient Greek drama, it refers to the central character, the hero or heroine, in a literary work.

realism The literary period in America following the Civil War is usually called the Age of Realism. Realism depicts the directly observable in everyday life. Realistic writers seek to *present* characters and situations as they would appear to a careful observer, not as they are imagined or created by the author. After 1865, American writers became increasingly interested in the sources of power and force, and in the means to survival and success, in an increasingly materialistic society. For writers of this period, realism was a literary mode to express a *naturalistic* philosophy. (See also *naturalism, verisimilitude.*)

rhetoric From Ancient Greece, the art of persuasion in speech or writing achieved through logical thought and skillful use of language.

rhetorical question A question posed in the course of an *argument* to provoke thought or to introduce a line of reasoning.

romance A novel or tale that includes elements of the supernatural, heroic adventure, or romantic passion. Hawthorne's *The Scarlet Letter* is a romance, not because it is a love story but because it goes beyond *verisimilitude* in dramatizing elements of demonic and mystical forces in the characters and their lives.

satire A form or style that uses elements of irony, ridicule, exaggeration, understatement, sarcasm, humor, or absurdity to criticize human behavior or a society. All satire is **ironic** (see *irony*) in that meaning or theme is conveyed in the discrepancy between what is said and what is meant, between what is and what should be, and between what appears and what truly is. Although satire is often entertaining, its purpose is serious and meant to provoke thought or judgment. The verses of Alexander Pope and many poems by e. e. cummings are satiric. In prose, much of the writing of Mark Twain is satire; *Huckleberry Finn* is the most striking example. Other American writers of satire include Sinclair Lewis, Edith Wharton, Aldous Huxley, Joseph Heller, Kurt Vonnegut, and Tom Wolfe. Popular television programs such as *The Daily Show*, *South Park*, and *The Simpsons* are also good examples of satire.

short story This form is distinguished from most novels not simply by length but by its focus on few characters and a central, revealing incident. In stories, however, there is as much variety in narrative point of view, subject, and technique as there is in novels. Edgar Allan Poe characterized the short story as "a short prose narrative, requiring from a half-hour to one or two hours in its perusal."

soliloquy A form of *monologue* in which a character expresses thoughts and feelings aloud but does not address them to anyone else or intend other characters in the work to hear them. In essence, the audience for a play is secretly listening in on a character's innermost thoughts. Macbeth's reflection on "Tomorrow, and tomorrow, and tomorrow . . ." is the best-known soliloquy in the play.

speaker The narrative voice in a literary work (see *persona*). Also, the character who speaks in a *dramatic monologue*.

symbol Most generally, anything that stands for or suggests something else. Language itself is symbolic: sounds and abstract written forms may be arranged to stand for virtually any human thought or experience. In literature, symbols are not Easter eggs, or mushrooms—they are not "hidden meanings." Symbols are real objects and *concrete* images that lead us to *think about* what is suggested. They organize a wide variety of ideas into single acts of understanding. They embody not single "meanings" but suggest whole areas of meaning.

theme Roughly analogous to *thesis* in an essay, this is an observation about human experience or an idea central to a work of literature. The *subject* of a work is in the specific setting, characters, and plot. Theme in a work of fiction is what is meaningful and significant to human experience generally. Themes are the ideas and truths that transcend the specific characters and plot. Shakespeare's *Macbeth* is about an ambitious nobleman who, encouraged by his equally ambitious wife, murders the king of Scotland in order to become king himself. The themes in *Macbeth* include the power of ambition to corrupt even those who are worthy and the mortal consequences of denying what is fundamental to one's nature.

thesis The central point, a statement of position in a formal or logical argument. Also used to refer to the topic or controlling idea of an essay. Use of the term *thesis* implies elaboration by reasons and examples.

tone The attitude of the writer toward the subject and toward the reader. (See the discussion in Chapter 4, page 52, and a glossary of Terms for Writing, page 68.)

transition A link between ideas or sections in a work. In prose arguments, single words such as *first, second, moreover,* and *therefore* or phrases such as *in addition, on the other hand,* and *in conclusion* serve as transitions. In fiction, a brief passage or chapter may serve as a transition. In *The Great Gatsby*, the narrator pauses from time to time to "fill in" the reader and to account for the passage of time between the dramatic episodes that make up the novel's main plot.

turning point In drama and fiction, the moment or episode in a plot when the action is moved toward its inevitable conclusion.

verisimilitude A literal quality in fiction and drama of being "true to life," of representing that which is real or actual. Verisimilitude in fiction is often achieved through specific, vivid description and dialogue; first-person narration also creates the effect of verisimilitude. In drama, it may be achieved through means of set, costumes, and lighting that are realistic in all their details.

STRUCTURE AND LANGUAGE IN POETRY

allegory A narrative, in prose or verse, in which abstract ideas, principles, human values, or states of mind are **personified**. The purpose of the allegory is to illustrate the significance of the ideas by dramatizing them. *Parable* and *fable* are particular kinds of allegory, in which a moral is illustrated in the form of a story.

alliteration The repetition of initial consonant sounds in words and syllables is one of the first patterns of sound a child creates; for example, "ma-ma; pa-pa." The stories of Dr. Seuss are told in alliteration and **assonance**. Poets use alliteration for its rich musical effect: "Fish, flesh, and fowl commend all summer long/Whatever is begotten, born, and dies" (Yeats); for humor: "Where at, with blade, with bloody, blameful blade/He bravely broached his boiling bloody breast" (Shakespeare); and to echo the sense of the lines: "The iron tongue of midnight hath told twelve" (Shakespeare).

allusion A reference to a historical event, to Biblical, mythological, or literary characters and incidents with which the reader is assumed to be familiar. Allusion may, with few words, enrich or extend the meaning of a phrase, idea, or image. Allusion may also be used for ironic effect. In his poem "Out, out . . ." Robert Frost expects the reader to recall from Macbeth's final soliloquy the line, "Out, out brief candle!" Such expressions as "a Herculean task" or "Achilles heel," are also forms of allusion.

ambiguity Denotes uncertainty of meaning. In literature and especially in poetry, we speak of intentional ambiguity, the use of language and images to suggest more than one meaning at the same time.

assonance The repetition of vowel sounds among words that begin or end with different consonants.

ballads Narrative poems, sometimes sung, that tell dramatic stories of individual episodes and characters.

blank verse Unrhymed *iambic pentameter*, usually in "paragraphs" of verse instead of stanzas. Shakespeare's plays are composed primarily in blank verse. For example, from *Macbeth* (Act I, Scene 5):

> Your face, my Thane, is as a book where men
> May read strange matters. To beguile the time,
> Look like the time; bear welcome in your eye,
> Your hand, your tongue; look like the innocent flower,
> But be the serpent under't . . .

connotation The feelings, attitudes, images, and associations of a word or expression. Connotations are usually said to be "positive" or "negative."

couplet Two lines of verse with similar meter and end ryhme. Couplets generally have self-contained ideas as well, so they may function as stanzas within a poem. In the English (Shakespearean) *sonnet*, the couplet serves as a conclusion. You will also discover that many scenes in Shakespeare's plays end with rhymed couplets: "Away, and mock the time with fairest show/False face must hide what the false heart doth know." (*Macbeth* Act I, Scene 7)

denotation That which a word actually names, identifies, or "points to." Denotation is sometimes referred to as "the dictionary definition" of a word.

dramatic monologue A poem in which a fictional character, at a critical or dramatic point in life, addresses a particular "audience," which is identifiable but silent. In the course of the monologue, we learn a great deal, often ironically, about the character who is speaking and the circumstances that have led to the speech. Robert Browning is the best-known 19th-century poet to compose dramatic monologues; "My Last Duchess" is a famous example. In the 20th century, such poets as Kenneth Fearing, E. A. Robinson, T. S. Eliot ("The Love Song of J. Alfred Prufrock"), Robert Frost, and Amy Lowell composed well-known dramatic monologues.

elegy A meditative poem mourning the death of an individual.

epic A long narrative poem often centering on a heroic figure who represents the fate of a great nation or people. *The Iliad* and *The Odyssey* of Homer, *The Aeneid* of Vergil, and the Anglo-Saxon *Beowulf* are well-known epics. Milton's *Paradise Lost* and Dante's *Divine Comedy* are examples of epic narratives in which subjects of great human significance are dramatized. *Omeros*, by Derek Walcott, is a contemporary example of an epic poem.

figurative language The intentional and imaginative use of words and comparisons that are not literal but that create original, vivid, and often unexpected images and associations. Figurative language is also called *metaphorical language.* (See *metaphor* and *simile.*)

free verse A poem written in free verse develops images and ideas in patterns of lines without specific metrical arrangements or formal rhyme. Free verse is distinguished from prose, however, because it retains such poetic elements as assonance, alliteration, and figurative language. The poetry of Walt Whitman and e. e. cummings offers striking examples. The poem "View with a Grain of Sand" on page 11 is also an example of free verse.

hyperbole An exaggerated expression (also called overstatement) for a particular effect, which may be humorous, satirical, or intensely emotional. Hyperbole is the expression of folktales and legends and, of course, of lovers: Romeo says to Juliet, "there lies more peril in thine eye/Than twenty of their swords." Hyperbole is often the expression of any overwhelming feeling. After he murders King Duncan, Macbeth looks with horror at his bloody hands: "Will all great Neptune's ocean wash this blood/Clean from my hand . . . ?" In her sleepwalking scene, Lady Macbeth despairs that "All the perfumes of Arabia will not sweeten this little hand." And everyone of us has felt, "I have mountains of work to do!"

iambic pentameter The basic meter of English speech: "I think I know exactly what you need/and yet at times I know that I do not." Formally, it identifies verse of ten syllables to the line, with the second, fourth, sixth, eighth, and tenth accented. There is, however, variation in the stresses within lines to reflect natural speech—and to avoid a "sing-song" or nursery rhyme effect. It is the meter in which most of the dialogue in Shakespeare's plays is composed (see *blank verse*).

image Images and imagery are the heart of poetry. Although the term suggests only something that is visualized, an image is the re-creation through language of *any* experience perceived directly through the senses.

internal rhyme A pattern in which a word or words within a line rhyme with the word that ends it. Poets may also employ internal rhyme at irregular intervals over many lines.

irony In general, a tone or figure of speech in which there is a discrepancy—a striking difference or contradiction—between what is expressed and what is meant or expected. Irony may be used to achieve a powerful effect indirectly. In satire, for example, it may be used to ridicule or criticize.

metaphor A form of analogy. Metaphorical expression is the heart of poetry. Through metaphor, a poet discovers and expresses a similarity between dissimilar things. The poet uses metaphor to imaginatively find common qualities between things we would not normally or literally compare. As a figure of speech, metaphor is said to be implicit or indirect, in contrast to simile where the comparison is expressed directly. In his final soliloquy, which begins "Tomorrow, and tomorrow, and tomorrow . . ." Macbeth creates a series of metaphors to express the meaninglessness of his own life: "Life's but a walking shadow, a poor player . . . it is a tale told by an idiot . . ." When we say, "the trip was a nightmare . . . ," or that "the meeting turned into a circus . . . ," we are speaking in metaphor.

meter and rhythm Rhythm refers to the pattern of movement in a poem. As music has rhythm, so does poetry. Meter refers to specific patterns of stressed and unstressed syllables. (See *imabic pentameter*.)

ode A meditation or celebration of a specific subject. Traditional odes addressed "elevated" ideas and were composed in elaborate stanza forms. Keats's "Ode to a Nightingale" and "Ode to Autumn" are particularly fine examples. Modern odes may address subjects either serious or personal. One well-known contemporary ode is Pablo Neruda's "Ode to My Socks."

onomatopoeia The use of words whose sound reflects their sense. "Buzz," "hiss," and "moan" are common examples.

oxymoron Closely related to *paradox*, oxymoron is a figure of speech in which two contradictory or sharply contrasting terms are paired for emphasis or ironic effect. Students' favorite examples include "jumbo shrimp" and "army intelligence." Poets have written of the "wise fool," a "joyful sadness," or an "eloquent silence."

paradox An expression, concept, or situation whose literal statement is contradictory, yet which makes a truthful and meaningful observation. Consider the widely used expression, "less is more," for example. Shakespeare's play *Macbeth* opens with a series of paradoxes to establish the moral atmosphere in which "foul is fair." John Donne's famous poem "Death Be Not Proud" ends with the paradox "Death thou shalt die."

personification A form of metaphor or simile in which nonhuman things—objects, plants and animals, forces of nature, abstract ideas—are given human qualities. Examples include "Pale flakes . . . come feeling for our faces . . ." (Owen); "Time . . . the thief of youth," (Milton); and "Blow winds, and crack your cheeks! Blow! Rage!" (Shakespeare).

prose poem This form appears on the page in the sentences and paragraphs of prose yet its effect is achieved through rhythm, images, and patterns of sound associated with poetry. The poetry of Karl Shapiro offers many excellent examples.

quatrain A stanza of four lines. The quatrain is the most commonly used stanza form in English poetry. Quatrains may be rhymed, *abab, aabb, abba,* for example, or they may be unrhymed.

rhyme In general, any repetition of identical or similar sounds among words that are close enough together to form an audible pattern. Rhyme is most evident when it occurs at the ends of lines of metrical verse.

rhyme scheme A regular pattern of end rhyme in a poem. The rhyme scheme in Shakespeare's sonnets, for example, is *abab/cdcd/efef/gg.*

satire A form or style that uses elements of irony, ridicule, exaggeration, understatement, sarcasm, humor, or absurdity to criticize human behavior or a society. All satire is **ironic** in that meaning or theme is conveyed in the discrepancy between what is said and what is meant, between what is and what should be, between what appears and what truly is. Although satire is often entertaining, its purpose is serious and meant to provoke thought or judgment. The verse of Alexander Pope is often extended satire, and many poems by e. e. cummings are satiric.

simile An expression that is a direct comparison of two things. It uses such words as *like, as, as if, seems, appears.* For example, "A line of elms plunging and tossing like horses" (Theodore Roethke); "Mind in its purest play is like some bat" (Richard Wilbur); "I wandered lonely as a cloud" (William Wordsworth).

soliloquy A form of monologue found most often in drama. It differs from a dramatic monologue in that the speaker is alone, revealing thoughts and feelings to or for oneself that are intentionally unheard by other characters. In Shakespeare's plays, for example, the principal characters' reflections on how to act or questions of conscience are revealed in their soliloquies. Hamlet's "To be, or not to be . . ." is probably the most famous of dramatic soliloquies.

sonnet A poem of fourteen lines in *iambic pentameter* that may be composed of different patterns of stanzas and rhyme schemes. The most common forms are the English, or Shakespearean sonnet, which consists of three quatrains and a closing couplet, and the Italian sonnet, which consists of an *octave* of eight lines and a *sestet* of six lines.

speaker The narrative voice in a poem. Also, the character who speaks in a *dramatic monologue*.

stanza The grouping of lines within a poem. A stanza reflects the basic organization and development of ideas, much as paragraphs do in an essay. Many stanza patterns may have a fixed number of lines and a regular pattern of rhyme. Poets, however, often create stanzas of varying length and form within a single poem. A stanza that ends with a period, completing an idea or image, is considered "closed," whereas a stanza that ends with a comma or with no punctuation is called "open," indicating that there should be very little pause in the movement from one stanza to another.

symbol Most generally, anything that stands for or suggests something else. Language itself is symbolic: sounds and abstract written forms may stand for virtually any human thought or experience. Symbols are real objects and *concrete* images that lead us to *think about* what is suggested. Symbols organize a wide variety of ideas into single acts of understanding. They embody not single "meanings" but suggest whole areas of meaning.

understatement Expression in which something is presented as less important or significant than it really is. Understatement is often used for humorous, satiric, or *ironic* effect. Much of the satire in *Huckleberry Finn* stems from Huck's naive and understated observations. One particular form of understatement, actually a double negative, includes such expressions as "I was not uninterested," which really means "I was interested"; or "He was not without imagination," which really means "He had some imagination."

TERMS FOR WRITING

anecdote A brief story or account of a single experience, often biographical, that illustrates something typical or striking about a person. Anecdotes, like parables, are effective as vivid, specific examples of a general observation or quality.

argument The development of reasons and examples to support a thesis; narrowly, to outline a position on an issue or problem with the intent to clarify or persuade. Argument is also used in a broad sense to refer to the way a writer develops any topic. See Chapter 2, page 22 for an explanation and examples of Argument, Part 2 of the Regents ELA Exam.

audience For the writer, this term refers to the intended reader. Awareness of an audience determines, for example, what the writer may assume a reader already knows, the level of diction, and the tone.

coherence A piece of writing has coherence when the logical relationship of ideas is evident and convincing. In a coherent discussion, statements and sections follow one another in a natural, even inevitable way. A coherent discussion hangs together; an incoherent one is scattered and disorganized.

description The expression in words of what is experienced by the senses. Good description recreates what is felt, seen, heard—sensed in any way. We also use the term describe to mean *identify, classify, characterize*, even for abstract ideas. Description permits readers to re-create the subject in their own imaginations.

diction Refers to word choice. Diction may be formal or informal, complex or simple, or elegant or modest, depending on the occasion and the audience. The language used in casual conversation is different from the language used in formal writing. The good writer uses language that is varied, precise, and vivid. The good writer has resources of language to suit a wide range of purposes. In the rubrics for the ELA Exam, diction is evaluated as use of "formal style and precise language."

exposition The development of a topic through examples, reasons, and details that explain, clarify, show, and instruct—the primary purpose of exposition is to convey information. Much of the writing assigned to students is referred to as expository writing. Through exposition, you can demonstrate what you have learned, discovered, understood, appreciated. The task for Part 3 of the Regents ELA Exam is a good example of what is meant by expository writing.

focus Refers to the way a writer concentrates and directs all the information, examples, ideas, and reasons in an essay on the specific topic.

narrative Because it tells a story, a narrative has chronological order. The narrative method is commonly used in exposition when examples are offered in a chronological development.

prompt A set of directions for a writing task; may also be a quote or passage meant to stimulate a piece of writing.

tone Refers to the attitude of the writer toward the subject and/or toward the reader. Tone may range from *harsh and insistent* to *gentle and reflective*. There is as much variety of tone in writing as there is in human feeling. Some pieces, essays of opinion for example, usually have a very distinct tone. Other works, especially in fiction or personal expression, may be more subtle and indirect in tone.

transition Words or phrases used to link ideas and sections in a piece of writing. Common transitions include *first, second . . . in addition . . . finally; on the other hand, moreover, consequently, therefore.* Transitions make the development of an argument clear.

unity In the narrowest sense, unity refers to focus: the ideas and examples are clearly related to the topic and to one another. In the largest sense, unity refers to a feature of our best writing. All elements—ideas, form, language, and tone—work together to achieve the effect of a complete and well-made piece.

A Guide to Proofreading for Common Errors

THE BASICS

Review your essays to make sure that you have begun sentences with capital letters and ended them with a period! Carelessness in this basic use of the conventions could lower your score if the test raters feel that you have not mastered this aspect of formal writing.

PUNCTUATION

COMMA USE

There is one general guideline to keep in mind for comma use: The primary function of the comma is to prevent confusion for your reader. The comma shows how separate parts of sentences are related to one another.

Introductory clauses and phrases need a comma. This makes it clear where the introduction ends and the main clause begins. Note the following examples:

> *"Though I have traveled all over the world, it is the smell of the tides and marshes of Beaufort County that identifies and shapes me."*

> *"Because I came to Beaufort County when I was a boy, my novels all smell of seawater."*
>
> —Pat Conroy

Use the comma in compound sentences with coordinating conjunctions *and, but, yet, so, or, for.* A compound sentence joins two or more independent clauses that could be expressed separately as simple sentences. *Note that the comma precedes the conjunction:*

"I walked slowly, for the detail on the beach was infinite."
—Ernie Pyle

"The luncheon hour was long past, and the two had their end of the vast terrace to themselves."
—Edith Wharton

A final suggestion: Use a comma only where you *hear* a clear need for one.

THE APOSTROPHE

Remember, the most common use of the apostrophe is to show possession.

The *novel's* major themes = The major themes **of the novel**
Fiction reveals *characters'* motives and actions = The motives **of the characters**
Shakespeare dramatizes *Macbeth's* struggle with his conscience and ambition.

Avoid the increasingly common error of using the apostrophe to show the plural.

Mark Twain wrote several **novels;** he did not write "novel's."
Holden Caulfield spends several **days** (not day's) in New York before going home.
Students in New York State are expected to read at least 25 **books** (not book's) per year.

GRAMMAR

SUBJECT/VERB AGREEMENT

Be sure to match subjects and verbs. Agreement is a form of consistency and is one of the most basic elements of grammar. When you learn to conjugate verbs, for example, you are applying the concept of agreement. Singular subjects take singular verbs; plural subjects take plural verbs.

He speaks/they speak; One is/many are

PRONOUN/ANTECEDENT AGREEMENT

Because pronouns replace nouns or other pronouns, they must agree with their singular or plural antecedents.

Evelyn is very grateful to *her parents* for *their* constant support and encouragement.

Most pronoun/antecedent errors arise when we use the indefinite pronouns *anyone, anybody, everyone, everybody, someone, somebody, no one,* and so on. These pronouns are singular because they refer to *individuals:*

Everybody is responsible for *his* own work.
Someone has left *her* books on the floor.
If *anyone* calls while I am out, please tell *him* or *her* that I will call back after lunch.

The common practice of replacing *him/her* with *them,* or *her/his* with *their,* solves the problem of choosing gender, but it is ungrammatical and illogical. The careful writer (and speaker) avoids these errors, or rewrites:

Please tell *anyone who calls* that I will return at noon.
Someone's books have been left on the floor.
Everyone has individual responsibility for the assignments.

SPELLING

You are, of course, expected to spell correctly common words, the key terms of your essay, and the names of authors, titles, and characters. An occasional misspelling in an on-demand piece of writing should not lower your score if all other elements are good.

Be especially careful to proofread for these very common errors—they mar the overall impression that your essay makes on the reader.

accept/except
To *accept* is to receive, take willingly, agree to:
I *accept* your offer, apology, invitation
To *except* is to exclude, to separate out:
I will *except* you from the requirement.
Except is also a preposition:
Everyone *except* him will be leaving on Tuesday.

affect/effect
To *affect* (v.) means to move, influence, or change.
To *affect* also means to put on an artificial quality of personality or character; an exaggerated or artificial person may be called *affected.*
The *effects* (n.) are the consequences or results.
To *effect* (v.) means to put into action, to complete—a plan or a change, for example.

could of/should of

You mean *could have/should have*.

Do not make this unfortunate confusion in the way words sound!

hear/here

You may put your things *here* on the table.

I cannot *hear* you with all the noise outside.

its/it's

it's = a contraction for *it is*

its = a possessive form; do not add an apostrophe

loose/lose

Be careful not to *lose* your ticket; it cannot be replaced.

The dog ran *loose* when the leash broke.

principal/principle

Lack of effort is often the *principal* reason for failure.

Many consider honesty a fundamental *principle* in their lives.

than/then

My sister is several years younger *than* I am.

You will answer multiple-choice questions, *then* complete your essays.

there/their/they're

There he goes! It is over *there*.

Students should bring *their* books to class everyday.

They're = *they are*

to/too/two

You will have *two* weeks *to* complete the reading assignment; do not put it off until it is *too* late.

who's/whose

Who's (who is) that coming down the hall?

Whose books are these lying on the floor?

Appendices

The New York State Learning Standards for English Language Arts

The following 11/12 grade-specific standards define end-of-year expectations and a cumulative progression designed to enable students to meet college and career readiness (CCR) expectations no later than the end of high school. The ELA/Regents Exam is designed to assess many (but not all) of the standards in each of the categories: Reading Literature, Reading Informational Texts, Writing, and Language. Note that the 2017 Revised Standards now include reading for Literature and reading for Informational Texts in a single set of standards (RL and RI).

2017 REVISED ELA STANDARDS FOR READING–Literature and Informational Texts (RL and RI)

11-12R1: Cite strong and thorough textual evidence to support analysis of what the text says explicitly/implicitly and make logical inferences, including determining where the text is ambiguous; develop questions for deeper understanding and for further exploration. (RI&RL)

11-12R2: Determine two or more themes or central ideas in a text and analyze their development, including how they emerge and are shaped and refined by specific details; objectively and accurately summarize a complex text. (RI&RL)

11-12R3: In literary texts, analyze the impact of author's choices. (RL) In informational texts, analyze a complex set of ideas or sequence of events and explain how specific individuals, ideas, or events interact and develop. (RI)

11-12R4: Determine the meaning of words and phrases as they are used in a text, including figurative and connotative meanings. Analyze the impact of specific word choices on meaning, tone, and mood, including words with multiple meanings. Analyze how an author uses and refines the meaning of technical or key term(s) over the course of a text. (RI&RL)

11-12R5: In literary texts, analyze how varied aspects of structure create meaning and affect the reader. (RL) In informational texts, analyze the impact and evaluate the effect structure has on exposition or argument in terms of clarity, persuasive/rhetorical technique, and audience appeal. (RI)

11-12R6: Analyze how authors employ point of view, perspective, and purpose to shape explicit and implicit messages (e.g., persuasiveness, aesthetic quality, satire, sarcasm, irony, or understatement). (RI&RL)

11-12R7: In literary texts, analyze multiple adaptations of a source text as presented in different formats (e.g., works of art, graphic novels, music, film, etc.), specifically evaluating how each version interprets the source. (RL) In informational texts, integrate and evaluate sources on the same topic or argument in order to address a question or solve a problem. (RI)

11-12R8: Delineate and evaluate an argument in applicable texts, applying a lens (e.g., constitutional principles, logical fallacy, legal reasoning, belief systems, codes of ethics, philosophies, etc.) to assess the validity or fallacy of key arguments, determining whether the supporting evidence is relevant and sufficient. (RI&RL)

11-12R9: Choose and develop criteria to evaluate the quality of texts. Make connections to other texts, ideas, cultural perspectives, eras, and personal experiences. (RI&RL)

WRITING STANDARDS GRADES 11/12 (W)

1. Write arguments to support claims in an analysis of substantive topics or texts, using valid reasoning and relevant and sufficient evidence.

2. Write informative/explanatory texts to examine and convey complex ideas and information clearly and accurately through the effective selection, organization, and analysis of content.

3. Write narratives to develop real or imagined experiences or events using effective technique, well-chosen details, and well-structured event sequences.

4. Produce clear and coherent writing in which the development, organization, and style are appropriate to task, purpose, and audience.

5. Develop and strengthen writing as needed by planning, revising, editing, rewriting, or trying a new approach.

6. Use technology, including the Internet, to produce and publish writing and to interact and collaborate with others.

7. Conduct short as well as more sustained research projects based on focused questions, demonstrating understanding of the subject under investigation.

8. Gather relevant information from multiple print and digital sources, assess the credibility and accuracy of each source, and integrate the information while avoiding plagiarism.

9. Draw evidence from literary or informational texts to support analysis, reflection, and research.

10. Write routinely over extended time frames (time for research, reflection, and revision) and shorter time frames (a single sitting or a day or two) for a range of tasks, purposes, and audiences.

11. Develop personal, cultural, textual, and thematic connections within and across genres as they respond to texts through written, digital, and oral presentations, employing a variety of media and genres.

LANGUAGE STANDARDS GRADES 11/12 (L)

Conventions of Standard English

1. Demonstrate command of the conventions of standard English grammar and usage when writing or speaking.

2. Demonstrate command of the conventions of standard English capitalization, punctuation, and spelling when writing.

Knowledge of Language

3. Apply knowledge of language to understand how language functions in different contexts, to make effective choices for meaning or style, and to comprehend more fully when reading or listening.

Vocabulary Acquisition and Use

4. Determine or clarify the meaning of unknown and multiple meaning words and phrases by using context clues, analyzing meaningful word parts, and consulting general and specialized reference materials, as appropriate.

5. Demonstrate understanding of figurative language, word relationships, and nuances in word meanings.

6. Acquire and use accurately a range of general academic and domain-specific words and phrases sufficient for reading, writing, speaking, and listening at the college and career readiness level; demonstrate independence in gathering vocabulary knowledge when considering a word or phrase important to comprehension or expression.

HOW IS THE REGENTS ELA EXAM SCORED?

WEIGHTING OF PARTS

Each of the three parts of the Regents Examination in English Language Arts has a number of raw score credits associated with the questions/tasks within that part. In order to ensure an appropriate distribution of credits across the test, each part is weighted.

For Part 1, each multiple-choice question is worth one point. The Part 2 essay is scored on a 6-point rubric then weighted × 4. The Part 3 Text Analysis is scored on a 4-point rubric and then weighted × 2.

As you can see, the Part 2 Argument Essay is the most heavily weighted section.

The table below shows the raw score credits, weighting factor, and weighted score credits for each part of the test.

Part	Maximum Raw Score Credits	Weighting Factor	Maximum Weighted Score Credits
Part 1	24	1	24
Part 2	6	4	24
Part 3	4	2	8
			Total 56

A student's final exam score is then determined in the conversion of the weighted score (of up to 56 points) on a scale of 0–100. Here is an example from a recent ELA exam:

SCORING RUBRICS FOR THE REGENTS ELA EXAM

Parts 2 and 3 of the Regents Examination in English Language Arts is scored using holistic rubrics. Part 2 is scored using a 6-credit rubric, and Part 3 is scored using a 4-credit rubric. Both rubrics reflect the demands called for by the Learning Standards for English Language Arts and Literacy through the end of Grade 11.

Regents Examination in English Language Arts—January 2017

Chart for Converting Total Weighted Raw Scores to Final Exam Scores (Scale Scores) (Use for the January 2017 examination only.)

Weighted Raw Score*	Scale Score	Performance Level	Weighted Raw Score*	Scale Score	Performance Level
56	100	5	27	55	2
55	99	5	26	52	1
54	99	5	25	48	1
53	98	5	24	45	1
52	97	5	23	42	1
51	96	5	22	38	1
50	95	5	21	35	1
49	95	5	20	31	1
48	94	5	19	27	1
47	92	5	18	24	1
46	91	5	17	20	1
45	90	5	16	17	1
44	89	5	15	14	1
43	88	5	14	11	1
42	87	5	13	9	1
41	86	5	12	8	1
40	85	5	11	7	1
39	83	4	10	6	1
38	81	4	9	5	1
37	80	4	8	4	1
36	79	4	7	4	1
35	76	3	6	3	1
34	74	3	5	2	1
33	71	3	4	2	1
32	69	3	3	1	1
31	66	3	2	1	1
30	65	3	1	1	1
29	61	2	0	0	1
28	58	2			

The conversion table is determined independently for each administration of the exam. You will find the conversion tables for each exam in the Answers Explained.

New York State Regents Examination in English Language Arts (Common Core)
Part 2 Rubric
Writing from Sources: Argument

Criteria	6 Essays at this Level	5 Essays at this Level	4 Essays at this Level	3 Essays at this Level	2 Essays at this Level	1 Essays at this Level
Content and Analysis: the extent to which the essay conveys complex ideas and information clearly and accurately in order to support claims in an analysis of the texts	-introduce a precise and insightful claim, as directed by the task -demonstrate in-depth and insightful analysis of the texts, as necessary to support the claim and to distinguish the claim from alternate or opposing claims	-introduce a precise and thoughtful claim, as directed by the task -demonstrate thorough analysis of the texts, as necessary to support the claim and to distinguish the claim from alternate or opposing claims	-introduce a precise claim, as directed by the task -demonstrate appropriate and accurate analysis of the texts, as necessary to support the claim and to distinguish the claim from alternate or opposing claims	-introduce a reasonable claim, as directed by the task -demonstrate some analysis of the texts, but insufficiently distinguish the claim from alternate or opposing claims	-introduce a claim -demonstrate confused or unclear analysis of the texts, failing to distinguish the claim from alternate or opposing claims	-do not introduce a claim -do not demonstrate analysis of the texts
Command of Evidence: the extent to which the essay presents evidence from the provided texts to support analysis	-present ideas fully and thoughtfully, making highly effective use of a wide range of specific and relevant evidence to support analysis -demonstrate proper citation of sources to avoid plagiarism when dealing with direct quotes and paraphrased material	-present ideas clearly and accurately, making effective use of specific and relevant evidence to support analysis -demonstrate proper citation of sources to avoid plagiarism when dealing with direct quotes and paraphrased material	-present ideas sufficiently, making adequate use of specific and relevant evidence to support analysis -demonstrate proper citation of sources to avoid plagiarism when dealing with direct quotes and paraphrased material	-present ideas briefly, making use of some specific and relevant evidence to support analysis -demonstrate inconsistent citation of sources to avoid plagiarism when dealing with direct quotes and paraphrased material	-present ideas inconsistently and/or inaccurately, in an attempt to support analysis, making use of some evidence that may be irrelevant -demonstrate little use of citations to avoid plagiarism when dealing with direct quotes and paraphrased material	-present little or no evidence from the texts -do not make use of citations

Criteria						
Coherence, Organization, and Style: the extent to which the essay logically organizes complex ideas, concepts, and information using formal style and precise language	-exhibit skillful organization of ideas and information to create a cohesive and coherent essay -establish and maintain a formal style, using sophisticated language and structure	-exhibit logical organization of ideas and information to create a cohesive and coherent essay -establish and maintain a formal style, using fluent and precise language and sound structure	-exhibit acceptable organization of ideas and information to create a coherent essay -establish and maintain a formal style, using precise and appropriate language and structure	-exhibit some organization of ideas and information to create a mostly coherent essay -establish but fail to maintain a formal style, using primarily basic language and structure	-exhibit inconsistent organization of ideas and information, failing to create a coherent essay -lack a formal style, using some language that is inappropriate or imprecise	-exhibit little organization of ideas and information -are minimal, making assessment unreliable -use language that is predominantly incoherent, inappropriate, or copied directly from the task or texts
Control of Conventions: the extent to which the essay demonstrates command of conventions of standard English grammar, usage, capitalization, punctuation, and spelling	-demonstrate control of conventions with essentially no errors, even with sophisticated language	-demonstrate control of the conventions, exhibiting occasional errors only when using sophisticated language	-demonstrate partial control, exhibiting occasional errors that do not hinder comprehension	-demonstrate emerging control, exhibiting occasional errors that hinder comprehension	-demonstrate a lack of control, exhibiting frequent errors that make comprehension difficult	-are minimal, making assessment of conventions unreliable

- An essay that addresses fewer texts than required by the task can be scored no higher than a 3.
- An essay that is a personal response and makes little or no reference to the task or texts can be scored no higher than a 1.
- An essay that is totally copied from the task and/or texts with no original student writing must be scored a 0.
- An essay that is totally unrelated to the task, illegible, incoherent, blank, or unrecognizable as English must be scored as a 0.

New York State Regents Examination in English Language Arts (Common Core)
Part 3 Rubric
Text Analysis: Exposition

Criteria	4 Responses at this Level	3 Responses at this Level	2 Responses at this Level	1 Responses at this Level
Content and Analysis: the extent to which the response conveys complex ideas and information clearly and accurately in order to respond to the task and support an analysis of the text	-introduce a well-reasoned central idea and a writing strategy that clearly establish the criteria for analysis -demonstrate a thoughtful analysis of the author's use of the writing strategy to develop the central idea	-introduce a clear central idea and a writing strategy that establish the criteria for analysis -demonstrate an appropriate analysis of the author's use of the writing strategy to develop the central idea	-introduce a central idea and/or a writing strategy -demonstrate a superficial analysis of the author's use of the writing strategy to develop the central idea	-introduce a confused or incomplete central idea or writing strategy and/or -demonstrate a minimal analysis of the author's use of the writing strategy to develop the central idea
Command of Evidence: the extent to which the response presents evidence from the provided text to support analysis	-present ideas clearly and consistently, making effective use of specific and relevant evidence to support analysis	-present ideas sufficiently, making adequate use of relevant evidence to support analysis	-present ideas inconsistently, inadequately, and/or inaccurately in an attempt to support analysis, making use of some evidence that may be irrelevant	-present little or no evidence from the text
Coherence, Organization, and Style: the extent to which the response logically organizes complex ideas, concepts, and information using formal style and precise language	-exhibit logical organization of ideas and information to create a cohesive and coherent response -establish and maintain a formal style, using precise language and sound structure	-exhibit acceptable organization of ideas and information to create a coherent response -establish and maintain a formal style, using appropriate language and structure	-exhibit inconsistent organization of ideas and information, failing to create a coherent response -lack a formal style, using language that is basic, inappropriate, or imprecise	-exhibit little or no organization of ideas and information -use language that is predominantly incoherent, inappropriate, or copied directly from the task or text -are minimal, making assessment unreliable

| Control of Conventions: the extent to which the response demonstrates command of conventions of standard English grammar, usage, capitalization, punctuation, and spelling | -demonstrate control of the conventions with infrequent errors | -demonstrate partial control of conventions with occasional errors that do not hinder comprehension | -demonstrate emerging control of conventions with some errors that hinder comprehension | -demonstrate a lack of control of conventions with frequent errors that make comprehension difficult
-are minimal, making assessment of conventions unreliable |

- A response that is a personal response and makes little or no reference to the task or text can be scored no higher than a 1.
- A response that is totally copied from the text with no original writing must be given a 0.
- A response that is totally unrelated to the task, illegible, incoherent, blank, or unrecognizable as English must be scored as a 0.

Regents ELA
Examinations
and Answers

Regents ELA Examination June 2016

English Language Arts

PART 1—Reading Comprehension

Directions (1–24): Closely read each of the three passages below. After each passage, there are several multiple-choice questions. Select the best suggested answer to each question and write its number in the space provided. You may use the margins to take notes as you read.

Reading Comprehension Passage A

. . .When the short days of winter came dusk fell before we had well
eaten our dinners. When we met in the street the houses had grown sombre.
The space of sky above us was the colour of ever-changing violet and towards
it the lamps of the street lifted their feeble lanterns. The cold air stung
(5) us and we played till our bodies glowed. Our shouts echoed in the silent
street. The career of our play brought us through the dark muddy lanes
behind the houses where we ran the gauntlet of the rough tribes[1] from the
cottages, to the back doors of the dark dripping gardens where odours arose
from the ashpits, to the dark odorous stables where a coach man smoothed
(10) and combed the horse or shook music from the buckled harness. When we
returned to the street light from the kitchen windows had filled the areas.
If my uncle was seen turning the corner we hid in the shadow until we had
seen him safely housed. Or if Mangan's sister came out on the doorstep
to call her brother in to his tea we watched her from our shadow peer up
(15) and down the street. We waited to see whether she would remain or go in

---

[1]tribes—gangs

and, if she remained, we left our shadow and walked up to Mangan's steps resignedly. She was waiting for us, her figure defined by the light from the half-opened door. Her brother always teased her before he obeyed and I stood by the railings looking at her. Her dress swung as she moved her body
(20) and the soft rope of her hair tossed from side to side.

Every morning I lay on the floor in the front parlour watching her door. The blind was pulled down to within an inch of the sash so that I could not be seen. When she came out on the doorstep my heart leaped. I ran to the hall, seized my books and followed her. I kept her brown figure always in
(25) my eye and, when we came near the point at which our ways diverged, I quickened my pace and passed her. This happened morning after morning. I had never spoken to her, except for a few casual words, and yet her name was like a summons to all my foolish blood. . . .

At last she spoke to me. When she addressed the first words to me I was
(30) so confused that I did not know what to answer. She asked me was I going to *Araby*. I forget whether I answered yes or no. It would be a splendid bazaar,[2] she said she would love to go.

"And why can't you?" I asked.

While she spoke she turned a silver bracelet round and round her wrist.
(35) She could not go, she said, because there would be a retreat[3] that week in her convent.[4] Her brother and two other boys were fighting for their caps and I was alone at the railings. She held one of the spikes, bowing her head towards me. The light from the lamp opposite our door caught the white curve of her neck, lit up her hair that rested there and, falling, lit up the
(40) hand upon the railing. It fell over one side of her dress and caught the white border of a petticoat, just visible as she stood at ease.

"It's well for you," she said.

"If I go," I said, "I will bring you something."

What innumerable follies laid waste my waking and sleeping thoughts
(45) after that evening! I wished to annihilate the tedious intervening days. I chafed against the work of school. At night in my bedroom and by day in the classroom her image came between me and the page I strove to read. The syllables of the word *Araby* were called to me through the silence in which my soul luxuriated and cast an Eastern enchantment over me. I asked for leave to
(50) go to the bazaar on Saturday night. My aunt was surprised and hoped it was not some Freemason[5] affair. I answered few questions in class. I watched my

---

[2]bazaar—fair
[3]retreat—a time set aside for prayer and reflection
[4]convent—religious school
[5]Freemason—a fraternal organization

master's face pass from amiability to sternness; he hoped I was not beginning to idle. I could not call my wandering thoughts together. I had hardly any patience with the serious work of life which, now that it stood between me and (55) my desire, seemed to me child's play, ugly monotonous child's play.

On Saturday morning I reminded my uncle that I wished to go to the bazaar in the evening. He was fussing at the hallstand, looking for the hatbrush, and answered me curtly:

"Yes, boy, I know." . . .

(60)   At nine o'clock I heard my uncle's latchkey in the halldoor. I heard him talking to himself and heard the hallstand rocking when it had received the weight of his overcoat. I could interpret these signs. When he was midway through his dinner I asked him to give me the money to go to the bazaar. He had forgotten.

(65)   "The people are in bed and after their first sleep now," he said.

I did not smile. My aunt said to him energetically: "Can't you give him the money and let him go? You've kept him late enough as it is." . . .

I held a florin[6] tightly in my hand as I strode down Buckingham Street towards the station. The sight of the streets thronged with buyers and glaring (70) with gas recalled to me the purpose of my journey. I took my seat in a third-class carriage of a deserted train. After an intolerable delay the train moved out of the station slowly. It crept onward among ruinous houses and over the twinkling river. At Westland Row Station a crowd of people pressed to the carriage doors; but the porters moved them back, saying that it was a special (75) train for the bazaar. I remained alone in the bare carriage. In a few minutes the train drew up beside an improvised wooden platform. I passed out on to the road and saw by the lighted dial of a clock that it was ten minutes to ten. In front of me was a large building which displayed the magical name. . . .

Remembering with difficulty why I had come I went over to one of the (80) stalls and examined porcelain vases and flowered tea-sets. At the door of the stall a young lady was talking and laughing with two young gentle men. I remarked their English accents and listened vaguely to their conversation. . . .

Observing me the young lady came over and asked me did I wish to buy anything. The tone of her voice was not encouraging; she seemed to have (85) spoken to me out of a sense of duty. I looked humbly at the great jars that stood like eastern guards at either side of the dark entrance to the stall and murmured:

"No, thank you."

---

[6]florin—coin

The young lady changed the position of one of the vases and went back
(90) to the two young men. They began to talk of the same subject. Once or twice
the young lady glanced at me over her shoulder.

I lingered before her stall, though I knew my stay was useless, to make
my interest in her wares seem the more real. Then I turned away slowly
and walked down the middle of the bazaar. I allowed the two pennies to
(95) fall against the sixpence in my pocket. I heard a voice call from one end
of the gallery that the light was out. The upper part of the hall was now
completely dark.

Gazing up into the darkness I saw myself as a creature driven and
derided by vanity; and my eyes burned with anguish and anger.

—James Joyce
excerpted from "Araby"
Dubliners, 1914
Grant Richards LTD.

1 The description of the neighborhood in lines 1 through 10 contributes to a mood of

  (1) indifference   (3) anxiety

  (2) gloom   (4) regret   1 _____

2 Which quotation from the text best illustrates the narrator's attitude toward Mangan's sister?

  (1) "we watched her from our shadow" (line 14)

  (2) "We waited to see whether she would remain or go in" (line 15)

  (3) "yet her name was like a summons" (lines 27 and 28)

  (4) "She asked me was I going to *Araby*" (lines 30 and 31)   2 _____

3 Lines 29 through 38 reveal Mangan's sister's

  (1) disinterest   (3) disappointment

  (2) silliness   (4) tension   3 _____

4 Lines 44 through 55 help to develop the idea that the narrator has

  (1) recognized that his priorities have changed

  (2) determined the academic focus of his studies

  (3) eliminated distractions from his daily routine

  (4) reassessed his relationship with his family   4 _____

5 The description of the narrator's train ride (lines 68 through 76) supports a theme of

  (1) confusion   (3) persecution

  (2) isolation   (4) deception   5 _____

6 The description in lines 83 through 91 suggests that the bazaar symbolizes

  (1) excessive greed   (3) false promise

  (2) future wealth   (4) lasting love   6 _____

7 It can be inferred from the text that the narrator's behavior is most guided by his

   (1) school experience
   (2) family situation
   (3) childhood memories
   (4) romantic feelings   7 _____

8 As used in line 99, the word "derided" most nearly means

   (1) taunted   (3) rewarded
   (2) restrained   (4) flattered   8 _____

9 Based on the text as a whole, the narrator's feelings of "anguish and anger" (line 99) are most likely a result of his having

   (1) ignored his opportunities
   (2) defended his family
   (3) realized his limitations
   (4) denied his responsibilities   9 _____

10 Which quotation best reflects a central theme of the text?

   (1) "Her brother and two other boys were fighting for their caps" (line 36)
   (2) " 'Can't you give him the money and let him go?' " (lines 66 and 67)
   (3) "It crept onward among ruinous houses and over the twinkling river" (lines 72 and 73)
   (4) "I lingered before her stall, though I knew my stay was useless" (line 92)   10 _____

Reading Comprehension Passage B

Assembly Line

In time's assembly line
Night presses against night.
We come off the factory night-shift
In line as we march towards home.
(5) Over our heads in a row
The assembly line of stars
Stretches across the sky.
Beside us, little trees
Stand numb in assembly lines.

(10) The stars must be exhausted
After thousands of years
Of journeys which never change.
The little trees are all sick,
Choked on smog and monotony,
(15) Stripped of their color and shape.
It's not hard to feel for them;
We share the same tempo and rhythm.

Yes, I'm numb to my own existence
As if, like the trees and stars
(20) —perhaps just out of habit
—perhaps just out of sorrow,
I'm unable to show concern
For my own manufactured fate.

—Shu Ting
from A *Splintered Mirror: Chinese Poetry from the*
Democracy Movement, 1991
translated by Carolyn Kizer
North Point Press

11 In the first stanza, a main idea is strengthened through the poet's use of

   (1) repetition   (3) allusion

   (2) simile   (4) understatement   11 _____

12 Line 17 contributes to a central idea by pointing out a parallel between .

   (1) profit and industrialization

   (2) humans and nature

   (3) recreation and production

   (4) sound and motion   12 _____

13 The structure and language of lines 20 and 21 suggests the narrator's

   (1) bitterness   (3) selfishness

   (2) determination   (4) uncertainty   13 _____

14 The phrase "manufactured fate" (line 23) emphasizes the narrator's

   (1) resignation to life

   (2) desire for control

   (3) hope for change

   (4) rejection of nature   14 _____

Reading Comprehension Passage C

. . .Memory teaches me what I know of these matters. The boy reminds the adult. I was a bilingual child, but of a certain kind: "socially disadvantaged," the son of working-class parents, both Mexican immigrants. . . .

(5)   In public, my father and mother spoke a hesitant, accented, and not always grammatical English. And then they would have to strain, their bodies tense, to catch the sense of what was rapidly said by *los gringos*. At home, they returned to Spanish. The language of their Mexican past sounded in counterpoint to the English spoken in public. The words would
(10) come quickly, with ease. Conveyed through those sounds was the pleasing, soothing, consoling reminder that one was at home.

During those years when I was first learning to speak, my mother and father addressed me only in Spanish; in Spanish I learned to reply. By contrast, English (*inglés*) was the language I came to associate with gringos,
(15) rarely heard in the house. I learned my first words of English overhearing my parents speaking to strangers. At six years of age, I knew just enough words for my mother to trust me on errands to stores one block away—but no more.

I was then a listening child, careful to hear the very different sounds
(20) of Spanish and English. Wide-eyed with hearing, I'd listen to sounds more than to words. First, there were English (*gringo*) sounds. So many words still were unknown to me that when the butcher or the lady at the drugstore said something, exotic polysyllabic sounds would bloom in the midst of their sentences. Often the speech of people in public seemed to me very loud,
(25) booming with confidence. The man behind the counter would literally ask, "What can I do for you?" But by being so firm and clear, the sound of his voice said that he was a gringo; he belonged in public society. There were also the high, nasal notes of middle-class American speech—which I rarely am conscious of hearing today because I hear them so often, but could not
(30) stop hearing when I was a boy. Crowds at Safeway or at bus stops were noisy with the birdlike sounds of *los gringos*. I'd move away from them all—all the chirping chatter above me.

My own sounds I was unable to hear, but I knew that I spoke English poorly. My words could not extend to form complete thoughts. And the
(35) words I did speak I didn't know well enough to make distinct sounds. (Listeners would usually lower their heads to hear better what I was trying to say.) But it was one thing for *me* to speak English with difficulty; it was

more troubling to hear my parents speaking in public: their high-whining
vowels and guttural[1] consonants; their sentences that got stuck with "eh"
(40) and "ah" sounds; the confused syntax; the hesitant rhythm of sounds so
different from the way gringos spoke. I'd notice, moreover, that my parents'
voices were softer than those of gringos we would meet.

I am tempted to say now that none of this mattered. (In adulthood
I am embarrassed by childhood fears.) And, in a way, it didn't matter very
(45) much that my parents could not speak English with ease. Their linguistic
difficulties had no serious consequences. My mother and father made
themselves understood at the county hospital clinic and at government
offices. And yet, in another way, it mattered very much. It was unsettling to
hear my parents struggle with English. Hearing them, I'd grow nervous, and
(50) my clutching trust in their protection and power would be weakened. . . .

But then there was Spanish: *español*, the language rarely heard away
from the house; *español*, the language which seemed to me therefore a
private language, my family's language. To hear its sounds was to feel myself
specially recognized as one of the family, apart from *los otros*.[2] A simple
(55) remark, an inconsequential comment could convey that assurance. My
parents would say something to me and I would feel embraced by the sounds
of their words. Those sounds said: *I am speaking with ease in Spanish. I am
addressing you in words I never use with* los gringos. *I recognize you as
someone special, close, like no one outside. You belong with us. In the family.*
(60) *Ricardo.*

At the age of six, well past the time when most middle-class children
no longer notice the difference between sounds uttered at home and
words spoken in public, I had a different experience. I lived in a world
compounded of sounds. I was a child longer than most. I lived in a magical
(65) world, surrounded by sounds both pleasing and fearful. I shared with my
family a language enchantingly private—different from that used in the city
around us. . . .

If I rehearse here the changes in my private life after my Americanization,
it is finally to emphasize a public gain. The loss implies the gain. The
(70) house I returned to each afternoon was quiet. Intimate sounds no longer
greeted me at the door. Inside there were other noises. The telephone
rang. Neighborhood kids ran past the door of the bedroom where I was
reading my schoolbooks—covered with brown shopping-bag paper.

---

[1]guttural—throaty
[2]los otros—the others

Once I learned the public language, it would never again be easy for me to
(75) hear intimate family voices. More and more of my day was spent hearing
words, not sounds. But that may only be a way of saying that on the day I
raised my hand in class and spoke loudly to an entire roomful of faces, my
childhood started to end. . . .

—Richard Rodriguez
excerpted from "Aria: A Memoir of a Bilingual Childhood"
The American Scholar, Winter 1981
The Phi Beta Kappa Society

15 The phrase "the boy reminds the adult" in the first paragraph establishes the narrator's

(1) mood   (3) creativity
(2) perspective   (4) disposition   15 _____

16 The use of the word "counterpoint" in line 9 helps to develop a central idea by presenting

(1) differing memories
(2) opposing principles
(3) contrasting cultures
(4) conflicting philosophies   16 _____

17 The use of figurative language in lines 20 and 21 demonstrates the narrator's

(1) eagerness to learn
(2) desire for recognition
(3) frustration with authority
(4) anxiety about adulthood   17 _____

18 The use of the word "public" in line 27 emphasizes the narrator's feeling of

(1) accomplishment   (3) satisfaction
(2) disillusionment   (4) separation   18 _____

19 The description of the narrator speaking English in lines 33 through 37 emphasizes his inability to

(1) communicate effectively
(2) understand the culture
(3) distinguish between languages
(4) express emotions   19 _____

20 In lines 44 through 49 the narrator's reaction to his parents' "linguistic difficulties" (lines 45 and 46) reveals his

(1) low expectations   (3) educational concerns
(2) conflicting feelings   (4) hostile thoughts   20 _____

21 Lines 51 through 60 contribute to a central idea in the text by focusing on the

  (1) narrator's sense of security
  (2) family's economic status
  (3) family's traditional beliefs
  (4) narrator's feeling of confusion   21 _____

22 Which quotation best reflects the narrator's overall experience with language?

  (1) "The words would come quickly, with ease" (lines 9 and 10)
  (2) "I'd listen to sounds more than to words" (lines 20 and 21)
  (3) "My own sounds I was unable to hear, but I knew that I spoke English poorly" (lines 33 and 34)
  (4) "Hearing them, I'd grow nervous" (line 49)   22 _____

23 The phrase "the loss implies the gain" (line 69) contributes to a central idea in the text by indicating that when the narrator speaks English comfortably he is

  (1) disconnected from his family
  (2) distressed by hearing English sounds
  (3) uninterested in his school work
  (4) undeterred from making new friends   23 _____

24 The narrator's tone in lines 75 through 78 suggests

  (1) distrust   (3) confidence
  (2) respect   (4) intolerance   24 _____

PART 2—Argument Response

Directions: Closely read each of the *four* texts on pages 98 through 107 and write a source-based argument on the topic below. You may use the margins to take notes as you read and scrap paper to plan your response. Write your argument on a separate sheet of paper.

Topic: Should celebrities become the voice of humanitarian causes?

Your Task: Carefully read each of the *four* texts provided. Then, using evidence from at least *three* of the texts, write a well-developed argument regarding whether or not celebrities should become the voice of humanitarian causes. Clearly establish your claim, distinguish your claim from alternate or opposing claims, and use specific, relevant, and sufficient evidence from at least *three* of the texts to develop your argument. Do *not* simply summarize each text.

Guidelines:

Be sure to

- Establish your claim regarding whether or not celebrities should become the voice of humanitarian causes.
- Distinguish your claim from alternate or opposing claims.
- Use specific, relevant, and sufficient evidence from at least *three* of the texts to develop your argument.
- Identify each source that you reference by text number and line number(s) or graphic (for example: Text 1, line 4 or Text 2, graphic).
- Organize your ideas in a cohesive and coherent manner.
- Maintain a formal style of writing.
- Follow the conventions of standard written English.

Texts:

Text 1—The Celebrity Solution

Text 2—Ethics of Celebrities and Their Increasing Influence in 21st Century Society

Text 3—Do Celebrity Humanitarians Matter?

Text 4—The Rise of the Celebrity Humanitarian

Text 1

The Celebrity Solution

  In 2004, Natalie Portman, then a 22-year-old fresh from college,
went to Capitol Hill to talk to Congress on behalf of the Foundation for
International Community Assistance, or Finca, a microfinance organization
for which she served as "ambassador." She found herself wondering what
(5) she was doing there, but her colleagues assured her: "We got the meetings
because of you." For lawmakers, Natalie Portman was not simply a young
woman—she was the beautiful Padmé from "Star Wars." "And I was like,
'That seems totally nuts to me, '" Portman told me recently. [*sic*] It's the way
it works, I guess. I'm not particularly proud that in our country I can get a
(10) meeting with a representative more easily than the head of a nonprofit can."
  Well, who is? But it is the way it works. Stars—movie stars, rock stars,
sports stars—exercise a ludicrous influence over the public consciousness.
Many are happy to exploit that power; others are wrecked by it. In recent
years, stars have learned that their intense presentness in people's daily lives
(15) and their access to the uppermost realms of politics, business and the media
offer them a peculiar kind of moral position, should they care to use it. And
many of those with the most leverage—Bono and Angelina Jolie and Brad Pitt
and George Clooney and, yes, Natalie Portman—have increasingly chosen
to mount that pedestal. Hollywood celebrities have become central players
(20) on deeply political issues like development aid, refugees and government-
sponsored violence in Darfur.
  Activists on these and other issues talk about the political power of stars
with a mixture of bewilderment and delight. But a weapon that powerful is
bound to do collateral damage. Some stars, like George Clooney, regard the
(25) authority thrust upon them with wariness; others, like Sean Penn or Mia
Farrow, an activist on Darfur, seize the bully pulpit with both hands. "There
is a tendency," says Donald Steinberg, deputy president of the International
Crisis Group, which seeks to prevent conflict around the world, "to treat
these issues as if it's all good and evil." Sometimes you need the rallying cry,
(30) but sometimes you need to accept a complex truth. . . .
  An entire industry has sprung up around the recruitment of celebrities
to good works. Even an old-line philanthropy like the Red Cross employs
a "director of celebrity outreach." Oxfam has a celebrity wrangler in Los
Angeles, Lyndsay Cruz, on the lookout for stars who can raise the charity's
(35) profile with younger people. In addition to established figures like Colin
Firth and Helen Mirren, Oxfam is affiliated with Scarlett Johansson, who has

visited South Asia (where the organization promotes girls' education) and is scheduled to go to Mali. Cruz notes that while "trendy young people" are attracted to the star of "Match Point" and "Lost in Translation," Johansson
(40) had "great credibility with an older audience because she's such a great actress." . . .

Microfinance is a one-star cause. Though for some reason the subject appeals to female royalty, including Queen Rania of Jordan and Princess Maxima of the Netherlands, Natalie Portman is the only member of
(45) Hollywood royalty who has dedicated herself to it. Perhaps this is because microfinance is a good deal more complicated than supplying fresh water to parched villages, and a good deal less glamorous than confronting the janjaweed[1] in Darfur. The premise of microfinance is that very poor people should have access to credit, just as the middle class and the rich do. They
(50) typically don't have such access because banks that operate in the developing world view the poor as too great a credit risk, and the processing cost of a $50 loan is thought to wipe out much of the potential profit. But small nonprofit organizations found that tiny loans could not only raise the incomes of the rural and small-town poor but also, unlike aid and other handouts, could
(55) help make them self-sufficient. And they found as well that if they harnessed the communities' own social bonds to create group support, repayment rates among the very poor could be higher than among the more well-off. (Indeed, commercial banks, apparently having recognized their error, have now begun to extend loans to the poor.) The idea of microfinance is thus to
(60) introduce the poor to capitalism. This is not, it's true, star material. . . .

Theres no question that causes do a great deal for the brand identity of the stars and the sponsors who embrace them. But what, exactly, do stars do for causes? They raise money, of course. But that is often less important than raising consciousness, as Natalie Portman has done. John Prendergast,
(65) a longtime activist on African issues and the chairman of Enough, an organization that brings attention to atrocities around the world, says: "Celebrities are master recruiters. If you're trying to expand beyond the already converted, there's no better way to do instant outreach than to have a familiar face where people want to know more about what they're doing in
(70) their personal lives." People come to see Natalie Portman, and they go away learning about microfinance. . . .

—James Traub
excerpted from "The Celebrity Solution"
www.nytimes.com, March 9, 2008

---

[1]janjaweed—militia

Text 2

Ethics of Celebrities and Their Increasing
Influence in 21st Century Society

The global influence of celebrities in the 21st century extends far beyond the entertainment sector. During the recent Palestinian presidential elections, the Hollywood actor Richard Gere broadcast a televised message to voters in the region and stated,

(5)   Hi, I'm Richard Gere, and I'm speaking for the entire world. (Richard Gere, actor)

Celebrities in the 21st century have expanded from simple product endorsements to sitting on United Nations committees, regional and global conflict commentators and international diplomacy. The Russian parliament

(10) is debating whether to send a global celebrity to its International Space Station. The celebrities industry is undergoing, "mission creep", or the expansion of an enterprise beyond its original goals.

There has always been a connection between Hollywood and politics, certainly in the USA. However, global celebrities in the 21st century are

(15) involved in proselytising[1] about particular religions, such as Scientology, negotiating with the Taliban in Afghanistan and participating in the Iraqi refugee crisis. The Hollywood actor, Jude Law's attempt to negotiate with the Taliban in Afghanistan was not successful; but the mere fact that Jude Law tried, and that it was discussed widely over the global internet, shows the

(20) expansion of celebrities' domain in today's society. The global entertainment industry, especially based in Hollywood, has vastly exceeded their original mandate in society. . . .

How is it that celebrities in the 21st century are formulating foreign aid policy, backing political bills or affecting public health debates? Traditionally,

(25) the economic value or market price of the entertainment industry and its various components was seen as intangible and difficult to measure. Movie stars and films, artists and the quality of art is often seen as difficult to measure in terms of value and price without the role of expert opinions. But global internet-driven 21st century seems to be driven by a general growth

(30) of the idea that celebrity can be measured in a tangible way. . . .

The 21st century's internet society seems to thrive on a harmonious three-way relationship among celebrities, audiences and fame addiction. The global internet in turns [sic] moulds this three-way relationship and accelerates its dissemination[2] and communication. This in turn allows

---

[1]proselytising—trying to persuade or recruit others
[2]dissemination—wide distribution

(35) celebrities in the 21st century to "mission creep", or expand and accelerate their influence into various new areas of society. This interaction of forces is shown in Figure 1. . . .

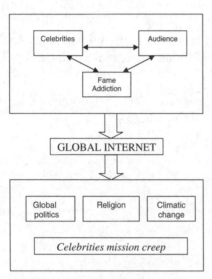

**Figure 1. Celebrities' mission creep
in the 21st century.**

In turn, the global popularity of internet-based social networking sites such as MySpace or individual blogspots all show the need to discuss events, but
(40) also things that are famous (Choi and Berger, 2009). Traditionally, celebrities were seen as people that needed to be seen from afar and while keeping one's distance. In this sense, celebrities were similar to art pieces, better to be seen from a distance (Halpern, 2008; Hirsch, 1972; Maury and Kleiner, 2002). This traditional distance has been reduced due to global technologies
(45) in communications. Celebrities, and famous people in turn, help to bring people, including adults, together in conversation and social interaction. The global role of the internet in the 21st century society will further accelerate such social and psychological trends throughout today's global knowledge-based society. Global internet communications have increased the availability
(50) of "fame" and access to the lives of celebrities, which in turn will further accelerate the global influence of celebrities in the 21st century society. . . .

—Chong Ju Choi and Ron Berger
excerpted from "Ethics of Celebrities and
Their Increasing Influence in 21st Century Society"
Journal of Business Ethics, 2009
www.idc.ac.il

References

Choi, C.J. and R. Berger: 2009, 'Ethics of Internet, Global Community, Fame Addiction', *Journal of Business Ethics* (forthcoming).

Halpern, J.: 2008, *Fame Junkies* (Houghton Mifflin, New York).

Hirsch, P.: 1972, 'Processing Fads and Fashions: An Organisation Set Analysis of Cultural Industry Systems', *American Journal of Sociology* 77 (1), 45–70.

Maury, M. and D. Kleiner: 2002, 'E-Commerce, Ethical Commerce?', *Journal of Business Ethics* 36 (3), 21–32.

Text 3

Do Celebrity Humanitarians Matter?

    . . .Recent years have seen a growth industry for celebrities engaged in humanitarian activities. The website *Look to the Stars* has calculated that over 2,000 charities have some form of celebrity support. UNICEF has dozens of "Goodwill Ambassadors" and "Advocates" such as Angelina Jolie
(5) and Mia Farrow. Celebrities have entered forums for global governance to pressure political leaders: George Clooney has spoken before the United Nations while Bob Geldof, Bono, and Sharon Stone have attended summits like DAVOS[1] and the G8[2] to discuss third world debt, poverty, and refugees. In the U.S. policy arena, [Ben] Affleck joins Nicole Kidman, Angelina Jolie,
(10) and other celebrities who have addressed the U.S. Congress on international issues.[3] The increase in celebrity involvement has spurred debate in academic circles and mainstream media. Celebrity humanitarianism is alternately lauded for drawing media attention and fostering popular engagement and criticized on a number of ethical grounds. According to *Mother Jones*, Africa
(15) is experiencing a "recolonization" as celebrities from the U.S. and UK lay claim to particular countries as recipients of their star power: South Africa (Oprah), Sudan (Mia Farrow), and Botswana (Russell Simmons). As the involvement of American celebrities in humanitarian causes grows, let us consider the activities of Affleck and his Eastern Congo Initiative [ECI].

Celebrity Humanitarians
(20)   Affleck can be considered a "celebrity humanitarian," a celebrity figure who has moved beyond his/her day job as an entertainer to delve into the areas of foreign aid, charity, and development. These activities can involve fundraising, hosting concerts and events, media appearances, and engaging in advocacy. Celebrities are distinguished by their unique ability to
(25) attract and engage diverse audiences ranging from their fan base and the media to political elites and philanthropists. Celebrity humanitarians often play an important bridging role, introducing Northern publics to issues in the developing world. They also use their star power to gain access to policy-making circles to effect social and political change. Since 1980, the U.S.
(30) Congress has seen the frequency of celebrity witnesses double to around

---

[1]DAVOS—an annual meeting of The World Economic Forum, hosted in Davos-Klosters, Switzerland, on global partnership
[2]G8—A group of 8 industrialized nations that hold a yearly meeting to discuss global issues
[3]ProQuest, "Quick Start: Congressional Hearing Digital Collections: Famous (Celebrity) Witnesses," *http://proquest.libguides.com/quick_start_hearings/famouscelebs*

20 a year with most celebrity appearances taking place before committees
addressing domestic issues. Interestingly, fewer than 5 percent of celebrity
witnesses testify before committees dealing with foreign relations, where
celebrity humanitarians push the United States to address global concerns.[4]

(35)　　　The rise and influence of celebrity humanitarians activate debates
on the consequences of their involvement. For some academics and
practitioners, celebrities are welcome figures in humanitarianism: educating
the public on global issues, raising funds, and using their populist appeal to
draw attention to policy-making arenas. For others, celebrity humanitarians
(40) are highly problematic figures who dilute debates, offer misguided policy
proposals, and lack credibility and accountability. Celebrity humanitarianism
privileges and invests the celebrity figure with the responsibility of speaking
on behalf of a "distant other" who is unable to give input or consent for their
representation. Stakeholders in the developing world unwittingly rely on
(45) the celebrity humanitarian as their communicator, advocate, and fundraiser.
Finally, celebrities are held to be self-serving, engaging in humanitarian
causes to burnish[5] their careers. . . .

Celebrity humanitarians should do their homework to earn credibility
while also respecting their bounded roles as celebrity figures. As a celebrity
(50) humanitarian, Affleck's proposals are based on serious preparation: spending
years to gain an in-depth understanding, consulting with professionals,
narrowing his advocacy efforts to a single region, and enduring the scrutiny of
the cameras and the blogosphere. Besides this self-education, his credibility
is based on ECI's dual mission of re-granting and policymaking. Since ECI
(55) has operations and partnerships in the DRC [Democratic Republic of the
Congo], the content of Affleck's writings and Congressional testimonies are
grounded in the realities of the DRC, peppered with first-hand accounts,
and supported by statistics and other research. However, there are limits
to his knowledge—Affleck is not a development expert or on-the-ground
(60) professional; his day job and main career lie elsewhere. And while the
decision to found an organization suggests that Affleck's commitment to
the DRC will extend beyond his nascent[6] efforts, rumors that he may seek
political office distort this image.

Celebrity humanitarians must find a way to avoid diverting resources
(65) and attention. Rather than bring his star power and ample financial
support to existing Congolese organizations, ECI furnished a platform for

---

[4]See Demaine, L.J., n.d. Navigating Policy by the Stars: The Influence of Celebrity Entertainers on Federal Lawmaking. *Journal of Law & Politics*, 25 (2), 83–143
[5]burnish—improve or enhance
[6]nascent—beginning

Affleck's advocacy and leadership that amplifies his voice over those of the Congolese. Nor was ECI crafted inside eastern Congo but in the offices of a strategic advisory firm based in Seattle. ECI is privately funded by a
(70) network of financial elites and does not rely on means-tested grant cycles or public support. While Affleck has received multiple awards in the short period he has been a celebrity humanitarian, his star power also distracts us from the people who work in the field of humanitarianism on a daily basis and rarely receive such recognition.[7] And by concentrating attention and
(75) money for Affleck's issue of Eastern Congo, other causes and countries may go unnoticed. . . .

—Alexandra Cosima Budabin
excerpted and adapted from "Do Celebrity Humanitarians Matter?"
www.carnegiecouncil.org, December 11, 2014

---

[7]Marina Hyde, "Angelina Jolie, Paris Hilton, Lassie and Tony Blair: here to save the world," The Guardian, 27 November 2014 *http://www.theguardian.com/lifeandstyle/ lostinshowbiz/2014/nov/27/angelina-jolie-paris-hilton-tony-blair-lassie-save-the-childrenaward? CMP=share_btn_fb*

Text 4

The Rise of the Celebrity Humanitarian

. . .One of the most effective methods of attracting a wide, although perhaps not a deep, following is the use of a celebrity humanitarian: An A-Lister who has delved into areas of foreign aid, charity and international development. The United Nations is the leader in this attention getting
(5) ploy, with at least 175 celebrities on the books as goodwill ambassadors[1] for one cause or another. Some celebrities even leverage their star power to promote their very own foundations and philanthropic projects.

It's a mutually beneficial relationship, really. Hollywood's elite get to wield their unique ability to engage diverse audiences, and the power of
(10) celebrity is put to good use effecting change—whether it's out of the good of their hearts, or because their publicists insist.

There is some downside that comes with publicly linking a campaign to a celebrity. For some, celebrity humanitarians are problematic figures[2] who dilute debates, offer misguided policy proposals, and lack credibility
(15) and accountability. Take Scarlett Johansson, who became embroiled in a scandal after partnering with soft drink maker SodaStream, which operated a factory in occupied Palestinian territory. This alliance was in direct conflict with her seven-year global ambassador position for Oxfam, which opposes all trade with the occupied territories. In the end, she stepped down from
(20) her role with Oxfam, stating a fundamental difference of opinion.

Moreover, if the star's popularity takes a hit, it can affect the reception of the cause. For example, when Lance Armstrong's popularity plummeted in the wake of doping allegations, it tarnished the brand of the Livestrong Foundation,[3] the nonprofit he founded to support people affected by cancer.
(25) Livestrong does, however, continue today, after cutting ties with Armstrong and undergoing a radical rebranding.

Even so, the following big names substantiate the idea that celebrity involvement brings massive amounts of attention and money to humanitarian causes and that, usually, this [sic] is a good thing. . . .
(30)   Bono participates in fundraising concerts like Live 8, and has cofounded several philanthropies, like the ONE Campaign and Product (RED). He also created EDUN, a fashion brand that strives to stimulate trade in Africa

[1]Bunting, Madeline. "The Issue of Celebrities and Aid Is Deceptively Complex"
http://www.theguardian.com, Dec. 17, 2010
[2]Budabin, Alexandra Cosima. "Do Celebrity Humanitarians Matter?"
http://www.carnegiecouncil.org, December 11, 2014
[3]Gardner, Eriq. "Livestrong Struggles After Lance Armstrong's Fall" *http://www.hollywoodreporter.com*, 7/25/2013

by sourcing production there. He has received three nominations for the Nobel Peace Prize, was knighted by the United Kingdom in 2007, and was
(35) named Time's 2005 Person of the Year. . . .

Popular singer Akon may not be as famous for his philanthropic work as Angelina Jolie or Bono, but he is in a unique position to help, as he has deep roots in the areas in which he works: He was raised in Senegal in a community without electricity, which inspired his latest project, Akon
(40) Lighting Africa. He also founded the Konfidence Foundation, raising awareness of conditions in Africa and providing underprivileged African youth access to education and other resources. . . .

In weighing the pros and cons of celebrity activism, perhaps [Ben] Affleck himself summed it up best in an essay reflecting on the constraints
(45) and possibilities of his own engagement:

"It makes sense to be skeptical about celebrity activism. There is always suspicion that involvement with a cause may be doing more good for the spokesman than he or she is doing for the cause. . .but I hope you can separate whatever reservations you may have from what is unimpeachably
(50) important."

—Jenica Funk
excerpted and adapted from "The Rise of the Celebrity Humanitarian"
www.globalenvision.org, January 29, 2015

PART 3—Text-Analysis Response

Your Task: Closely read the text on pages 109 through 111 and write a well-developed, text-based response of two to three paragraphs. In your response, identify a central idea in the text and analyze how the author's use of *one* writing strategy (literary element or literary technique or rhetorical device) develops this central idea. Use strong and thorough evidence from the text to support your analysis. Do *not* simply summarize the text. You may use the margins to take notes as you read and scrap paper to plan your response. Write your response on a separate sheet of paper.

Guidelines:

Be sure to

- Identify a central idea in the text.
- Analyze how the author's use of *one* writing strategy (literary element or literary technique or rhetorical device) develops this central idea. Examples include: characterization, conflict, denotation/connotation, metaphor, simile, irony, language use, point-of-view, setting, structure, symbolism, theme, tone, etc.
- Use strong and thorough evidence from the text to support your analysis.
- Organize your ideas in a cohesive and coherent manner.
- Maintain a formal style of writing.
- Follow the conventions of standard written English.

Text

It was my father who called the city the Mansion on the River. He was talking about Charleston, South Carolina, and he was a native son, peacock proud of a town so pretty it makes your eyes ache with pleasure just to walk down its spellbinding, narrow streets. Charleston was my father's
(5)　ministry, his hobbyhorse, his quiet obsession, and the great love of his life. His bloodstream lit up my own with a passion for the city that I've never lost nor ever will. I'm Charleston-born, and bred. The city's two rivers, the Ashley and the Cooper, have flooded and shaped all the days of my life on this storied[1] peninsula.
(10)　　I carry the delicate porcelain beauty of Charleston like the hinged shell of some soft-tissued mollusk. My soul is peninsula-shaped and sun-hardened and river-swollen. The high tides of the city flood my consciousness each day, subject to the whims and harmonies of full moons rising out of the Atlantic. I grow calm when I see the ranks of palmetto trees pulling guard duty on the
(15)　banks of Colonial Lake or hear the bells of St. Michael's calling cadence[2] in the cicada-filled trees along Meeting Street. Deep in my bones, I knew early that I was one of those incorrigible[3] creatures known as Charlestonians. It comes to me as a surprising form of knowledge that my time in the city is more vocation than gift; it is my destiny, not my choice. I consider it a high
(20)　privilege to be a native of one of the loveliest American cities, not a high-kicking, glossy, or lipsticked city, not a city with bells on its fingers or brightly painted toenails, but a ruffled, low-slung city, understated and tolerant of nothing mismade or ostentatious.[4] Though Charleston feels a seersuckered, tuxedoed view of itself, it approves of restraint far more than vainglory.[5]
(25)　　As a boy, in my own backyard I could catch a basket of blue crabs, a string of flounder, a dozen redfish, or a net full of white shrimp. All this I could do in a city enchanting enough to charm cobras out of baskets, one so corniced and filigreed[6] and elaborate that it leaves strangers awed and natives self-satisfied. In its shadows you can find metalwork as delicate as
(30)　lace and spiral staircases as elaborate as yachts. In the secrecy of its gardens you can discover jasmine and camellias and hundreds of other plants that look embroidered and stolen from the Garden of Eden for the sheer love of richness and the joy of stealing from the gods. In its kitchens, the stoves are

---

[1]storied—told of in history
[2]cadence—rhythmic recurrence of sound
[3]incorrigible—cannot be reformed
[4]ostentatious—showy
[5]vainglory—excessive pride
[6]corniced and filigreed—architecturally decorated

lit up in happiness as the lamb is marinating in red wine sauce, vinaigrette is
(35) prepared for the salad, crabmeat is anointed with sherry, custards are baked
in the oven, and buttermilk biscuits cool on the counter.

Because of its devotional, graceful attraction to food and gardens and
architecture, Charleston stands for all the principles that make living well
both a civic virtue and a standard. It is a rapturous, defining place to grow up.
(40) Everything I reveal to you now will be Charleston-shaped and Charleston-
governed, and sometimes even Charleston-ruined. But it is my fault and
not the city's that it came close to destroying me. Not everyone responds
to beauty in the same way. Though Charleston can do much, it can't always
improve on the strangeness of human behavior. But Charleston has a high
(45) tolerance for eccentricity and bemusement.[7] There is a tastefulness in its
gentility[8] that comes from the knowledge that Charleston is a permanent
dimple in the understated skyline, while the rest of us are only visitors. . . .

I turned out to be a late bloomer, which I long regretted. My parents
suffered needlessly because it took me so long to find my way to a place at
(50) their table. But I sighted the early signs of my recovery long before they
did. My mother had given up on me at such an early age that a comeback
was something she no longer even prayed for in her wildest dreams. Yet in
my anonymous and underachieving high school career, I laid the foundation
for a strong finish without my mother noticing that I was, at last, up to some
(55) good. I had built an impregnable castle of solitude for myself and then set
out to bring that castle down, no matter how serious the collateral damage
or who might get hurt.

I was eighteen years old and did not have a friend my own age. There
wasn't a boy in Charleston who would think about inviting me to a party or
(60) to come out to spend the weekend at his family's beach house.

I planned for all that to change. I had decided to become the most
interesting boy to ever grow up in Charleston, and I revealed this secret to
my parents.

Outside my house in the languid[9] summer air of my eighteenth year, I
(65) climbed the magnolia tree nearest to the Ashley River with the agility that
constant practice had granted me. From its highest branches, I surveyed
my city as it lay simmering in the hot-blooded saps of June while the sun
began to set, reddening the vest of cirrus clouds that had gathered along
the western horizon. In the other direction, I saw the city of rooftops and

---

[7]bemusement—bewilderment
[8]gentility—refinement
[9]languid—without energy

(70) columns and gables that was my native land. What I had just promised my
parents, I wanted very much for them and for myself. Yet I also wanted it
for Charleston. I desired to turn myself into a worthy townsman of such a
many-storied city.

Charleston has its own heartbeat and fingerprint, its own mug shots
(75) and photo ops and police lineups. It is a city of contrivance,[10] of blueprints;
devotion to pattern that is like a bent knee to the nature of beauty itself.
I could feel my destiny forming in the leaves high above the city. Like
Charleston, I had my alleyways that were dead ends and led to nowhere,
but mansions were forming like jewels in my bloodstream. Looking down,
(80) I studied the layout of my city, the one that had taught me all the lures
of attractiveness, yet made me suspicious of the showy or the makeshift. I
turned to the stars and was about to make a bad throw of the dice and try to
predict the future, but stopped myself in time.

A boy stopped in time, in a city of amber-colored life, that possessed the
(85) glamour forbidden to a lesser angel.

—Pat Conroy
excerpted from *South of Broad*, 2009
Nan A. Talese

---

[10]contrivance—invention

Regents ELA Answers June 2016

English Language Arts

Answer Key

PART 1

1. **2**	9. **3**	17. **1**
2. **3**	10. **4**	18. **4**
3. **3**	11. **1**	19. **1**
4. **1**	12. **2**	20. **2**
5. **2**	13. **4**	21. **1**
6. **3**	14. **1**	22. **2**
7. **4**	15. **2**	23. **1**
8. **1**	16. **3**	24. **3**

PART 2   *See Answers and Explanations*

PART 3   *See Answers and Explanations*

Regents ELA Examination in English Language Arts-June 2016

Chart for Converting Total Weighted Raw Scores to Final Exam Scores (Scale Scores) (Use for the June 2016 examination only.)

Weighted Raw Score*	Scale Score	Performance Level		Weighted Raw Score*	Scale Score	Performance Level
56	100	5		27	60	2
55	99	5		26	57	2
54	98	5		25	55	2
53	97	5		24	51	1
52	96	5		23	47	1
51	95	5		22	44	1
50	94	5		21	40	1
49	93	5		20	37	1
48	93	5		19	33	1
47	92	5		18	29	1
46	91	5		17	25	1
45	90	5		16	22	1
44	89	5		15	18	1
43	88	5		14	15	1
42	87	5		13	11	1
41	86	5		12	9	1
40	85	5		11	8	1
39	83	4		10	7	1
38	82	4		9	6	1
37	81	4		8	5	1
36	79	4		7	4	1
35	78	3		6	3	1
34	76	3		5	3	1
33	74	3		4	2	1
32	72	3		3	2	1
31	70	3		2	1	1
30	67	3		1	1	1
29	65	3		0	0	1
28	62	2				

The conversion table is determined independently for each administration of the exam.

Answers Explained

PART 1—Reading Comprehension

Multiple-Choice Questions

Passage A

1. **2** "gloom." Of the choices, this is the best answer: the houses are "sombre," the light of the street lamps is "feeble," the air is biting cold, and the street is silent.

2. **3** "yet her name was like a summons [to all my foolish blood]." This line concludes the narrator's gradual revelation of his silent attraction to Mangan's sister: he watches for her daily, and when she appears, "my heart leaped." None of the other choices suggests the narrator's feelings.

3. **3** "disappointment." At line 32 Mangan's sister says that "she would love to go" and explains that she must attend a retreat at her school instead. The images of Mangan's sister turning the bracelet on her arm and bowing her head toward the narrator are also subtle indications of her disappointment. This answer best expresses Mangan's sister's feelings.

4. **1** "recognized that his priorities have changed." In this passage, the narrator reveals that he no longer cares to do well in school and that he "had hardly any patience with the serious work of life." What he had considered priorities before he now regards as "ugly, monotonous child's play."

5. **2** "isolation." The narrator takes his seat on the "deserted train" and "remained alone in the bare carriage." These details emphasize how alone the narrator feels on his journey to the bazaar.

6. **3** "false promise." In this passage, the narrator discovers that there is nothing here for him to buy, the young lady at the stand knows he is not a likely customer, and that his stay "was useless." There is no exotic and romantic world to be found in the bazaar; instead, the narrator finds only tea sets and vases he could not possibly afford or even want to buy for Mangan's sister.

7. **4** "romantic feelings." Romantic here refers both to the narrator's attraction to Mangan's sister and to the idea of *Araby* (the bazaar) as a distant place of exotic attraction and escape from the gloom of the Dublin neighborhood where they live.

8. **1** "taunted." Other synonyms for "derided" include "ridiculed," "mocked," and "scorned." The narrator feels foolish and ashamed for acting on his romantic notions. None of the other choices expresses the narrator's feelings here.

9. **3** "realized his limitations." This phrase best expresses the narrator's feelings. This phrase sums up the narrator's recognition of his foolish and naïve behavior cited in the questions above.

10. **4** "I lingered before her stall, though I knew my stay was useless." This line also best expresses the theme of the story. Note how the details cited in questions 6–9 lead to the answer to this question.

Passage B

11. **1** "repetition." The opening line reveals the key metaphor in the poem, but the main idea is strengthened through repetition, notably of "night" and "assembly line." There are no examples of simile, allusion, or understatement in the stanza, and metaphor is not offered as a choice.

12. **2** "humans and nature." The central idea in the second stanza is that "the stars must be exhausted" by years of unchanging work (journeys) and by choking smog and monotony. In line 17, the poet asserts that "We share" the same exhaustion, sickness, and loss of individuality ("their color and shape"). None of the other choices is suggested by the images in this stanza.

13. **4** "uncertainty." In lines 20–21, repetition of the phrases beginning with "perhaps" establishes the sense of uncertainty in the poet's voice. There is also a strong feeling of bitterness and regret in the poem, but the question focuses on the language in these two lines: "uncertainty" is the best answer among these choices.

14. **1** "resignation to life." The images in the last stanza reveal the poet's acceptance of a life that is manufactured and fated: he is numb to his existence and "unable to show concern." None of the other choices is suggested in these lines.

Passage C

15. **2** "perspective." The first sentence establishes Rodriguez's perspective in this passage: the memory of boyhood will "remind the adult" of how through language he grew out of his protected but linguistically limiting childhood.

16. **3** "contrasting cultures." In this paragraph, Rodriguez recalls how his parents struggled in the public world of English speakers but could recover, at home, the ease and comfort that speaking their native Spanish gave them. The contrast here is in cultures, not in memories, principles, or philosophies.

17. **1** "eagerness to learn." "Wide-eyed with hearing" is a lovely metaphor to describe how eager Rodriguez was to distinguish first the differences in sound between English and Spanish and to understand how the sounds of a language conveyed meaning even before he knew the words. The image of one who is wide-eyed conveys a sense of wonder and openness to take in something new.

18. **4** "separation." This paragraph further develops the contrast between the comfort and cultural ease of life at home and the challenges of interactions in the public, English-speaking world. How Rodriguez overcame this "separation" is the key theme of the passage.

19. **1** "communicate effectively." These lines are a vivid description of what it is like to try to communicate before one has sufficient language skills: he could not "form complete thoughts . . . make distinct [English] sounds"; and listeners struggled to hear what he was trying to say. This is the best answer among the choices.

20. **2** "conflicting feelings." The narrator claims at first that "it didn't matter much that my parents could not speak English with ease." "And yet . . . it mattered very much" because he found it unsettling and became nervous about a loss in their "protection and power."

21. **1** "narrator's sense of security." In this paragraph, Rodriguez describes the reassurance he would feel in hearing the sounds of the language of their life in private: he feels "recognized as one of the family . . . *someone special*." He felt "embraced by the sounds of their words." These are all feelings of security. None of the other choices expresses the feelings in this paragraph.

22. **2** "I'd listen to sounds more than to words." Throughout the passage, Rodriguez emphasizes the importance of sounds as he grows up and ultimately learns to speak fluent English. It is the sounds of Spanish that console and reassure him; it is the sounds of English in public that signal a different culture. He tells us toward the end of the passage that, "I lived in a world compounded of sounds." This is the best answer to the question.

23. **1** "disconnected from his family." In the final paragraph, Rodriguez describes the change, the loss, of "intimate sounds" at home: now the sounds are noises from life outside. He is hearing words, the words of public language. The disconnection from his family occurs as "my childhood started to end."

24. **3** "confidence." The act of raising his hand in class and speaking loudly, "to an entire roomful of faces," is a vivid image of the boy confident in expressing himself in the public world of English. None of the other choices captures the significance of what Rodriguez tells us here.

PART 2—Argument Response

Sample Essay Response

In recent years especially, there has been growing concern for conditions in third-world societies and the welfare of their people. Numerous non-profit organizations have been established to address the humanitarian issues in said societies through fundraising and charity. However, these organizations must grab people's attention to raise what they need to help other people in needy situations. What better way to do that than to use celebrities to promote the cause? There is a debate regarding the ethics of using celebrities to promote non-profit organizations, however. While some may believe that celebrities should not be the voice for humanitarian causes, I emphatically believe that celebrities should become the voice of such causes for two compelling reasons.

First, I believe that celebrities should be the voice of humanitarian causes because they can be actively involved by donating their money and their time. According to "The Celebrity Solution," "the premise of microfinance is that very poor people should have access to credit, just as the middle class and the rich do." (Text 1, lines 48–49) The article states that the support of microfinance projects by the actress Natalie Portman means poor people will benefit immensely.

"People come to see Natalie Portman, and they go away learning about microfinance." (Text 1, lines 70–71) According to the article "Do Celebrity Humanitarians Matter?" "celebrities are welcome figures in humanitarianism: educating the public on global issues, raising funds, and using their populist appeal to draw attention to policy-making arenas." (Text 3, lines 37–39) Basically the article is stating that celebrities can be directly involved in promoting and being dedicated to their causes by educating the public and raising money through concerts or other events.

However, "Do Celebrity Humanitarians Matter?" also claims that "For others, celebrity humanitarians are highly problematic figures who dilute debates, offer misguided policy proposals, and lack credibility and accountability." (Text 3, lines 39–41) I disagree with the previous statement because I believe celebrities can easily become educated themselves about a cause through their own research.

Secondly, celebrities have the ability to use their popularity to draw attention to a humanitarian cause. As "The Rise of the Celebrity Humanitarian" puts it, "Hollywood's elite get to wield their unique ability to engage diverse audiences, and the power of celebrity is put to good use effecting change." (Text 4, lines 8–10) Basically the article states that celebrities can influence change by using their popularity. With the use of social media on the rise, celebrities have a powerful means of connecting with the people to promote a cause. According to

"Ethics of Celebrities and Their Increasing Influence in 21st Century Society," *"[c]elebrities and famous people in turn, help to bring people, including adults, together in conversation and social interaction." (Text 2, lines 45–46) This means that through the use of the Internet, celebrities can get the public involved in their cause. However, Text 4 also argues, "if the star's popularity takes a hit, it can affect the reception of the cause." (Text 4, lines 21–22) Although this has been known to happen, in the case of Lance Armstrong for example, humanitarian causes can recover from their celebrity spokesperson's decline in popularity and find a new voice for the cause.*

    I emphatically believe that celebrities should be the voice for humanitarian causes. Celebrities have an uncanny ability to draw attention to a cause, which in turn would undoubtedly benefit those in need.

Analysis

This essay offers a good example of the argument supporting the role of celebrities in humanitarian causes. The opening paragraph outlines the issue and clearly establishes the writer's position: first, with a rhetorical question, "What better way . . . than to use celebrities to promote the cause?" and then with a forceful assertion of the controlling idea: "I emphatically believe that celebrities should become the voice of such causes for two compelling reasons." The reference to a debate over the ethics of using celebrities for humanitarian causes at the beginning establishes that opposing views will be acknowledged.

    The argument is organized clearly, with a paragraph devoted to each of the writer's claims. Key points are developed and supported with relevant references to all four texts: some give support to the writer's point of view and some offer opportunities to refute opposing arguments. Development is minimal but adequate; the conclusion is less forcefully expressed than the body of the argument is. The overall strategy of argument is sound, however, and the writer demonstrates control of the conventions. This argument would merit a high score.

(See pages 79–80 for the scoring guidelines.)

PART 3—Text-Analysis Response

Sample Essay Response

In this passage, the author depicts Charleston, South Carolina, as an understated and beautiful place where anything is possible. The author feels that Charleston has the power to shape people and have an ever-lasting influence on their lives. This idea of Charleston's power is developed through the author's use of figurative language.

The author is in awe of Charleston's beauty and subtle power. In lines 31–32, imagery is used when Charleston's gardens are described as containing "plants that look embroidered and stolen from the Garden of Eden." This description emphasizes how delicate and cared for Charleston is because embroidery involves delicate and intricate work. Also, by comparing something in Charleston to the Garden of Eden, it is elevated and placed on a holy level. Additionally, the author uses metaphor on lines 46–47 when he states that "Charleston is a permanent dimple in the understated skyline, while the rest of us are only visitors." This emphasizes Charleston's permanence and subtle power. While people may come and go, Charleston is forever. Lastly, Charleston is personified at line 74 when it is given "its own heartbeat and fingerprint."

By giving Charleston life-like qualities, the author dramatizes the city's power. Charleston is elevated by being compared to a human. The author feels blessed and honored to have grown up in a place like Charleston, and this passage shows its significant and omnipresent force in his life.

Analysis

This richness of language and passionate feelings of the author give students a number of ways to discuss this passage. Point of view is an obvious choice, as are diction, tone, and theme. This writer chose figurative language as a focus for analysis and offers excellent examples of imagery, metaphor, and personification. The essay has a clear plan of development: the opening paragraph expresses the overall theme of the passage and establishes the writer's controlling idea. The second paragraph offers three relevant examples of figurative language, and each is illustrated with an appropriate quote from the passage. Note too that the examples are developed in order of their significance to the overall theme. The final paragraph is a strong statement of how the figurative language supports the author's theme. The writing is clear and demonstrates the writer's control of the conventions. This response would merit a high score.

(See pages 81–82 for the scoring guidelines.)

Regents ELA Examination August 2016

English Language Arts

PART 1—Reading Comprehension

Directions (1–24): Closely read each of the three passages below. After each passage, there are several multiple-choice questions. Select the best suggested answer to each question and write its number in the space provided. You may use the margins to take notes as you read.

Reading Comprehension Passage A

. . .Three years in London had not changed Richard, although it had changed the way he perceived the city. Richard had originally imagined London as a gray city, even a black city, from pictures he had seen, and he was surprised to find it filled with color. It was a city of red brick and white
(5) stone, red buses and large black taxis, bright red mailboxes and green grassy parks and cemeteries. . . .

Two thousand years before, London had been a little Celtic village on the north shore of the Thames, which the Romans had encountered, then settled in. London had grown, slowly, until, roughly a thousand years later, it
(10) met the tiny Royal City of Westminster immediately to the west, and, once London Bridge had been built, London touched the town of Southwark directly across the river; and it continued to grow, fields and woods and marshland slowly vanishing beneath the flourishing town, and it continued to expand, encountering other little villages and hamlets as it grew, like
(15) Whitechapel and Deptford to the east, Hammersmith and Shepherd's Bush to the west, Camden and Islington in the north, Battersea and Lambeth across the Thames to the south, absorbing all of them, just as a pool of mercury encounters and incorporates smaller beads of mercury, leaving only their names behind.

(20)   London grew into something huge and contradictory. It was a good place, and a fine city, but there is a price to be paid for all good places, and a price that all good places have to pay.

After a while, Richard found himself taking London for granted; in time, he began to pride himself on having visited none of the sights of (25) London (except for the Tower of London, when his Aunt Maude came down to the city for a weekend, and Richard found himself her reluctant escort).

But Jessica changed all that. Richard found himself, on otherwise sensible weekends, accompanying her to places like the National Gallery and the Tate Gallery, where he learned that walking around museums too (30) long hurts your feet, that the great art treasures of the world all blur into each other after a while, and that it is almost beyond the human capacity for belief to accept how much museum cafeterias will brazenly charge for a slice of cake and a cup of tea. . . .

Richard had been awed by Jessica, who was beautiful, and often quite (35) funny, and was certainly going somewhere. And Jessica saw in Richard an enormous amount of potential, which, properly harnessed by the right woman, would have made him the perfect matrimonial accessory. If only he were a little more focused, she would murmur to herself, and so she gave him books with titles like *Dress for Success* and *A Hundred and Twenty-* (40) *Five Habits of Successful Men*, and books on how to run a business like a military campaign, and Richard always said thank you, and always intended to read them. In Harvey Nichols's men's fashion department she would pick out for him the kinds of clothes she thought that he should wear—and he wore them, during the week, anyway; and, a year to the day after their first (45) encounter, she told him she thought it was time that they went shopping for an engagement ring.

"Why do you go out with her?" asked Gary, in Corporate Accounts, eighteen months later. "She's terrifying."

Richard shook his head. "She's really sweet, once you get to know her."
(50)   Gary put down the plastic troll doll he had picked up from Richard's desk. "I'm surprised she still lets you play with these." . . .

It was a Friday afternoon. Richard had noticed that events were cowards: they didn't occur singly, but instead they would run in packs and leap out at him all at once. Take this particular Friday, for example. It was, as (55) Jessica had pointed out to him at least a dozen times in the last month, the most important day of his life. So it was unfortunate that, despite the Post-it note Richard had left on his fridge door at home, and the other Post-it note he had placed on the photograph of Jessica on his desk, he had forgotten about it completely and utterly.

(60)   Also, there was the Wandsworth report, which was overdue and taking up most of his head. Richard checked another row of figures; then he noticed that page 17 had vanished, and he set it up to print out again; and another page down, and he knew that if he were only left alone to finish it . . . if, miracle of miracles, the phone did not ring. . . . It rang. He thumbed (65) the speakerphone.

"Hello? Richard? The managing director needs to know when he'll have the report."

Richard looked at his watch. "Five minutes, Sylvia. It's almost wrapped up. I just have to attach the P & L projection."

(70)   "Thanks, Dick. I'll come down for it." Sylvia was, as she liked to explain, "the MD's PA," [Managing Director's Personal Assistant] and she moved in an atmosphere of crisp efficiency. He thumbed the speaker phone off; it rang again, immediately. "Richard," said the speaker, with Jessica's voice, "it's Jessica. You haven't forgotten, have you?"

(75)   "Forgotten?" He tried to remember what he could have forgotten. He looked at Jessica's photograph for inspiration and found all the inspiration he could have needed in the shape of a yellow Post-it note stuck to her forehead.

"Richard? Pick up the telephone."

(80)   He picked up the phone, reading the Post-it note as he did so. "Sorry, Jess. No, I hadn't forgotten. Seven P.M., at Ma Maison Italiano. Should I meet you there?"

"Jessica, Richard. Not Jess." She paused for a moment. "After what happened last time? I don't think so. You really could get lost in your own (85) backyard, Richard." . . .

"I'll meet you at your place," said Jessica. "We can walk down together."

"Right, Jess. Jessica—sorry."

"You *have* confirmed our reservation, haven't you, Richard."

"Yes," lied Richard earnestly. The other line on his phone had begun to (90) ring. "Jessica, look, I. . ."

"Good," said Jessica, and she broke the connection. He picked up the other line.

"Hi Dick. It's me, Gary." Gary sat a few desks down from Richard. He waved. "Are we still on for drinks? You said we could go over the Merstham (95) account."

"Get off the bloody phone, Gary. Of course we are." Richard put down the phone. There was a telephone number at the bottom of the Post-it note; Richard had written the Post-it note to himself, several weeks earlier. And he *had* made the reservation: he was almost certain of that. But he had not

(100) confirmed it. He had kept meaning to, but there had been so much to do
and Richard had known that there was plenty of time. But events run in
packs. . .

Sylvia was now standing next to him. "Dick? The Wandsworth report?"

"Almost ready, Sylvia. Look, just hold on a sec, can you?"

(105) He finished punching in the number, breathed a sigh of relief when
somebody answered. "Ma Maison. Can I help you?"

"Yes," said Richard. "A table for three, for tonight. I think I booked it.
And if I did I'm confirming the reservation. And if I didn't, I wondered if I
could book it. Please." No, they had no record of a table for tonight in the
(110) name of Mayhew. Or Stockton. Or Bartram—Jessica's surname. And as for
booking a table. . .

They had put down the phone.

"Richard?" said Sylvia. "The MD's waiting."

"Do you think," asked Richard, "they'd give me a table if I phoned back
(115) and offered them extra money?" . . .

—Neil Gaiman
excerpted and adapted from *Neverwhere*, 1997
Avon Books

1 The author most likely includes the description of London in lines 1 through 22 to

  (1) provide reasons for Richard's dislike of the city
  (2) highlight opportunities for Richard's career in the city
  (3) convey a sense of Richard's frustration with the city
  (4) illustrate the nature of Richard's life in the city   1 _____

2 The figurative language used in lines 17 to 19 reinforces the

  (1) growth of the city
  (2) problems with development
  (3) increase in isolation
  (4) history of the towns   2 _____

3 The narrator uses lines 27 through 33 to help the reader understand Richard's

  (1) continuous efforts to save money while on dates
  (2) willingness to tolerate undesirable situations to please others
  (3) overall acceptance of cultural experiences in the city
  (4) affection for newfound experiences when shared with others   3 _____

4 In the context of the text as a whole, which statement regarding lines 47 through 49 is true?

  (1) Gary is jealous of Richard because he has a girlfriend.
  (2) Gary has a moody temperament and hides his feelings.
  (3) Richard has a plan and wishes to keep it a secret.
  (4) Richard is in a state of denial regarding his relationship.   4 _____

5 How do lines 52 through 54 contribute to the characterization of Richard?

  (1) by portraying him as inefficient at organizing his time
  (2) by indicating that he works well under pressure
  (3) by describing him as likely to succeed
  (4) by suggesting that he is unmotivated in his job   5 _____

6 The narrator's description of Sylvia as moving "in an atmosphere of crisp efficiency" (lines 71 and 72) presents a

(1) shift   (3) contrast

(2) possibility   (4) solution   6 _____

7 Lines 79 through 85 contribute to a central idea by highlighting Jessica's

(1) domineering nature

(2) compassionate side

(3) lack of responsibility

(4) sense of humor   7 _____

8 The narrator's use of dialogue in lines 79 through 96 enhances a mood of

(1) satisfaction   (3) confidence

(2) stress   (4) remorse   8 _____

9 Richard's question in lines 114 and 115 reveals his

(1) subtle refinement   (3) honest gratitude

(2) suppressed hostility   (4) quiet desperation   9 _____

10 Which quote best reflects a central theme in the text?

(1) "London grew into something huge and contradictory . . . and a price that all good places have to pay." (lines 20 through 22)

(2) "Richard checked another row of figures . . . and he set it up to print out again;" (lines 61 and 62)

(3) "Richard looked at his watch. 'Five minutes, Sylvia. It's almost wrapped up. I just have to attach the P & L projection.' " (lines 68 and 69)

(4) "He finished punching in the number, breathed a sigh of relief when somebody answered. 'Ma Maison. Can I help you?' " (lines 105 and 106)   10 _____

Reading Comprehension Passage B

We Are Many

Of the many men whom I am, whom we are,
I cannot settle on a single one.
They are lost to me under the cover of clothing.
They have departed for another city.

(5) When everything seems to be set
to show me off as a man of intelligence,
the fool I keep concealed on my person
takes over my talk and occupies my mouth.

On other occasions, I am dozing in the midst
(10) of people of some distinction,
and when I summon my courageous self,
a coward completely unknown to me
swaddles[1] my poor skeleton
in a thousand tiny reservations.

(15) When a stately home bursts into flames,
instead of the fireman I summon,
an arsonist bursts on the scene,
and he is I. There is nothing I can do.
What must I do to distinguish myself?
(20) How can I put myself together?

All the books I read
lionize[2] dazzling hero figures,
always brimming with self-assurance.
I die with envy of them;
(25) and, in films where bullets fly on the wind,
I am left in envy of the cowboys,
left admiring even the horses.

---

[1]swaddles—wraps   [2]lionize—glorify

But when I call upon my dashing being,
out comes the same old lazy self,
(30) and so I never know just who I am,
nor how many I am, nor who we will be being.
I would like to be able to touch a bell
and call up my real self, the truly me,
because if I really need my proper self,
(35) I must not allow myself to disappear.

While I am writing, I am far away;
and when I come back, I have already left.
I should like to see if the same thing happens
to other people as it does to me,
(40) to see if as many people are as I am,
and if they seem the same way to themselves.
When this problem has been thoroughly explored,
I am going to school myself so well in things
that, when I try to explain my problems,
(45) I shall speak, not of self, but of geography.

—Pablo Neruda
from *We Are Many*, 1970
translated by Alastair Reid
Grossman Publishers

11 The overall purpose of the figurative language in lines 12 through
  14 is to show the narrator's

   (1) contempt for self-reliance
   (2) desire for adventure
   (3) lack of self-confidence
   (4) jealousy of writers   11 _____

12 A primary function of the questions in lines 19 and 20 is to

   (1) introduce the narrator's biases
   (2) challenge the narrator's beliefs
   (3) clarify the narrator's dilemma
   (4) explain the narrator's decision   12 _____

13 The contradictions presented throughout the poem serve to illustrate the relationship between

   (1) society's conflicts and the narrator's reaction
   (2) the narrator's sensibilities and his determination
   (3) society's expectations and the narrator's possibilities
   (4) the narrator's idealism and his reality   13 _____

14 The solution proposed in lines 42 through 45 can best be described as

   (1) balanced   (3) inappropriate
   (2) universal   (4) unrealistic   14 _____

Reading Comprehension Passage C

. . .By natural design, dogs' ears have evolved to hear certain kinds of sounds. Happily, that set of sounds overlaps with those we can hear and produce: if we utter it, it will at least hit the eardrum of a nearby dog. Our auditory range is from 20 hertz to 20 kilohertz: from the lowest pitch on
(5) the longest organ pipe to an impossibly squeaky squeak. We spend most of our time straining to understand sounds between 100 hertz and 1 kilohertz, the range of any interesting speech going on in the vicinity. Dogs hear most of what we hear and then some. They can detect sounds up to 45 kilohertz, much higher than the hair cells of our ears bother to bend to. Hence the
(10) power of the dog whistle, a seemingly magical device that makes no apparent sound and yet perks the ears of dogs for blocks around. We call this sound "ultrasonic," since it's beyond our ken,[1] but it is within the sonic range for many animals in our local environment. Don't think for a moment that apart from the occasional dog whistle, the world is quiet for dogs up at those high
(15) registers. Even a typical room is pulsing with high frequencies, detectable by dogs constantly. Think your bedroom is quiet when you rise in the morning? The crystal resonator used in digital alarm clocks emits a never-ending alarm of high-frequency pulses audible to canine ears. Dogs can hear the navigational chirping of rats behind your walls and the bodily vibrations of
(20) termites within your walls. That compact fluorescent light you installed to save energy? You may not hear the hum, but your dog probably can.

The range of pitches we are most intent on are those used in speech. Dogs hear all sounds of speech, and are nearly as good as we are at detecting a change of pitch—relevant, say, for understanding statements, which end
(25) in a low pitch, versus questions, which in English end in a raised pitch: "Do you want to go for a walk(?)" With the question mark, this sentence is exciting to a dog with experience going on walks with humans. Without it, it is simply noise. Imagine the confusion generated by the recent growth of "up-talking," speech that ends every sentence with the sound of a question?
(30)   If dogs understand the stress and tones—the *prosody*—of speech, does this hint that they understand language? This is a natural but vexed[2] question. Since language use is one of the most glaring differences between the human animal and all other animals, it has been proposed as the ultimate, incomparable criterion for intelligence. This raises serious hackles[3] in some
(35) animal researchers (not thought of as a hackled species, ironically), who have

---

[1]ken—recognition [2]vexed—problematic [3]raises serious hackles—arouses anger

set about trying to demonstrate what linguistic ability animals have. Even those researchers who may agree that language is necessary for intelligence have nonetheless added reams of results to the growing pile of evidence of linguistic ability in non-human animals. All parties agree, though, (40) that there has been no discovery of a humanlike language—a corpus[4] of infinitely combinable words that often carry many definitions, with rules for combining words into meaningful sentences—in animals.

This is not to say that animals might not understand some of our language use, even if they don't produce it themselves. There are, for (45) instance, many examples of animals taking advantage of the communicative system of nearby unrelated animal species. Monkeys can make use of nearby birds' warning calls of a nearby predator to themselves take protective action. Even an animal who deceives another animal by mimicry—which some snakes, moths, and even flies can do—is in some way using another (50) species's [*sic*] language.

The research with dogs suggests that they do understand language—to a limited degree. On the one hand, to say that dogs understand *words* is a misnomer. Words exist in a language, which itself is product of a culture; dogs are participants in that culture on a very different level. Their framework (55) for understanding the application of the word is entirely different. There is, no doubt, more to the words of their world than Gary Larson's *Far Side* comics suggest: eat, walk, and fetch. But he is on to something, insofar as these are organizing elements of their interaction with us: we circumscribe the dog's world to a small set of activities. Working dogs seem miraculously (60) responsive and focused compared to city pets. It is not that they are innately more responsive or focused, but that their owners have added to their vocabularies types of things to do.

One component in understanding a word is the ability to discriminate it from other words. Given their sensitivity to the prosody of speech, dogs do (65) not always excel at this. Try asking your dog on one morning to *go for a walk*; on the next, ask if your dog wants to *snow forty locks* in the same voice. If everything else remains the same, you'll probably get the same, affirmative reaction. The very first sounds of an utterance seem to be important to dog perception, though, so changing the swallowed consonants for articulated (70) ones and the long vowels for short ones—*ma for a polk?*—might prompt the confusion merited by this gibberish. Of course humans read meaning into prosody, too. English does not give the prosody of speech syntactical leverage but it is still part of how we interpret "what has just been said."

---

[4]corpus—collection

If we were more sensitive to the *sound* of what we say to dogs, we might
(75) get better responses from them. High-pitched sounds mean something
different than low sounds; rising sounds contrast with falling sounds. It is
not accidental that we find ourselves cooing to an infant in silly, giddy
tones (called *motherese*)—and might greet a wagging dog with similar baby
talk. Infants can hear other speech sounds, but they are more interested
(80) in motherese. Dogs, too, respond with alacrity[5] to baby talk—partially
because it distinguishes speech that is directed *at* them from the rest of the
continuous yammering above their heads. Moreover, they will come more
easily to high-pitched and repeated call requests than to those at a lower
pitch. What is the ecology behind this? High-pitched sounds are naturally
(85) interesting to dogs: they might indicate the excitement of a tussle or the
shrieking of nearby injured prey. If a dog fails to respond to your reasonable
suggestion that he come *right now*, resist the urge to lower and sharpen
your tone. It indicates your frame of mind—and the punishment that might
ensue for his prior uncooperativeness. Correspondingly, it is easier to get a
(90) dog to *sit* on command to a longer, descending tone rather than repeated,
rising notes. Such a tone might be more likely to induce relaxation, or
preparation for the next command from their talky human. . . .

—Alexandra Horowitz
excerpted from *Inside of a Dog*, 2010
Scribner

---

[5]alacrity—eagerness

15 Lines 1 through 13 introduce the central idea of the passage by

(1) explaining how ear structure affects sound
(2) describing various frequencies dogs hear
(3) explaining various ways humans hear
(4) describing how dog whistle tones differ   15 _____

16 Lines 22 through 26 best support the idea that

(1) dogs cannot learn to obey human signals
(2) human actions are difficult for dogs to interpret
(3) humans can verbally communicate with dogs
(4) dogs can learn complex human language   16 _____

17 Based on lines 22 through 29, humans can possibly confuse dogs by

(1) speaking to dogs in a nonsense language
(2) giving dogs only direct commands
(3) making gestures when speaking to dogs
(4) altering the intonation of familiar words   17 _____

18 Lines 30 through 34 that language use is an indicator of

(1) higher-level thinking
(2) basic survival instinct
(3) increased emotional response
(4) problem-solving skills   18 _____

19 In lines 39 through 42, the author states there is agreement that non-human animals cannot

(1) master complicated directions
(2) duplicate human sound pitches
(3) create human sentence structures
(4) interpret foreign languages   19 _____

20 The primary function of the examples in lines 44 through 50 is to show how some animals can

(1) imitate behavior and sound
(2) foster community and diversity
(3) transform from prey to predator
(4) compromise freedom for safety   20 _____

21 The author uses the term "gibberish" in line 71 to emphasize the

   (1) importance of word order
   (2) complexity of spoken sounds
   (3) relevance of hidden gestures
   (4) necessity of voice and movement   21 _____

22 Which sentence best restates a central idea in lines 68 through 76?

   (1) High-pitched sounds often cause dogs to become agitated.
   (2) How we speak to dogs is more important than what we say.
   (3) Dogs must learn to interpret human speech early in life.
   (4) Dogs become distressed when they hear baby talk.   22 _____

23 The author's reference to "motherese" (line 78) helps to illustrate a connection between the

   (1) combinations of languages and the effects on listeners
   (2) volume of speech and possible misperception
   (3) importance of word choice and its impact on understanding
   (4) styles of spoken communication and likely responses   23 _____

24 The primary purpose of the text is to

   (1) explain a popular myth regarding dogs' behavior
   (2) promote a new method for working with dogs
   (3) educate people about dogs' experience with sound
   (4) present an alternative to traditional dog training   24 _____

PART 2—Argument Response

Directions Closely read each of the *four* texts on pages 137 through 145 and write a source-based argument on the topic below. You may use the margins to take notes as you read and scrap paper to plan your response. Write your argument on a separate sheet of paper.

Topic: Should the United States government create strict sugar regulations?

Your Task: Carefully read each of the *four* texts provided. Then, using evidence from at least *three* of the texts, write a well-developed argument regarding whether or not the United States government should create strict sugar regulations. Clearly establish your claim, distinguish your claim from alternate or opposing claims, and use specific, relevant, and sufficient evidence from at least *three* of the texts to develop your argument. Do *not* simply summarize each text.

Guidelines:

Be sure to

- Establish your claim regarding whether or not the United States government should create strict sugar regulations.
- Distinguish your claim from alternate or opposing claims.
- Use specific, relevant, and sufficient evidence from at least *three* of the texts to develop your argument.
- Identify each source that you reference by text number and line number(s) or graphic (for example: Text 1, line 4 or Text 2, graphic).
- Organize your ideas in a cohesive and coherent manner.
- Maintain a formal style of writing.
- Follow the conventions of standard written English.

Texts:

Text 1—FDA Urged to Regulate Sugar in Drinks

Text 2—Sugar Should Be Regulated As Toxin, Researchers Say

Text 3—The Toxic Truth About Sugar

Text 4—Sugar Taxes Are Unfair and Unhealthy

Text 1

FDA Urged to Regulate Sugar in Drinks

WASHINGTON—The US Food and Drug Administration [FDA] should regulate the amount of added sugars in soda and other sweetened beverages to reverse the obesity epidemic, a Washington-based nutrition activist group urged in a petition signed by Harvard School of Public Health
(5) researchers, the Boston Public Health Commission, and others.

"The FDA considers sugar to be a safe food at the recommended level of consumption, but Americans are consuming two to three times that much," Michael Jacobson, executive director of the Center for Science in the Public Interest, which filed the petition, said at a press briefing on Wednesday. He
(10) added that the average American consumes 78 pounds of added sugars each year, mostly from high fructose corn syrup prevalent in sugary sodas, sports drinks, and fruit punch. . . .

Over the past half-century, Americans have dramatically increased their intake of sugary drinks, and research suggests this has contributed to
(15) the obesity epidemic and a rise in related diseases such as type 2 diabetes, heart disease, and a variety of cancers.

"The evidence is very robust that when we eat more sugar we gain weight and when we eat less, we lose weight," said Dr. Walter Willett, chairman of nutrition at the Harvard School of Public Health, who also spoke at the
(20) briefing. "Each 12-ounce serving of soda a person consumes each day raises type 2 diabetes risk by 10 to 15 percent, and many Americans are consuming five or six servings."

While the FDA has the authority to set limits on ingredients on its "generally recognized as safe" list, it has not done so for many of them,
(25) including table sugar and high fructose corn syrup.

Jeffrey Senger, former acting chief counsel of the FDA who is now a partner at the law firm Sidley Austin, said it is unlikely the agency would act to restrict sugar. "Any food, if it's abused, can be unhealthy," he said. "Sugar isn't the same thing as arsenic. It's not a food that's inherently unsafe." . . .

(30) She [FDA spokeswoman, Shelly Burgess] confirmed that the latest petition was received and would be reviewed by FDA officials, but added that the FDA was not aware of any evidence highlighting added safety risks from high fructose corn syrup compared with other sugars such as honey, table sugar, or molasses.

(35)   That suggests that the agency might have a hard time requiring Coke or Pepsi to limit their products to 10 grams of added sugar per serving—what many public health specialists recommend—without also requiring the same limits on cereal, baked goods, and other processed foods.

      "To limit the amount of added sugars in beverages, the FDA would
(40) need to establish that there is enough scientific evidence to justify limiting these ingredients and to go through a rulemaking process that allows for public comment," said Miriam Guggenheim, a partner in the food and beverage practice at Covington & Burling LLP in Washington, D.C.

      Taking a firm position against government regulations to limit added
(45) sugars, the American Beverage Association, which represents soft drink manufacturers, pointed out in a statement on its website that companies have already made efforts to reduce sugar in sweetened beverages.

      "Today about 45 percent of all non-alcoholic beverages purchased have zero calories," the group said, "and the overall average number of calories
(50) per beverage serving is down 23 percent since 1998." . . .

      About half of Americans consume sugary beverages on any given day, according to the latest data from the federal Centers for Disease Control and Prevention, and consumption of sugary beverages has increased among children and adults over the past 30 years.

—Deborah Kotz
excerpted and adapted from "FDA Urged to Regulate Sugar in Drinks"
http://www.bostonglobe.com, February 14, 2013

Text 2

Sugar Should Be Regulated As Toxin, Researchers Say

A spoonful of sugar might make the medicine go down. But it also makes blood pressure and cholesterol go up, along with your risk for liver failure, obesity, heart disease and diabetes.

Sugar and other sweeteners are, in fact, so toxic to the human body that
(5) they should be regulated as strictly as alcohol by governments worldwide, according to a commentary in the current issue of the journal Nature by researchers at the University of California, San Francisco (UCSF).

The researchers propose regulations such as taxing all foods and drinks that include added sugar, banning sales in or near schools and placing age
(10) limits on purchases.

Although the commentary might seem straight out of the Journal of Ideas That Will Never Fly, the researchers cite numerous studies and statistics to make their case that added sugar—or, more specifically, sucrose, an even mix of glucose and fructose found in high-fructose corn syrup and in
(15) table sugar made from sugar cane and sugar beets—has been as detrimental to society as alcohol and tobacco.

Sour words about sugar

. . .Many researchers are seeing sugar as not just "empty calories," but rather a chemical that becomes toxic in excess. At issue is the fact that glucose from complex carbohydrates, such as whole grains, is safely metabolized by
(20) cells throughout the body, but the fructose element of sugar is metabolized primarily by the liver. This is where the trouble can begin—taxing the liver, causing fatty liver disease, and ultimately leading to insulin resistance, the underlying causes of obesity and diabetes.

Added sugar, more so than the fructose in fiber-rich fruit, hits the liver
(25) more directly and can cause more damage—in laboratory rodents, anyway. Some researchers, however, remained unconvinced of the evidence of sugar's toxic effect on the human body at current consumption levels, as high as they are.

Economists to the rescue

[Robert] Lustig, a medical doctor in UCSF's Department of Pediatrics,
(30) compares added sugar to tobacco and alcohol (coincidentally made from
sugar) in that it is addictive, toxic and has a negative impact on society, thus
meeting established public health criteria for regulation. Lustig advocates a
consumer tax on any product with added sugar.

Among Lustig's more radical proposals are to ban the sale of sugary
(35) drinks to children under age 17 and to tighten zoning laws for the sale
of sugary beverages and snacks around schools and in low-income areas
plagued by obesity, analogous to alcoholism and alcohol regulation.

Economists, however, debate as to whether a consumer tax—such as
a soda tax proposed in many U.S. states—is the most effective means of
(40) curbing sugar consumption. Economists at Iowa State University led by
John Beghin suggest taxing the sweetener itself at the manufacturer level,
not the end product containing sugar.

This concept, published last year in the journal Contemporary
Economic Policy, would give companies an incentive to add less sweetener
(45) to their products. After all, high-fructose corn syrup is ubiquitous[1] in food
in part because it is so cheap and serves as a convenient substitute for more
high-quality ingredients, such as fresher vegetables in processed foods.

Some researchers argue that saturated fat, not sugar, is the root cause
of obesity and chronic disease. Others argue that it is highly processed foods
(50) with simple carbohydrates. Still others argue that it is a lack of physical
exercise. It could, of course, be a matter of all these issues.

—Christopher Wanjek
excerpted and adapted from "Sugar Should Be
Regulated As Toxin, Researchers Say"
http://www.livescience.com, February 1, 2012

---

[1]ubiquitous—present everywhere

Text 3

The Toxic Truth About Sugar

. . .No Ordinary Commodity

In 2003, social psychologist Thomas Babor and his colleagues published a landmark book called *Alcohol: No Ordinary Commodity*, in
which they established four criteria, now largely accepted by the public-
health community, that justify the regulation of alcohol—unavoidability (or
(5) pervasiveness throughout society), toxicity, potential for abuse and negative
impact on society. Sugar meets the same criteria, and we believe that it
similarly warrants some form of societal intervention.

First, consider unavoidability. Evolutionarily, sugar as fruit was available to
our ancestors for only a few months a year (at harvest time), or as honey, which
(10) was guarded by bees. But in recent years, sugar has been added to virtually
every processed food, limiting consumer choice. Nature made sugar hard to
get; man made it easy. In many parts of the world, people are consuming an
average of more than 500 calories per day from added sugar alone.

Now, let's consider toxicity. A growing body of epidemiological and
(15) mechanistic[1] evidence argues that excessive sugar consumption affects
human health beyond simply adding calories. Importantly, sugar induces
all of the diseases associated with metabolic syndrome. This includes:
hypertension (fructose increases uric acid, which raises blood pressure);
high triglycerides and insulin resistance through synthesis of fat in the liver;
(20) diabetes from increased liver glucose production combined with insulin
resistance; and the ageing process, caused by damage to lipids, proteins and
DNA [deoxyribonucleic acid] through non-enzymatic binding of fructose to
these molecules. It can also be argued that fructose exerts toxic effects on
the liver similar to those of alcohol. This is no surprise, because alcohol is
(25) derived from the fermentation of sugar. Some early studies have also linked
sugar consumption to human cancer and cognitive decline.

Sugar also has a clear potential for abuse. Like tobacco and alcohol, it
acts on the brain to encourage subsequent intake. There are now numerous studies examining the dependence-producing properties of sugar
(30) in humans. Specifically, sugar dampens the suppression of the hormone
ghrelin, which signals hunger to the brain. It also interferes with the normal
transport and signalling of the hormone leptin, which helps to produce the

---

[1]epidemiological and mechanistic—evidence based on the study of the causes, incidence, and treatment of diseases

feeling of satiety.[2] And it reduces dopamine signalling in the brain's reward centre, thereby decreasing the pleasure derived from food and compelling
(35) the individual to consume more.

Finally, consider the negative effects of sugar on society. Passive smoking and drink-driving fatalities provided strong arguments for tobacco and alcohol control, respectively. The long-term economic, health-care and human costs of metabolic syndrome place sugar overconsumption in the
(40) same category. The United States spends $65 billion in lost productivity and $150 billion on health-care resources annually for co-morbidities[3] associated with metabolic syndrome. Seventy-five per cent of all US health-care dollars are now spent on treating these diseases and resultant disabilities. Because 75% of military applicants are now rejected for obesity-related reasons, the
(45) past three US surgeons general and the chairman of the US Joint Chiefs of Staff have declared obesity a "threat to national security."

How to Intervene

How can we reduce sugar consumption? After all, sugar is natural. Sugar is a nutrient. Sugar is pleasure. So is alcohol, but in both cases, too much of a good thing is toxic. It may be helpful to look to the many generations of
(50) international experience with alcohol and tobacco to find models that work. So far, evidence shows that individually focused approaches, such as school-based interventions that teach children about diet and exercise, demonstrate little efficacy.[4] Conversely, for both alcohol and tobacco, there is robust evidence that gentle 'supply side' control strategies which stop far short of
(55) all-out prohibition—taxation, distribution controls, age limits—lower both consumption of the product and accompanying health harms. Successful interventions all share a common end-point: curbing availability. . . .

---

[2]satiety—fullness
[3]co-morbidities—diseases that occur simultaneously
[4]efficacy—power to produce an effect

DEADLY EFFECT Excessive consumption of fructose can cause many of the same health problems as alcohol.	
Chronic ethanol exposure	**Chronic fructose exposure**
Hematologic disorders	
Electrolyte abnormalities	
Hypertension	Hypertension (uric acid)
Cardiac dilatation	
Cardiomyopathy	Myocardial infarction (dyslipidemia, insulin resistance)
Dyslipidemia	Dyslipidemia (de novo lipogenesis)
Pancreatitis	Pancreatitis (hypertriglyceridemia)
Obesity (insulin resistance)	Obesity (insulin resistance)
Malnutrition	Malnutrition (obesity)
Hepatic dysfunction (alcoholic steatohepatitis)	Hepatic dysfunction (non-alcoholic steatohepatitis)
Fetal alcohol syndrome	
Addiction	Habituation, if not addiction

The Possible Dream

Government-imposed regulations on the marketing of alcohol to young people have been quite effective, but there is no such approach to sugar-
(60) laden products. Even so, the city of San Francisco, California, recently instituted a ban on including toys with unhealthy meals such as some types of fast food. A limit—or, ideally, ban—on television commercials for products with added sugars could further protect children's health. . . .

Ultimately, food producers and distributors must reduce the amount of
(65) sugar added to foods. But sugar is cheap, sugar tastes good, and sugar sells, so companies have little incentive to change. Although one institution alone can't turn this juggernaut[5] around, the US Food and Drug Administration could "set the table" for change. To start, it should consider removing fructose from the Generally Regarded as Safe (GRAS) list, which allows food
(70) manufacturers to add unlimited amounts to any food. Opponents will argue that other nutrients on the GRAS list, such as iron and vitamins A and D, can also be toxic when over-consumed. However, unlike sugar, these substances have no abuse potential. Removal from the GRAS list would send a powerful signal to the European Food Safety Authority and the rest of the world. . . .

—Robert H. Lustig, Laura A. Schmidt, and Claire D. Brindis
excerpted and adapted from "The Toxic Truth About Sugar"
Nature, February 2, 2012

---

[5]juggernaut—powerful force

Text 4

Sugar Taxes Are Unfair and Unhealthy

If the regulatory discussion about sugar is going to be based on science, rather than science fiction, it needs to move beyond kicking the soda can.

Conventional wisdom says draconian[1] regulation—specifically, a high tax—on sugary drinks and snacks reduces unhealthy consumption, and
(5) thereby improves public health. There are many reasons, however, why high sugar taxes are at best unsuccessful, and at worst economically and socially harmful.

Research finds that higher prices don't reduce soda consumption, for example. No scientific studies demonstrate a difference either in aggregate[2]
(10) soda consumption or in child and adolescent Body Mass Index [BMI] between the two thirds of states with soda taxes and those without such taxes.

The study that did find taxes might lead to a moderate reduction in soda consumption also found this had no effect on adolescent obesity, as
(15) the reduction was completely offset by increases in consumption of other calorific drinks.

Economic research finds sugar taxes are a futile instrument in influencing the behavior and habits of the overweight and the obese. Why do sugar taxes fail? Those consumers who strongly prefer unhealthy foods
(20) continue to eat and drink according to their individual preferences until such time as it becomes prohibitively expensive to do so.

Demand for food is largely insensitive to price. A 10 percent increase in price reduces consumption by less than 1 percent. Applied to soda, this means that to reduce consumption by 10 percent, the tax rate on sugary
(25) drinks would need to be 100 percent!

A sugar tax also has undesirable social and economic consequences. This tax is economically regressive, as a disproportionate share of the tax is paid by low earners, who pay a higher proportion of their incomes in sales tax and also consume a disproportionate share of sugary snacks and drinks.
(30)   Such taxes also have perverse, unintended consequences. Taxes on sugary snacks lead many consumers to replace the taxed food with equally unhealthy foods. Poorer consumers react to higher food prices not by

---

[1]draconian—severe
[2]aggregate—total

changing their diets but by consuming even fewer healthy foods, such as fruits and vegetables, and eating more processed foods. For instance, taxes
(35) levied specifically on sugar content increase saturated fat consumption.

Sugar taxes have failed where they've been tried, and are unfair and unhealthy. Given that there's no compelling evidence they'll improve public health, we can't justify using the tax code to shape the sweetness of our dietary choices.

—Patrick Basham
excerpted and adapted from "Sugar Taxes Are Unfair and Unhealthy"
http://www.usnews.com, March 30, 2012

PART 3—Text-Analysis Response

Your Task: Closely read the text on pages 147 through 149 and write a well-developed, text-based response of two to three paragraphs. In your response, identify a central idea in the text and analyze how the author's use of *one* writing strategy (literary element or literary technique or rhetorical device) develops this central idea. Use strong and thorough evidence from the text to support your analysis. Do *not* simply summarize the text. You may use the margins to take notes as you read and scrap paper to plan your response. Write your response on a separate sheet of paper.

> **Guidelines:**
>
> > **Be sure to**
> >
> > - Identify a central idea in the text.
> > - Analyze how the author's use of *one* writing strategy (literary element or literary technique or rhetorical device) develops this central idea. Examples include: characterization, conflict, denotation/connotation, metaphor, simile, irony, language use, point-of-view, setting, structure, symbolism, theme, tone, etc.
> > - Use strong and thorough evidence from the text to support your analysis.
> > - Organize your ideas in a cohesive and coherent manner.
> > - Maintain a formal style of writing.
> > - Follow the conventions of standard written English.

Text

. . .In the air now, I feel a new excitement, a slight surge of energy,
a new light of a new dawn. This anticipation is like grass in the path of a
distant approaching thunderstorm. I feel that the "spirit line" out of our
complacencies in art has been drawn. A fresh expression of our passions,
(5) our joys and pains is in the making. A new generation of interpretations
of our legends and stories, strengths and weaknesses as Navajo people are
replacing the images of stoic[1] tribalism that so pervaded our recent art
history. To paraphrase another artist, "realness instead of redness." I feel as
do other young fine artists of the northern reservation, that there is much
(10) potential for individual expression of beauty, of power, of mysteries to be
created within the perimeter of our culture in this time. But what inspires
us young Navajo artists to create these interpretations of our culture?
What force drives us to seek fresher means of expression? We all have
our reasons and means to do this. It may be money, it may be recognition
(15) or self-satisfaction. For me, it is a means of confronting myself, my fears
and mysteries. A means of coming to terms with childhood phobias and a
recognition of my strength and weaknesses in this day. In Navajo society, it is
necessary to journey that road to self-discovery. To attain a spiritual growth,
we will have to go beyond the world we retreat into. We must recognize
(20) and acknowledge this new high tech world, yet still maintain an identity. We
must draw a line beyond which we don't venture. Be able to compromise
wisely and know how much to expose of ourselves. Know ourselves and our
past, yet still have faith in the future. We are a segment of a society that
has been thrust into the 20th century all within 30 years. We will not allow
(25) ourselves to become casualties in this collision of cultures. The art that we
represent must be flexible and adaptable, like the nature of our grandfather,
if it is to survive, lest we become brittle and blow away like shells of dry
piñon nuts. The art that we represent, like the role of the medicine man
of today, must help in creating a positive evolution into this new era for
(30) our people and those coming after us. It will scream of tomorrow, yet be
dressed in the truth of our past. I believe this to be a collective therapy for
us, for our culture and our art. . . .

    When I was around four years old, I traveled with my grandmother
to the foot of the Sacred Mountain of the West. During this time, she told
(35) me many things. She told me that we are responsible in maintaining and
nurturing a good identity with our grandparents every single day. Each day

---

[1]stoic—calm and uncomplaining

before the sun rises, we should greet the new coming day with pollen and
re-affirm our relationship with it. To a young piñon tree, we greet "*Yá'áhtééh
shima'sáni*" (Hello, my grandmother); to a young juniper tree; "*Yá'áhtééh
(40) shí'cheii*" (hello, my grandfather). In this manner, we bring new light and
life to our world. At this age I learned to feel, see and smell my world. I still
associate lots of pieces of past experiences, painful and pleasant, to these
subtleties. There are few things more pleasant than waking up in the morning
to see dew on blades of grass, or to hear rolling of the thunder as dark clouds
(45) gather on spring days. To smell wet sand and hear the raindrops dancing on
parched ground. The cornstalks weeping for joy. Forming figures from clay
and feeling like a god. The soft crunching sound in the snow as I make my
way home with a rabbit or two on moonlit winters [*sic*] night, or even being
momentarily lost in a blizzard. To feel as a tumbleweed rolling across rough
(50) landscape, to see the last ray of sunlight hitting the mesa after an autumn
day, light reflecting off a distant passing car makes me feel vulnerable and
sad at times. These past feelings and experiences, associated with time and
places, I regard as a reservoir of my inspiration.

Like most young Navajos my age, we spent many winter nights gathered
(55) around our father, listening to stories passed down through generations. We
sat in expectation as we journeyed up from the womb of the Mother in
creation stories. We sat mesmerized by coyote stories. Laughing at his antics
and frightened by his cruelties. We sat in awe as First Man and First Woman
brought forth life upon the Fourth World. We journey back from the west,
(60) the home of Changing Woman, into the midst of the Four Sacred Mountains
after the creation of our clans. "Slayer of Enemies" and "Born for Water,"
the hero and savior of the fourth world, came alive for us these nights. I felt
the pain of their fathers' testing in the roaring fire of the hearth. Their war
with the Monster Gods raged as the snow storm dusted outside our door,
(65) snow sifting through the cracks of the door. Shadows leaping on cribbed
wall of the *hooghan*[2] brought to life the animal beings as the shoe game was
created. As the nights wore on, the youngest ones of us fell asleep where
we sat. My mother's spindle scratching the floor set the tempo of these late
night journeys . . . back. From these sources I draw my inspirations. I am
(70) humbled by its beauty and strengthened by its power. With great respect,
I relive this in every creation, every all-night Blessingway chant and every
vision of glory upon this land. With good intentions, I recreate this in every
piece of art: intentions of preserving and passing on, intentions of sharing

---

[2]hooghan—traditional dwelling of the Navajo people

and inviting all good-willed people for the sake of us as American Indians in
(75) general, as Navajos in particular and the beauty of our culture. This culture through art, in whatever form, however expressed, will endure. . . .

—Shonto W. Begay
excerpted from "The View From The Mesa: A Source of Navajo Creativity"
Anii Ánáádaalyaa'Ígíí (Recent ones that are made), 1988
Wheelright Museum of the American Indian

Regents ELA Answers August 2016

English Language Arts

Answer Key

PART 1

1. 4	9. 4	17. 4
2. 1	10. 1	18. 1
3. 2	11. 3	19. 3
4. 4	12. 3	20. 1
5. 1	13. 4	21. 2
6. 3	14. 2	22. 2
7. 1	15. 2	23. 4
8. 2	16. 3	24. 3

PART 2   *See Answers and Explanations*

PART 3   *See Answers and Explanations*

Regents Examination in English Language Arts—August 2016

Chart for Converting Total Weighted Raw Scores to Final Exam Scores (Scale Scores) (Use for the August 2016 examination only.)

Weighted Raw Score*	Scale Score	Performance Level		Weighted Raw Score*	Scale Score	Performance Level
56	100	5		27	55	2
55	99	5		26	52	1
54	99	5		25	49	1
53	98	5		24	45	1
52	97	5		23	42	1
51	96	5		22	38	1
50	96	5		21	35	1
49	95	5		20	31	1
48	94	5		19	27	1
47	93	5		18	24	1
46	92	5		17	20	1
45	91	5		16	17	1
44	90	5		15	13	1
43	89	5		14	10	1
42	88	5		13	9	1
41	87	5		12	8	1
40	85	5		11	7	1
39	84	4		10	6	1
38	82	4		9	5	1
37	81	4		8	4	1
36	79	4		7	4	1
35	77	3		6	3	1
34	74	3		5	2	1
33	72	3		4	2	1
32	69	3		3	1	1
31	67	3		2	1	1
30	65	3		1	1	1
29	61	2		0	0	1
28	58	2				

The conversion table is determined independently for each administration of the exam.

Answers and Explanations

PART 1—Reading Comprehension

Passage A

1. **4** "illustrate the nature of Richard's life in the city." The reader is meant to understand from the description of London that Richard perceives the city as colorful, huge, and contradictory, but he is unchanged by it. We learn in the passage that Richard took the city for granted and made no effort to visit the sights. The images of a vibrant city that has grown and changed over time are meant to contrast with Richard's passive and indifferent nature.

2. **1** "growth of the city." The image in lines 17 through 19, ". . . a pool of mercury encounters and incorporates smaller beads of mercury . . . " reinforces the way London expanded by absorbing what had once been separate small villages and towns.

3. **2** "willingness to tolerate undesirable situations to please others." Richard "learns" from his excursions with Jessica that going to museums means tired feet, boredom, and expensive cafeterias. He tolerates these discomforts because he is "awed by Jessica" and is easily led by her.

4. **4** "Richard is in a state of denial regarding his relationship." Gary sees how controlling Jessica is and wonders why Richard puts up with her. Gary says to Richard, "She's terrifying." Richard's panic over the dinner reservation suggests that he may indeed be afraid to disappoint Jessica. None of the other choices is suggested in the text.

5. **1** "by portraying him as inefficient at organizing his time." Richard's feeling that events have a way of piling up and hitting him all at once is a vivid image of what happens to someone who is disorganized and who tends to let things go until the last minute. The text does not suggest that Richard works well under pressure or is likely to succeed. He may be unmotivated by his job, but he seems to be unmotivated by almost everything. These lines best describe Richard's lack of focus and attention to what needs to get done.

6. **3** "contrast." Sylvia's atmosphere of "crisp efficiency" offers a vivid contrast to all that we know about Richard in the text. This is the best answer among the choices.

7. **1** "domineering nature." In these lines, we hear Jessica ordering Richard to pick up the phone, insisting that he might have forgotten their date, and correcting him when he calls her "Jess." There is little in this text to suggest compassion, irresponsibility, or a sense of humor in Jessica.

8. **2** "stress." In this passage, we see Richard juggling two phone lines and being reminded that, not only has he forgotten to make an important dinner reservation, but he has made a commitment to have drinks and work with Gary that evening. His manager is also waiting for a report due in the next five minutes. "Stressful" best describes this scene.

9. **4** "quiet desperation." Richard has run out of ways to meet Jessica's expectations for that evening. He had obviously forgotten to make the reservation weeks before, and he knows he will pay a heavy price for his failure. None of the other choices captures Richard's state of mind here.

10. **1** "London grew into something huge and contradictory . . . ." These lines from the opening of the passage establish the setting and mood of the story. Richard lives in, " . . . a good place and a fine city," but he is overwhelmed by the variety of forces at work in his life.

Passage B

11. **3** "lack of self-confidence." The image of the narrator's "courageous self" wrapped in self-doubt and hesitation ("reservations") by a cowardly self is best described as a lack of self-confidence. None of the other choices is suggested by that image.

12. **3** "clarify the narrator's dilemma." The narrator's predicament or quandary is in determining which of the many selves, or aspects of character, is his "proper self." The narrator is asking the universal question, "Who am I?" This is a dilemma because he cannot seem to find "my real self, the truly me . . . ." The poem reveals little about the narrator's biases or beliefs, and there is no decision revealed in these lines.

13. **4** "the narrator's idealism and his reality." Among these choices, this is the best way to describe the contradictions in the narrator's view of himself. He believes that he has courageous, intelligent, and bold selves (his idealism), but, instead of acting as a man of intelligence, he acts the fool. In situations demanding courage, he is cowardly. He envies heroic figures, but when he needs to be confident and daring, " . . . out comes the same old lazy self (reality)."

14. **2** "universal." Note that in the preceding lines, the narrator declares that his solution will be, " . . . to see if the same thing happens/to other people." The narrator plans a thorough exploration of other people's experiences in order to find a way to explain his problems, to find his "real self."

Passage C

15. **2** "describing various frequencies dogs hear." These lines first outline and compare the range of sounds that can be heard by humans and by dogs. These details support the central idea that, "Dogs hear most of what we hear and then some." These lines are not about *how* dogs and humans hear, but about which range of frequencies each can hear.

16. **3** "humans can verbally communicate with dogs." What these lines establish is that when they hear humans speak, dogs recognize changes in pitch and tone, not necessarily the meaning of specific words. It is that recognition of patterns in sound that allow humans to communicate verbally with dogs. None of the other choices is supported in the passage.

17. **4** "altering the intonation of familiar words." This idea is an elaboration on the ideas in the question above. Because dogs recognize intonation, the pattern in a question for example, they could be confused if something they heard sounded like a familiar question, even when the words were expressing no such thing.

18. **1** "higher-level thinking." These lines include the declaration that language use distinguishes humans from all other animals, and that language use is viewed as an, " . . . incomparable criterion for intelligence." The passage is asserting that language use implies higher-level thinking.

19. **3** "create human sentence structures." This passage acknowledges that there is considerable disagreement among researchers about the extent of linguistic ability in non-human animals, but asserts that, "All parties agree . . ." there is no discovery of the ability in animals to combine " . . . words into meaningful sentences." None of the other choices applies to these lines.

20. **1** "imitate behavior and sound." This passage offers examples of how animals can recognize warning signals in bird cries or can trap prey by using deceptive gestures. These forms of communication are, " . . . in some way using another specie's language."

21. **2** "complexity of spoken sounds." The key term in this answer is "sounds." This section of the text emphasizes the importance of how dogs understand the sound and pattern of what we say more than recognizing specific words. If an utterance sounds familiar but the actual words (sounds) are meaningless (gibberish), the dog may confuse it with an utterance he has understood in the past. This passage does not refer to word order, hidden gestures, or movement.

22. **2** "How we speak to dogs is more important than what we say." The first and last paragraphs of the text do point out how dogs respond to high-pitched sounds, but the central idea in lines 63–71 is that dogs are sensitive to how we speak, to the rhythm and tone of voice in what they hear. The other choices are not supported by the text.

23. **4** "styles of spoken communication and likely responses." The term "motherese" identifies the often babbling, cooing sounds we use in communicating with infants. The author points out that dogs also respond to "baby talk," especially because they perceive that it is actually being directed at them. This passage is further demonstration of the importance of manner and style in spoken communication.

24. **3** "educate people about dogs' experience with sound." Note that the first sentence of the passage establishes dogs' capacity to hear and respond to sounds as the central idea; the examples that follow are illustrations of how dogs perceive the world and human communication through tone, rhythm, and pitch level.

PART 2—Argument Response

Sample Essay Response

Should the government create strict sugar regulations to protect its citizens from serious health problems? I definitely believe the U.S. government has the responsibility to ensure safe food for its people. It must regulate the production, labeling, and availability of sugary foods and drinks.

Critics of the claim say it's not sugar itself that creates health risks but a person's decision to drink and eat sugar-heavy products. As Jeffrey Senger, a former attorney for the FDA remarked, "Sugar isn't the same thing as arsenic. It's not a food that's inherently unsafe." (Text 1, lines 28–29) In addition, an FDA spokesperson placed sugar and high fructose corn syrup in the same category as honey and molasses. (Text 1, lines 33–34) Opponents of regulation, therefore, place blame and responsibility on the people instead of on the companies that produce these sweetened products. This text explains why it would be difficult for the FDA to set limits on sugar.

However, recent scientific research shows just how dangerous sugar in any form is to a person's health, especially since the average person in America consumes 78 pounds of sugar in one year. (Text 1, lines 10–11) Fructose "is metabolized primarily by the liver, . . . taxing the liver, causing fatty liver disease, and ultimately leading to insulin resistance." (Text 2, lines 20–22) The graphic from Text 3 further illustrates the very serious damage that excessive fructose intake creates: "hypertension, pancreatitis, obesity, malnutrition, hepatic dysfunction," and even possible addiction. As the number of potential ill effects of sugar consumption rises, the case for government regulation is strengthened. Text 3 compares the effects of sugar consumption to alcohol and tobacco use in its damaging effects on people. Why wouldn't the government take similar steps to regulate sugar?

Besides being a personal health issue, sugar consumption is having effects on the U.S. economy. As the health of individuals becomes compromised, so are employment, health-care costs, and the military in the U.S. Lost time at work due to sugar-related disease is "$65 billion in lost productivity." Add to that the $150 billion spent on health-care resources for obesity every year. (Text 3, lines 40–41) Sugar is even being called "a threat to national security," because "75% of military applicants are now rejected for obesity-related reasons." (Text 3, lines 44–46)

Clearly, the government must take steps to strictly regulate the consumption of sugar. Sugary drinks and foods must be banned from schools and commercials, taxes should be placed on companies that continue to produce and market high-sugar products, and education about the dangers of excess sugar must be emphasized. This issue has gone beyond that of personal responsibility; it is having a negative impact on the country as a whole. The U.S. government must take action to protect its citizens from the deadly consequences of high-sugar products.

Analysis

This response is a good example of an argument developed with evidence from texts. The introduction restates the topic in the form of a rhetorical question, which also suggests the line of reasoning to follow: "Should the government create strict sugar regulations to protect its citizens from serious health problems?" The introduction could be improved if more details to establish the context were included, but the argument that follows is well developed.

    The organization is clear. The second paragraph acknowledges one of the key arguments against regulation. The paragraph that follows offers several examples of the health risks of sugar consumption and closes with another effective rhetorical question: "Why wouldn't the government take similar steps to regulate sugar?" The paragraph that follows further develops the argument with examples of economic costs. The conclusion summarizes the argument for regulation, proposes specific regulatory actions, and rejects the opposing view that personal responsibility is a sufficient response. The supporting details come from three of the texts and are accurately cited. This response would merit a high score.

(See pages 79–80 for the scoring guidelines.)

PART 3—Text-Analysis Response

Sample Essay Response

The central idea of this text is that when two cultures collide, a more primitive culture must adapt to the new culture while maintaining its own cultural identity. This text was written in the perspective of an American Indian artist whose artwork displays the culture of the Navajo people. The artist recognizes the difficulty for the Navajo people to transition and adapt to a new and advanced culture, therefore he uses his artwork to help his people cope with the change. The artist understands that if the Navajo culture is not perpetuated in artwork, it will be lost to a new culture.

The artist develops this central idea through the literary technique of figurative language. In lines 28 to 30 the artist states, "The art that we represent, like the role of the medicine man of today, must help in creating a positive evolution in this new era for our people and those coming after us." The artist uses a simile to compare contemporary Navajo artwork to the role of a present day medicine man: art that looks to the future yet is "dressed in the truth of our past . . ." is like "a collective therapy." The artwork that is created still incorporates the culture that the Navajo people are accustomed to, making it easier for them to adapt to the new culture while maintaining their own cultural identity. In line 21, the artist states, "We must draw a line beyond which we do not venture." Here, the artist is describing his artwork with a line in the form of a metaphor. This comparison shows a sense of boundary, where the artwork of the Navajo people would show an adaptation to the new culture, but not too much to where they lose their cultural identity. In lines 26 to 28, the artist states, "the art that we represent must be flexible and adaptable . . . if it is to survive, lest we become brittle and blow away like shells of dry pinion nuts." Here, the artist uses a simile to show that the culture of the Navajo people will disappear—blow away like dry shells—if it does not remain true to its own cultural identity as it adapts to the new culture.

Analysis

This passage offers several possibilities for a thoughtful response, including vivid imagery in the author's descriptions of his childhood experiences, effective use of tone, voice, and point of view. This writer chose to analyze the author's use of figurative language in developing the central idea of the passage.

    The first paragraph gives an excellent paraphrase of the central idea, outlines the context, and clearly establishes the author's point of view. The significance of figurative language is developed in the second paragraph, with relevant quotes and accurate representations of the author's views. The organization of the essay is clear and the style is appropriately formal, with no significant errors in the conventions. This response would merit a high score.

(See pages 81–82 for the scoring guidelines.)

Regents ELA Examination June 2017

English Language Arts

PART 1—Reading Comprehension

Directions (1–24): Closely read each of the three passages below. After each passage, there are several multiple-choice questions. Select the best suggested answer to each question and write its number in the space provided. You may use the margins to take notes as you read.

Reading Comprehension Passage A

  I received one morning a letter, written in pale ink on glassy, bluelined note-paper, and bearing the postmark of a little Nebraska village. This communication, worn and rubbed, looking as if it had been carried for some days in a coat pocket that was none too clean, was from my uncle Howard,
(5) and informed me that his wife had been left a small legacy by a bachelor relative, and that it would be necessary for her to go to Boston to attend to the settling of the estate. He requested me to meet her at the station and render her whatever services might be necessary. On examining the date indicated as that of her arrival, I found it to be no later than tomorrow. He
(10) had characteristically delayed writing until, had I been away from home for a day, I must have missed my aunt altogether. . . .
  Whatever shock Mrs. Springer [the landlady] experienced at my aunt's appearance, she considerately concealed. As for myself, I saw my aunt's battered figure with that feeling of awe and respect with which we behold
(15) explorers who have left their ears and fingers north of Franz-Joseph-Land,[1]

---

[1]Franz-Joseph-Land—Russian archipelago of 191 islands in the Arctic Ocean

or their health somewhere along the Upper Congo. My Aunt Georgiana had
been a music teacher at the Boston Conservatory, somewhere back in the
latter sixties [1860s]. One summer, while visiting in the little village among
the Green Mountains where her ancestors had dwelt for generations,
(20) she had kindled the callow[2] fancy of my uncle, Howard Carpenter, then
an idle, shiftless boy of twenty-one. When she returned to her duties in
Boston, Howard followed her, and the upshot of this infatuation was that
she eloped with him, eluding the reproaches of her family and the criticism
of her friends by going with him to the Nebraska frontier. Carpenter, who,
(25) of course, had no money, took up a homestead in Red Willow County, fifty
miles from the railroad. There they had measured off their land themselves,
driving across the prairie in a wagon, to the wheel of which they had tied
a red cotton handkerchief, and counting its revolutions. They built a dug-
out in the red hillside, one of those cave dwellings whose inmates so often
(30) reverted to primitive conditions. Their water they got from the lagoons
where the buffalo drank, and their slender stock of provisions was always at
the mercy of bands of roving Indians. For thirty years my aunt had not been
farther than fifty miles from the homestead.

I owed to this woman most of the good that ever came my way in my
(35) boyhood, and had a reverential[3] affection for her. During the years when I
was riding herd for my uncle, my aunt, after cooking the three meals— the
first of which was ready at six o'clock in the morning—and putting the six
children to bed, would often stand until midnight at her ironing board, with
me at the kitchen table beside her, hearing me recite Latin declensions and
(40) conjugations, gently shaking me when my drowsy head sank down over a
page of irregular verbs. It was to her, at her ironing or mending, that I read
my first Shakspere, and her old text-book on mythology was the first that
ever came into my empty hands. She taught me my scales and exercises on
the little parlour organ which her husband had bought her after fifteen years
(45) during which she had not so much as seen a musical instrument. She would
sit beside me by the hour, darning and counting, while I struggled with the
"Joyous Farmer." She seldom talked to me about music, and I understood
why. Once when I had been doggedly beating out some easy passages from
an old score of *Euryanthe* I had found among her music books, she came up

---

[2]callow—naive
[3]reverential—with great honor and respect

(50) to me and, putting her hands over my eyes, gently drew my head back upon her shoulder, saying tremulously, "Don't love it so well, Clark, or it may be taken from you." . . .

At two o'clock the Symphony Orchestra was to give a Wagner program, and I intended to take my aunt; though, as I conversed with her, I grew
(55) doubtful about her enjoyment of it. I suggested our visiting the Conservatory and the Common before lunch, but she seemed altogether too timid to wish to venture out. She questioned me absently about various changes in the city, but she was chiefly concerned that she had forgotten to leave instructions about feeding half-skimmed milk to a certain weakling calf, "old Maggie's
(60) calf, you know, Clark," she explained, evidently having forgotten how long I had been away. She was further troubled because she had neglected to tell her daughter about the freshly-opened kit of mackerel[4] in the cellar, which would spoil if it were not used directly. . . .

The first number [of the concert] was the *Tannhauser*[5] overture. When
(65) the horns drew out the first strain of the Pilgrim's chorus, Aunt Georgiana clutched my coat sleeve. Then it was I first realized that for her this broke a silence of thirty years. With the battle between the two motives,[6] with the frenzy of the Venusberg theme and its ripping of strings, there came to me an overwhelming sense of the waste and wear we are so powerless
(70) to combat; and I saw again the tall, naked house on the prairie, black and grim as a wooden fortress; the black pond where I had learned to swim, its margin pitted with sun-dried cattle tracks; the rain gullied clay banks about the naked house, the four dwarf ash seedlings where the dish-cloths were always hung to dry before the kitchen door. The world there was the flat
(75) world of the ancients; to the east, a cornfield that stretched to daybreak; to the west, a corral that reached to sunset; between, the conquests of peace, dearer-bought than those of war. . . .

Her lip quivered and she hastily put her handkerchief up to her mouth. From behind it she murmured, "And you have been hearing this ever
(80) since you left me, Clark?" Her question was the gentlest and saddest of reproaches. . . .

The deluge of sound poured on and on; I never knew what she found in the shining current of it; I never knew how far it bore her, or past what happy islands. From the trembling of her face I could well believe that
(85) before the last number she had been carried out where the myriad graves

---

[4]kit of mackerel—container of fish
[5]*Tannhauser*—an opera by Richard Wagner
[6]motives—recurrent musical phrases

are, into the grey, nameless burying grounds of the sea; or into some world of death vaster yet, where, from the beginning of the world, hope has lain down with hope and dream with dream and, renouncing, slept. . . .

(90) I spoke to my aunt. She burst into tears and sobbed pleadingly. "I don't want to go, Clark, I don't want to go!"

I understood. For her, just outside the concert hall, lay the black pond with the cattle-tracked bluffs; the tall, unpainted house, with weathercurled boards, naked as a tower; the crook-backed ash seedlings where the dishcloths hung to dry; the gaunt, moulting turkeys picking up refuse about the
(95) kitchen door.

—Willa Cather
excerpted and adapted from "A Wagner Matinée"
Youth and the Bright Medusa, April 1920

1 A primary function of the first paragraph is to

    (1) establish the reason for the meeting
    (2) create an atmosphere of mystery
    (3) identify preferences of the narrator's aunt
    (4) reveal flaws in the narrator's character   1 _____

2 In lines 1 through 11, the commentary about the letter implies that the narrator believes his uncle is

    (1) uncomfortable with changes
    (2) careless about details
    (3) angry with his wife
    (4) disappointed at his decision   2 _____

3 The details in lines 16 through 24 suggest that in her youth Aunt Georgiana was

    (1) courageous yet hesitant
    (2) compassionate yet critical
    (3) resourceful yet cautious
    (4) intelligent yet impulsive   3 _____

4 Lines 32 and 33, "For thirty years my aunt had not been farther than fifty miles from the homestead" reinforces a sense of

    (1) discomfort   (3) isolation
    (2) happiness   (4) affection   4 _____

5 Which statement from the passage best explains the narrator's "reverential affection" (line 35) for his Aunt Georgiana?

    (1) "It was to her, at her ironing or mending, that I read my first Shakspere" (lines 41 and 42)
    (2) " 'Don't love it so well, Clark, or it may be taken from you' " (lines 51 and 52)
    (3) "Her lip quivered and she hastily put her handkerchief up to her mouth" (line 78)
    (4) "I never knew how far it bore her, or past what happy islands" (lines 83 and 84)   5 _____

6 Lines 43 through 45 develop a central theme by

   (1) recalling the husband's generosity in supporting the narrator's music lessons

   (2) suggesting that the narrator resented his music lessons

   (3) emphasizing the role of discipline in developing Aunt Georgiana's musical talent

   (4) implying that Aunt Georgiana missed having music in her life   6 _____

7 In lines 47 and 48, when the narrator states that he "understood why," he is implying that his Aunt Georgiana

   (1) knew little about current musical trends

   (2) avoided talking about his musical skills

   (3) realized what she has given up

   (4) needed some recognition of her ability   7 _____

8 Lines 57 through 63 contribute to a central idea by depicting Aunt Georgiana's

   (1) concern for daily responsibilities

   (2) desire for cultural experiences

   (3) fear of future separations

   (4) fixation on painful memories   8 _____

9 The author's choice of how to end the story (lines 89 through 95) places emphasis on Aunt Georgiana's

   (1) bleak future   (3) domestic skills

   (2) unusual lifestyle   (4) hostile attitude   9 _____

10 Which quotation best reflects the narrator's realization resulting from Aunt Georgiana's visit?

   (1) "He requested me to meet her at the station and render her whatever services might be necessary" (lines 7 and 8)

   (2) "At two o'clock the Symphony Orchestra was to give a Wagner program, and I intended to take my aunt" (line 53)

   (3) "there came to me an overwhelming sense of the waste and wear we are so powerless to combat" (lines 78 and 79)

   (4) "sound poured on and on; I never knew what she found in the shining current of it" (lines 82 and 83)   10 _____

Reading Comprehension Passage B

Mi Historia[1]

My red pickup choked on burnt oil
as I drove down Highway 99.[2]
In wind-tattered garbage bags
I had packed my whole life:
(5) two pairs of jeans, a few T-shirts,
and a pair of work boots.
My truck needed work, and through
the blue smoke rising from under the hood,
I saw almond orchards, plums,
(10) the raisins spread out on paper trays,
and acres of Mendota cotton my mother picked as a child.

My mother crawled through the furrows
and plucked cotton balls that filled
the burlap sack she dragged,
(15) shoulder-slung, through dried-up bolls,
husks, weevils, dirt clods,
and dust that filled the air with thirst.
But when she grew tired,
she slept on her mother's burlap,
(20) stuffed thick as a mattress,
and Grandma dragged her over the land
where time was told by the setting sun. . . .

History cried out to me from the earth,
in the scream of starling flight,
(25) and pounded at the hulls of seeds to be set free.
History licked the asphalt with rubber,
sighed in the windows of abandoned barns,

---

[1]Mi Historia—Spanish for "my history"
[2]Highway 99—the highway that runs through California's fertile Central Valley where generations of farmworkers have settled and been employed

slumped in the wind-blasted palms,
groaned in the heat, and whispered its soft curses.
(30) I wanted my own history—not the earth's,
nor the history of blood, nor of memory,
and not the job found for me at Galdini Sausage.
I sought my own—a new bruise to throb hard
as the asphalt that pounded the chassis of my truck.

—David Dominguez
from *Work Done Right*, 2003
The University of Arizona Press

11 The poet's purpose in referencing "Highway 99" in line 2 is most likely to establish

    (1) a connection with the narrator's cultural heritage
    (2) a criticism of the valley's agricultural economy
    (3) an understanding of the narrator's difficult childhood
    (4) an emphasis on the region's diverse landscape   11 _____

12 The second stanza reveals that the narrator's overall point of view is influenced by

    (1) his experience working on farms
    (2) his nostalgia for farm life
    (3) the labor of his relatives
    (4) the expectations of his family   12 _____

13 The personification in lines 23 through 29 stresses history's desire to be

    (1) repeated   (3) comforted
    (2) forgotten   (4) heard   13 _____

14 The figurative language in lines 33 and 34 implies the narrator

    (1) regrets leaving his past behind
    (2) understands that his future will have challenges
    (3) anticipates that his new life will be successful
    (4) thinks he made a wrong decision   14 _____

Reading Comprehension Passage C

In 1973, a book claiming that plants were sentient[1] beings that feel emotions, prefer classical music to rock and roll, and can respond to the unspoken thoughts of humans hundreds of miles away landed on the New York Times best-seller list for nonfiction. "The Secret Life of Plants," by
(5) Peter Tompkins and Christopher Bird, presented a beguiling mashup of legitimate plant science, quack experiments, and mystical nature worship that captured the public imagination at a time when New Age thinking was seeping into the mainstream. The most memorable passages described the experiments of a former C.I.A. polygraph expert named Cleve Backster,
(10) who, in 1966, on a whim, hooked up a galvanometer to the leaf of a dracaena, a houseplant that he kept in his office. To his astonishment, Backster found that simply by imagining the dracaena being set on fire he could make it rouse the needle of the polygraph machine, registering a surge of electrical activity suggesting that the plant felt stress. "Could the plant have been
(15) reading his mind?" the authors ask. "Backster felt like running into the street and shouting to the world, 'Plants can think!' " . . .

In the ensuing years, several legitimate plant scientists tried to reproduce the "Backster effect" without success. Much of the science in "The Secret Life of Plants" has been discredited. But the book had made
(20) its mark on the culture. Americans began talking to their plants and playing Mozart for them, and no doubt many still do. This might seem harmless enough; there will probably always be a strain of romanticism running through our thinking about plants. (Luther Burbank and George Washington Carver both reputedly talked to, and listened to, the plants they did such
(25) brilliant work with.) But in the view of many plant scientists "The Secret Life of Plants" has done lasting damage to their field. According to Daniel Chamovitz, an Israeli biologist who is the author of the recent book "What a Plant Knows," Tompkins and Bird "stymied[2] important research on plant behavior as scientists became wary[3] of any studies that hinted at parallels
(30) between animal senses and plant senses." Others contend that "The Secret Life of Plants" led to "self-censorship" among researchers seeking to explore the "possible homologies[4] between neurobiology[5] and phytobiology"[6]; that

---

[1]sentient—conscious
[2]stymied—prevented
[3]wary—cautious
[4]homologies—similarities
[5]neurobiology—the study of the nervous system
[6]phytobiology—the study of plants

is, the possibility that plants are much more intelligent and much more like us than most people think—capable of cognition,[7] communication, (35) information processing, computation, learning and memory. . . .

Indeed, many of the most impressive capabilities of plants can be traced to their unique existential[8] predicament as beings rooted to the ground and therefore unable to pick up and move when they need something or when conditions turn unfavorable. The "sessile life style," as plant biologists term (40) it, calls for an extensive and nuanced understanding of one's immediate environment, since the plant has to find everything it needs, and has to defend itself, while remaining fixed in place. A highly developed sensory apparatus is required to locate food and identify threats. Plants have evolved between fifteen and twenty distinct senses, including analogues of our five: (45) smell and taste (they sense and respond to chemicals in the air or on their bodies); sight (they react differently to various wavelengths of light as well as to shadow); touch (a vine or a root "knows" when it encounters a solid object); and, it has been discovered, sound. In a recent experiment, Heidi Appel, a chemical ecologist at the University of Missouri, found that, when (50) she played a recording of a caterpillar chomping a leaf for a plant that hadn't been touched, the sound primed the plant's genetic machinery to produce defense chemicals. Another experiment, done in Mancuso's[9] lab and not yet published, found that plant roots would seek out a buried pipe through which water was flowing even if the exterior of the pipe was dry, which (55) suggested that plants somehow "hear" the sound of flowing water. . . .

Scientists have since found that the tips of the plant roots, in addition to sensing gravity, moisture, light, pressure, and hardness, can also sense volume, nitrogen, phosphorus, salt, various toxins, microbes, and chemical signals from neighboring plants. Roots about to encounter an impenetrable (60) obstacle or a toxic substance change course before they make contact with it. Roots can tell whether nearby roots are self or other and, if other, kin or stranger. Normally, plants compete for root space with strangers, but, when researchers put four closely related Great Lakes searocket plants (*Cakile edentula*) in the same pot, the plants restrained their usual competitive (65) behaviors and shared resources.

---

[7]cognition—understanding
[8]existential—relating to existence
[9]Mancuso—Stefano Mancuso, Italian plant physiologist

Somehow, a plant gathers and integrates all this information about its environment, and then "decides"—some scientists deploy the quotation marks, indicating metaphor at work; others drop them—in precisely what direction to deploy its roots or its leaves. Once the definition of "behavior"
(70) expands to include such things as a shift in the trajectory[10] of a root, a reallocation of resources, or the emission of a powerful chemical, plants begin to look like much more active agents, responding to environmental cues in ways more subtle or adaptive than the word "instinct" would suggest. "Plants perceive competitors and grow away from them," Rick Karban, a
(75) plant ecologist at U.C. Davis, explained, when I asked him for an example of plant decision-making. "They are more leery of actual vegetation than they are of inanimate objects, and they respond to potential competitors before actually being shaded by them." These are sophisticated behaviors, but, like most plant behaviors, to an animal they're either invisible or really,
(80) really slow.

The sessile life style also helps account for plants' extraordinary gift for biochemistry, which far exceeds that of animals and, arguably, of human chemists. (Many drugs, from aspirin to opiates, derive from compounds designed by plants.) Unable to run away, plants deploy a complex molecular
(85) vocabulary to signal distress, deter or poison enemies, and recruit animals to perform various services for them. A recent study in *Science* found that the caffeine produced by many plants may function not only as a defense chemical, as had previously been thought, but in some cases as a psychoactive drug in their nectar. The caffeine encourages bees to remember a particular
(90) plant and return to it, making them more faithful and effective pollinators.

One of the most productive areas of plant research in recent years has been plant signalling. Since the early nineteen-eighties, it has been known that when a plant's leaves are infected or chewed by insects they emit volatile chemicals that signal other leaves to mount a defense. Sometimes
(95) this warning signal contains information about the identity of the insect, gleaned from the taste of its saliva. Depending on the plant and the attacker, the defense might involve altering the leaf's flavor or texture, or producing toxins or other compounds that render the plant's flesh less digestible to herbivores. When antelopes browse acacia trees, the leaves produce tannins
(100) that make them unappetizing and difficult to digest. When food is scarce and acacias are overbrowsed, it has been reported, the trees produce sufficient amounts of toxin to kill the animals. . . .

---

[10]trajectory—a path

All species face the same existential challenges—obtaining food, defending themselves, reproducing—but under wildly varying (105) circumstances, and so they have evolved wildly different tools in order to survive. Brains come in handy for creatures that move around a lot; but they're a disadvantage for ones that are rooted in place. Impressive as it is to us, self-consciousness is just another tool for living, good for some jobs, unhelpful for others. That humans would rate this particular adaptation so (110) highly is not surprising, since it has been the shining destination of our long evolutionary journey, along with the epiphenomenon of selfconsciousness that we call "free will." . . .

—Michael Pollan
excerpted from "The Intelligent Plant"
The New Yorker, December 23 & 30, 2013

15 The first paragraph conveys a sense of

   (1) caution   (3) excitement

   (2) accusation   (4) relief   15 _____

16 The details in the first paragraph serve mainly to establish the

   (1) relationship between plant science and musical trends

   (2) difference between houseplants and wild plants

   (3) importance of forensic science for theories of plant behavior

   (4) impact of early studies of plant behavior on current research   16 _____

17 The author uses the word "But" in line 19 to

   (1) express the controversial nature of "The Secret Life of Plants"

   (2) compare "The Secret Life of Plants" with "What a Plant Knows"

   (3) express the similarities between certain types of plants

   (4) compare the learning ability of particular types of plants   17 _____

18 A primary purpose of the details in lines 43 through 48 is to indicate a connection

   (1) among diverse plant species

   (2) among several independent studies

   (3) between humans and plants

   (4) between predators and prey   18 _____

19 The use of quotation marks in lines 67 and 69 acknowledges the presence of

   (1) deception   (3) confusion

   (2) debate   (4) resentment   19 _____

20 Lines 69 through 73 support a central idea suggesting that plants

   (1) resist cooperation   (3) produce sound

   (2) avoid modification   (4) possess intent   20 _____

21 The evidence provided in lines 86 through 90 demonstrates that plants may

   (1) develop symbiotic relationships
   (2) attack weaker organisms
   (3) waste essential resources
   (4) produce genetic mutations   21 _____

22 The term "plant signalling" (line 92) refers to the way plants

   (1) reproduce with similar species
   (2) protect themselves from predators
   (3) react to human contact
   (4) adapt themselves to climate   22 _____

23 The final paragraph contributes to a central idea by suggesting that

   (1) humans have acquired superior characteristics
   (2) species develop according to their own needs
   (3) plants would benefit from having self-awareness
   (4) scientists have dismissed important findings   23 _____

24 The text's credibility relies on the author's use of

   (1) order of importance
   (2) extended comparison
   (3) observable evidence
   (4) personal anecdotes   24 _____

PART 2—Argument Response

Directions: Closely read each of the *four* texts on pages 176 through 184 and write a source-based argument on the topic below. You may use the margins to take notes as you read and scrap paper to plan your response. Write your argument on a separate sheet of paper.

Topic: Should school recess be structured play?

Your Task: Carefully read each of the *four* texts provided. Then, using evidence from at least *three* of the texts, write a well-developed argument regarding whether or not school recess should be structured play. Clearly establish your claim, distinguish your claim from alternate or opposing claims, and use specific, relevant, and sufficient evidence from at least *three* of the texts to develop your argument. Do *not* simply summarize each text.

Guidelines:

Be sure to

- Establish your claim regarding whether or not school recess should be structured play.
- Distinguish your claim from alternate or opposing claims.
- Use specific, relevant, and sufficient evidence from at least *three* of the texts to develop your argument.
- Identify each source that you reference by text number and line number(s) or graphic (for example: Text 1, line 4 or Text 2, graphic).
- Organize your ideas in a cohesive and coherent manner.
- Maintain a formal style of writing.
- Follow the conventions of standard written English.

Texts:

Text 1—The Crucial Role of Recess in School

Text 2—Why Children Need More Unstructured Play

Text 3—Study Weighs Benefits of Organizing Recess

Text 4—Forget Goofing Around: Recess Has a New Boss

Text 1

The Crucial Role of Recess in School

. . .Structured recess is a recess based on structured play, during which games and physical activities are taught and led by a trained adult (teachers, school staff, or volunteers). Proponents[1] for structured recess note that children often need help in developing games and require suggestions and
(5) encouragement to participate in physical activities. Recently, policy makers and funding organizations have called for more opportunities for daily activity as a means to address childhood obesity. These statements have strengthened the argument to maintain or reinstate recess as an integral component of the school day. Although this new dimension to the recess
(10) debate has increased attention on its role, it also has created tension. Some have promoted recess time as a solution for increasing children's physical activity and combating obesity. If recess assumes such a role, then, like physical education, it will need to be planned and directed to ensure that all children are participating in moderately vigorous physical activity. Pediatric
(15) health care providers, parents, and school officials should be cognizant,[2] however, that in designing a structured recess, they will sacrifice the notion of recess as an unstructured but supervised break that belongs to the child; that is, a time for the child to make a personal choice between sedentary, physical, creative, or social options. However, there are many cited benefits
(20) of structured recess to consider, including:

- Older elementary children may benefit from game instruction and encouragement for total class inclusion.
- Children can be coached to develop interpersonal skills for appropriate conflict resolution.
(25)
- More children can actively participate in regular activity, irrespective of skill level.
- Anecdotally,[3] teachers have reported improved behavior and attention in the classroom after vigorous structured recess.

To be effective, structured recess requires that school personnel (or
(30) volunteers) receive adequate training so that they are able to address and encourage the diverse needs of all students. One aspect of supervision should be to facilitate social relationships among children by encouraging

---

[1]proponents—those who support
[2]cognizant—aware
[3]anecdotally—based on casual observation

inclusiveness in games. A problem arises when the structured activities of recess are promoted as a replacement for the child's physical education
(35) requirement. The replacement of physical education by recess threatens students' instruction in and acquisition of new motor skills, exploration of sports and rules, and a concept of lifelong physical fitness.

There are ways to encourage a physically active recess without necessarily adding structured, planned, adult-led games, such as offering
(40) attractive, safe playground equipment to stimulate free play; establishing games/boundaries painted on the playground; or instructing children in games, such as four square or hop-scotch. These types of activities can range from fully structured (with the adult directing and requiring participation) to partly unstructured (with adults providing supervision and initial instruction)
(45) to fully unstructured (supervision and social guidance). In structured, partly structured, or unstructured environments, activity levels vary widely on the basis of school policy, equipment provided, encouragement, age group, gender, and race. Consequently, the potential benefits of mandatory participation of all children in a purely structured recess must be weighed
(50) against the potential social and emotional trade-off of limiting acquisition of important developmental skills. Whichever style is chosen, recess should be viewed as a supplement to motor skill acquisition in physical education class. . . .

—Council on School Health
excerpted from "The Crucial Role of Recess in School,"
December 31, 2012
http://pediatrics.aapublications.org/

Text 2

Why Children Need More Unstructured Play

The nature of an average child's free time has changed. For the past 25 years kids have been spending decreasing amounts of time outdoors. The time that our kids do spend outdoors is frequently a part of an organized sports activity. Other activities taking up our children's time include indoor
(5) lessons and organized events such as music, art and dance lessons. Another big indoor activity, taking up to 7.5 hours a day of our children's time according to a Kaiser Family Foundation study, is electronic entertainment. Of course some of these activities bring joy and fulfillment to our kids, but, in return, time for unstructured play has decreased.

(10)   Unstructured play is that set of activities that children create on their own without adult guidance. Children naturally, when left to their own devices, will take initiative and create activities and stories in the world around them. Sometimes, especially with children past the toddler stage, the most creative play takes place outside of direct adult supervision. Unstructured free play
(15) can happen in many different environments, however, the outdoors may provide more opportunities for free play due to the many movable parts, such as sticks, dirt, leaves and rocks which lend themselves to exploration and creation.

Some parents find it challenging to provide unstructured play time for
(20) their kids. Letting our kids play without constant supervision, especially outside, can be even more difficult. It feels hard to balance reasonable concern, over-vigilance, and the desire to let our kids experience freedom and learn from their own mistakes and experiences. . . .

Why might we need to loosen up and get over some of our fears in
(25) order to get our kids outdoor unstructured play time? In the January 2005 *Archives of Pediatric and Adolescent Medicine*, Burdette and Whitaker wrote on the importance of free play. They argue that free play promotes intellectual and cognitive growth, emotional intelligence, and benefits social interactions. They describe how play involves problem solving which is one
(30) of the highest executive functions. ["]Children plan, organize, sequence, and make decisions,["] they explain. In addition, play requires attention to the game and, especially in the case of very young children, frequent physical activity. Unstructured play frequently comes from or results in exposure to the outdoors. Surveys of parents and teachers report that children's focus
(35) and attention are improved after outdoor physical activity and free play and some small studies suggest that time spent outdoors improves focus in children with ADHD [Attention Deficit Hyperactivity Disorder].

Socialization and emotional intelligence benefit through shared interactions and physical movement that take place during play. Children (40) must work together to decide which game to play, what agreeable rules are, and how to manage scenarios that invariably involve their differing perspectives. This "work" builds the social qualities that we all wish for our children: empathy, self-awareness, self-regulation, and flexibility. Emotional development is promoted along with physical health when people spend (45) time moving. In adults and older children physical activity has been well documented to decrease stress, anxiety, and depression, and to improve overall mood. Though the research is sparse in younger children, it seems likely that our youngest children benefit as well. Free play in toddlers and young children most frequently involves spurts of gross motor activity over (50) a period of time with multiple episodes of rest in between. Most children are smiling and laughing when they engage in play, and it is reasonable to assume that their mood is improved during and after play. . . .

—Avril Swan, MD
excerpted and adapted from "Why Children Need More
Unstructured Play" *www.kevinmd.com*, July 21, 2011

Text 3

Study Weighs Benefits of Organizing Recess

While an overwhelming number of elementary school principals believe in the power of recess to improve academic achievement and make students more focused in class, most discipline-related problems happen at school when kids cut loose at recess and lunch, according to surveys.

(5)   One of the solutions, according to a study released this week [2012] by the Robert Wood Johnson Foundation: more, and well-trained, staff on the playground.

The study examines an approach to creating more-structured recess time that is provided by Playworks, based in Oakland, Calif. It finds that the
(10) nonprofit organization's program can smooth the transition between recess and class time—giving teachers more time to spend on instruction—and can cut back on bullying in the schoolyard. Teachers in participating schools also reported that their students felt safer and more included at recess, compared with those at schools without the program. . . .

(15)   The most significant finding shows students who participate in a Playworks-structured recess transition from that to schoolwork more quickly than students in traditional recess, said Susanne James-Burdumy, an associate director of research at Mathematica Policy Research. "I think it is an exciting set of findings," Ms. James-Burdumy said. "This is one area
(20) where Playworks is aiming to have an impact: specifically trying to improve students' ability to focus on class activities."

The study found that, on average, teachers at participating schools needed about 2.5 fewer minutes of transition time between recess and learning time—a difference that researchers termed statistically significant.
(25) Over the course of a school year, that can add up to about a day of class time.

Scaling Up

The Robert Wood Johnson Foundation, also based in Princeton, has been funding Playworks since 2005. It helped the program expand from a few schools in Oakland to more than 300 schools in 23 cities, said Nancy Barrand, the foundation's senior adviser for program development. The goal
(30) is to expand into 27 cities and 750 schools.

"We're using a process of scaling where we've identified a successful, evidence-based model," Ms. Barrand said. Playworks "is a pretty common sense approach. It's really about the school environment and how you create a healthy school environment for the children," she continued. "If children
(35) are healthy and happy, they learn better."

Playworks founder and chief executive officer, Jill Vialet, said the idea came from a frustrated principal 15 years ago. The principal had been dealing with the same three students daily because of scuffles and mischief at recess that spilled over into their classes.

(40)   Ms. Vialet wondered whether creating a little structure at recess could quell some of those ongoing woes. She recalled her own days as a child when a municipal parks and recreation worker named Clarence made sure she—one of the few girls there—was included in the games at a District of Columbia park.

(45)   "I wanted to make sure every kid had a Clarence," she said. . . . The coaches map the area where students spend recess, setting boundaries for different activities, such as kickball. They help children pick teams using random measures, such as students' birth months, to circumvent emotionally scarring episodes of being chosen based on skill or popularity.

(50) If conflicts arise, coaches teach simple ways to settle disputes and preempt some quibbles by teaching games including rock-paper-scissors.

Forty percent of the surveyed teachers said students used the rock-paper-scissors game to resolve conflicts or make decisions when they were back in class.

(55)   Coaches get involved in the activities, which "makes it possible for kids who don't see themselves as super-sporty to get into the games themselves," Ms. Vialet said. "There's just enough structure for the kids to be successful."

Solving Own Problems
While adults need to be present and ready to intervene at recess if necessary, said Edward Miller, one of the founding partners of the New York

(60) City-based Alliance for Childhood, and Playworks provides that service, children should also have the opportunity for individual and small-group play. . . .

The Mathematica study found Playworks has a mixed effect on behaviors related to bullying: Teachers at schools with the program found that there

(65) was significantly less bullying and exclusionary behavior during recess than teachers at schools without it, but not a reduction in more general aggressive behavior. Playworks has no formal curriculum that addresses the problem, Ms. Vialet noted.

(70)   "Our coaches are functioning like the older kids in the play yard used to: teaching kids rules to games, intervening if there is conflict, norming[1] behaviors around inclusion," she said.

         However, researchers also found that teachers' and students' perception of aggression and bullying on the playground differed. While teachers observed that there was less name-calling, shoving of classmates,
(75)   and excluding of some students from games because of Playworks, students didn't, Mathematica's Ms. James-Burdumy said. . . .

—Nirvi Shah
excerpted and adapted from
"Study Weighs Benefits of Organizing Recess"
www.edweek.org, April 17, 2012

---

[1]norming—setting a standard

Text 4

Forget Goofing Around: Recess Has a New Boss

Newark—At Broadway Elementary School here, there is no more sitting around after lunch. No more goofing off with friends. No more doing nothing.

(5) Instead there is Brandi Parker, a $14-an-hour recess coach with a whistle around her neck, corralling children behind bright orange cones to play organized games. There she was the other day, breaking up a renegade game of hopscotch and overruling stragglers' lame excuses.

They were bored. They had tired feet. They were no good at running. "I don't like to play," protested Esmeilyn Almendarez, 11.

(10) "Why do I have to go through this every day with you?" replied Ms. Parker, waving her back in line. "There's no choice."

Broadway Elementary brought in Ms. Parker in January out of exasperation with students who, left to their own devices, used to run into one another, squabble over balls and jump-ropes or monopolize the blacktop

(15) while exiling their classmates to the sidelines. Since she started, disciplinary referrals at recess have dropped by three-quarters, to an average of three a week. And injuries are no longer a daily occurrence.

"Before, I was seeing nosebleeds, busted lips, and students being a danger to themselves and others," said Alejandro Echevarria, the principal.

(20) "Now, Coach Brandi does miracles with 20 cones and three handballs."

The school is one of a growing number across the country that are reining in recess to curb bullying and behavior problems, foster social skills and address concerns over obesity. They also hope to show children that there is good old-fashioned fun to be had without iPods and video games. . . .

(25) Although many school officials and parents like the organized activity, its critics say it takes away the only time that children have to unwind. . . .

Dr. Romina M. Barros, an assistant clinical professor at Albert Einstein College of Medicine in the Bronx who was an author of a widely cited study on the benefits of recess, published last year [2009] in the journal *Pediatrics*,

(30) says that children still benefit most from recess when they are let alone to daydream, solve problems, use their imagination to invent their own games and "be free to do what they choose to do."

Structured recess, Dr. Barros said, simply transplants the rules of the classroom to the playground.

(35) "You still have to pay attention," she said. "You still have to follow rules. You don't have that time for your brain to relax." . . .

Ms. Parker, 28, the coach at Broadway Elementary, had worked as a counselor for troubled teenagers in a group home in Burlington, N.C. Besides her work at recess, she visits each class once a week to play games (40) that teach lessons about cooperation, sportsmanship and respect.

"These are the things that matter in life: who you are as a human being at the core," she said. . . .

There are three 15-minute recesses, with more than 100 children at a time packed into a fenced-in basketball court equipped with nothing more (45) than a pair of netless hoops.

On a chilly morning, Ms. Parker shoveled snow off the blacktop so that the students could go outside after being cooped up in the cafeteria during recess in the previous week. She drew squares in blue and green chalk for a game called switch, a fast-paced version of musical chairs—without the (50) chairs. (She goes through a box of chalk a week.) Ms. Parker, who greets students with hugs and a cheerful "hello-hello," keeps the rules simple so that they can focus on playing rather than on following directions. "We're trying to get them to exert energy, to get it all out," she said. "They can be as loud as they want. I never tell them to be quiet unless I'm telling them (55) something." . . .

—Winnie Hu
excerpted and adapted from "Forget Goofing Around:
Recess Has a New Boss" *www.nytimes.com*, March 14, 2010

PART 3-Text Analysis Response

Your Task: Closely read the text on pages 186 through 188 and write a well-developed, text-based response of two to three paragraphs. In your response, identify a central idea in the text and analyze how the author's use of *one* writing strategy (literary element or literary technique or rhetorical device) develops this central idea. Use strong and thorough evidence from the text to support your analysis. Do *not* simply summarize the text. You may use the margins to take notes as you read and scrap paper to plan your response. Write your response on a separate sheet of paper.

Guidelines:

Be sure to

- Identify a central idea in the text.
- Analyze how the author's use of *one* writing strategy (literary element or literary technique or rhetorical device) develops this central idea. Examples include: characterization, conflict, denotation/connotation, metaphor, simile, irony, language use, point-of-view, setting, structure, symbolism, theme, tone, etc.
- Use strong and thorough evidence from the text to support your analysis.
- Organize your ideas in a cohesive and coherent manner.
- Maintain a formal style of writing.
- Follow the conventions of standard written English.

Text

The following excerpt from the memoir of a South Pole explorer includes quotations from his diary.

. . .Then came a fateful day—Wednesday, October 27. The position was lat. [latitude] 69° 5′ S., long. [longitude] 51° 30′ W. The temperature was −8.5° Fahr. [Fahrenheit], a gentle southerly breeze was blowing and the sun shone in a clear sky. "After long months of ceaseless anxiety and strain, after
(5) times when hope beat high and times when the outlook was black indeed, the end of the *Endurance* has come. But though we have been compelled to abandon the ship, which is crushed beyond all hope of ever being righted, we are alive and well, and we have stores and equipment for the task that lies before us. The task is to reach land with all the members of the Expedition.
(10) It is hard to write what I feel. To a sailor his ship is more than a floating home, and in the Endurance I had centred ambitions, hopes, and desires. Now, straining and groaning, her timbers cracking and her wounds gaping, she is slowly giving up her sentient[1] life at the very outset of her career. She is crushed and abandoned after drifting more than 570 miles in a north-
(15) westerly direction during the 281 days since she became locked in the ice. The distance from the point where she became beset[2] to the place where she now rests mortally hurt in the grip of the floes[3] is 573 miles, but the total drift through all observed positions has been 1186 miles, and probably we actually covered more than 1500 miles. We are now 346 miles from Paulet
(20) Island, the nearest point where there is any possibility of finding food and shelter. A small hut built there by the Swedish expedition in 1902 is filled with stores left by the Argentine relief ship. I know all about those stores, for I purchased them in London on behalf of the Argentine Government when they asked me to equip the relief expedition. The distance to the nearest
(25) barrier west of us is about 180 miles, but a party going there would still be about 360 miles from Paulet Island and there would be no means of sustaining life on the barrier. We could not take from here food enough for the whole journey; the weight would be too great.

---

[1]sentient—conscious
[2]beset—hemmed in
[3]floes—ice sheets

"This morning, our last on the ship, the weather was clear, with a gentle
(30)   south-southeasterly to south-south-westerly breeze. From the crow's-nest
there was no sign of land of any sort. The pressure was increasing steadily, and
the passing hours brought no relief or respite[4] for the ship. The attack of the
ice reached its climax at 4 p.m. The ship was hove[5] stern up by the pressure,
and the driving floe, moving laterally across the stern, split the rudder and
(35)   tore out the rudder-post and stern-post. Then, while we watched, the ice
loosened and the *Endurance* sank a little. The decks were breaking upwards
and the water was pouring in below. Again the pressure began, and at 5 p.m.
I ordered all hands on to the ice. The twisting, grinding floes were working
their will at last on the ship. It was a sickening sensation to feel the decks
(40)   breaking up under one's feet, the great beams bending and then snapping
with a noise like heavy gunfire. The water was overmastering the pumps,
and so to avoid an explosion when it reached the boilers I had to give orders
for the fires to be drawn[6] and the steam let down. The plans for abandoning
the ship in case of emergency had been made well in advance, and men and
(45)   dogs descended to the floe and made their way to the comparative safety of
an unbroken portion of the floe without a hitch. Just before leaving, I looked
down the engineroom skylight as I stood on the quivering deck, and saw the
engines dropping sideways as the stays and bed-plates gave way. I cannot
describe the impression of relentless destruction that was forced upon me
(50)   as I looked down and around. The floes, with the force of millions of tons of
moving ice behind them, were simply annihilating the ship." . . .

"To-night the temperature has dropped to –16° Fahr., and most of the
men are cold and uncomfortable. After the tents had been pitched I mustered
all hands and explained the position to them briefly and, I hope, clearly. I
(55)   have told them the distance to the barrier and the distance to Paulet Island,
and have stated that I propose to try to march with equipment across the ice
in the direction of Paulet Island. I thanked the men for the steadiness and
good morale they have shown in these trying circumstances, and told them
I had no doubt that, provided they continued to work their utmost and to
(60)   trust me, we will all reach safety in the end. Then we had supper, which the
cook had prepared at the big blubber stove, and after a watch[7] had been
set all hands except the watch turned in." For myself, I could not sleep.

---

[4]respite—rest
[5]hove—heaved
[6]drawn—closed
[7]watch—crewman who stays awake on guard all night

The destruction and abandonment of the ship was no sudden shock. The disaster had been looming ahead for many months, and I had studied my
(65) plans for all contingencies[8] a hundred times. But the thoughts that came to me as I walked up and down in the darkness were not particularly cheerful. The task now was to secure the safety of the party, and to that I must bend my energies and mental power and apply every bit of knowledge that experience of the Antarctic had given me. The task was likely to be long and
(70) strenuous, and an ordered mind and a clear programme were essential if we were to come through without loss of life. A man must shape himself to a new mark directly the old one goes to ground. . . .

—Sir Ernest Shackleton
excepted and adapted from *South*, 1920
The MacMillan Company

---

[8]contingencies—possibilities

Regents ELA Answers June 2017

English Language Arts

Answer Key

PART 1

1. **1**	9. **1**	17. **1**
2. **2**	10. **3**	18. **3**
3. **4**	11. **1**	19. **2**
4. **3**	12. **3**	20. **4**
5. **1**	13. **4**	21. **1**
6. **4**	14. **2**	22. **2**
7. **3**	15. **3**	23. **2**
8. **1**	16. **4**	24. **3**

PART 2   *See Answers and Explanations*

PART 3   *See Answers and Explanations*

Regents Examination in English Language Arts—June 2017

Chart for Converting Total Weighted Raw Scores to Final Exam Scores (Scale Scores) (Use for the June 2017 examination only.)

Weighted Raw Score*	Scale Score	Performance Level	Weighted Raw Score*	Scale Score	Performance Level
56	100	5	27	52	1
55	99	5	26	47	1
54	99	5	25	43	1
53	99	5	24	39	1
52	98	5	23	36	1
51	97	5	22	32	1
50	96	5	21	28	1
49	95	5	20	24	1
48	94	5	19	21	1
47	92	5	18	18	1
46	91	5	17	14	1
45	90	5	16	11	1
44	88	5	15	9	1
43	87	5	14	8	1
42	86	5	13	7	1
41	85	5	12	6	1
40	83	4	11	5	1
39	82	4	10	5	1
38	80	4	9	4	1
37	79	4	8	3	1
36	76	4	7	3	1
35	74	3	6	2	1
34	72	3	5	2	1
33	69	3	4	1	1
32	66	3	3	1	1
31	65	3	2	1	1
30	60	2	1	1	1
29	57	2	0	0	1
28	55	2			

The conversion table is determined independently for each administration of the exam.

Answers Explained

PART 1—Reading Comprehension

Multiple-Choice Questions

Passage A

1. **1** "establish the reason for the meeting." In this paragraph, the narrator describes the letter he received from his uncle and the request that he assist his aunt when she comes to Boston to receive a small inheritance. This passage is factual and straightforward in tone and reveals little about the narrator or his aunt.

2. **2** "careless about details." The narrator tells us that the letter showed signs of being carried in a pocket for several days, and that it arrived only the day before his aunt was to arrive. These details suggest that the uncle neglected to mail the letter in a timely way. None of the other choices is suggested in this paragraph.

3. **4** "intelligent yet impulsive." We learn in these lines that the narrator's aunt had been an accomplished music teacher in Boston when she met and eloped with the young Howard, ". . . an idle, shiftless [lacking ambition] boy of twenty-one." These lines indicate that both her parents and her friends were deeply opposed to this relationship. Aunt Georgiana's actions suggest that she was not very critical, hesitant, or cautious in her youth.

4. **3** "isolation." This passage describes a life with no money on a nearly barren prairie homestead of primitive conditions, which is ". . . fifty miles from the railroad." This detail at line 26 strongly suggests that Aunt Georgiana had been physically and emotionally isolated in the thirty years since she first arrived in Nebraska.

5. **1** "It was to her, at her ironing or mending, that I read my first Shakespere." In this section of the story, we learn that Aunt Georgiana gave the narrator his early encounters with classical education, coaching him in Latin, arithmetic, and music. The passage strongly implies that it was because of his aunt that the narrator had a life of possibilities beyond a Nebraska boyhood.

6. **4** "implying that Aunt Georgiana missed having music in her life." The image in these lines strongly suggests how important music once was in her life as she urges the narrator as a young boy to develop musical ability himself. None of the other choices are suggested in these lines.

7. **3** "realized what she has given up." Here the narrator indicates that he understood even as a boy how deeply his aunt felt the loss of music in her life. Among the choices, this is the most convincing description of the narrator's understanding.

8. **1** "concern for daily responsibilities." This passage describes the aunt's reluctance to visit various places in Boston because, before the concert, she is ". . . chiefly concerned about . . . a weakling calf . . . ," and a container of fish in the basement at home.

9. **1** "bleak future." The author closes the story with images of the life Aunt Georgiana will return to: "the tall, unpainted house . . . ," wash-cloths drying on the seedlings of trees, and gaunt turkeys pecking at, " . . . refuse about the kitchen door."

10. **3** "there came to me an overwhelming sense of the waste and wear we are so powerless to combat." The first two choices are simple statements of fact, and the fourth is a statement about what the narrator does not fully understand. What he does feel is the sense of loss—of "waste and wear"—in his aunt's life.

Passage B

11. **1** "a connection with the narrator's cultural heritage." The footnote identifies Highway 99 as the main route through California's Central Valley, where for generations migrant farm workers—historically from Mexico—have picked the crops. The poem ends with the poet's assertion that he will seek his own, and a different, life history. Note here how the title, "Mi Historia," contributes to the meaning of the poem.

12. **3** "the labor of his relatives." The second stanza of the poem offers vivid images of what that life was like for his mother and grandmother. Close reading reveals that his mother was picking cotton as a young child, who, ". . . when she grew tired/. . . slept on her mother's burlap." The grandmother is also in the field picking cotton. It is this "history" that the poet is determined not to live.

13. **4** "heard." The images in these lines are of the sounds the poet hears when, "History cried out to me . . . and pounded . . . sighed in the windows . . . groaned in the heat, and whispered its soft curses." None of the other choices describes the effect of the personification in these lines.

14. **2** "understands that his future will have challenges." The poet says his new life, will be a ". . .bruise to throb hard as the asphalt . . . ." His new "history" may be a life as hard as the one of his ancestors, but it will be of his own choice. The tone of voice in the last five lines does not suggest that the poet feels regret at leaving or that he has made a wrong decision, nor does he express confidence that he will necessarily be successful.

Passage C

15. **3** "excitement." This paragraph, about a once popular belief that plants had thoughts and emotions, closes with a description of Clive Backster's thrilling belief that he had proved, "Plants can think!" He is so excited, ". . . he felt like running into the street and shouting to the world . . . ."

16. **4** "impact of early studies of plant behavior on current research." The author describes the claims of a popular book on "The Secret Life of Plants" as " . . . a mashup of legitimate plant science, quack experiments, and mystical nature worship . . . ." Because this kind of thinking, "was seeping into the mainstream . . . ," many legitimate scientists later tried to reproduce Backster's experiment, but without success.

17. **1** "express the controversial nature of 'the Secret Life of Plants.'" Because "The Secret Life of Plants" "had made its mark on the culture" and people were "talking to their plants and playing Mozart for them," many plant scientists later believed that the book had "done lasting damage to their field." Because the science in Tompkins and Bird's work was formally discredited, later researchers were reluctant to explore any "parallels between animal senses and plant senses."

18. **3** "between humans and plants." This passage outlines the scientific view that plants have evolved " . . . between fifteen and twenty distinct senses, including analogues of our five . . . ." None of the other choices accurately describes the purpose of this passage.

19. **2** "debate." The terms "decides" and "behavior" are in quotes because they attribute human intentional acts to plants. This passage indicates that some scientists prefer to use these terms as metaphors, while others drop the quotation marks and describe plants as "active agents" in their behavior.

20. **4** "possess intent." In the preceding paragraphs, the author outlines a number of ways in which plants actively respond to their environment: they can emit chemicals to defend from insects; they can ". . . somehow 'hear' the sound of flowing water . . ." and they will "share or compete for resources" with neighboring plants.

21. **1** "develop symbiotic relationships." This item is an example of how the Regents Exam indirectly assesses vocabulary. The term "symbiotic" refers to a mutually beneficial relationship between or among plants and animals. These lines describe, for example, how the caffeine produced by many plants as a defense mechanism also ". . . encourages bees to remember [them] . . . , making [the bees] more faithful and effective pollinators."

22. **2** "protect themselves from predators." This paragraph presents examples of how, when chewed or infected, plants can "emit volatile chemicals that signal other leaves to mount a defense." Some plants or trees can produce "toxins or other compounds that render [them] . . . less digestible," even poisonous. None of the other choices accurately refers to the term "plant signalling."

23. **2** "species develop according to their own needs." This paragraph concludes with the observation that, "All species face the same existential challenges . . . , but under wildly varying circumstances, and so they have evolved wildly different tools in order to survive." This is the best choice to describe a central idea of the article, which is about the evolutionary adaptability of plants, not about the importance of brains and self-consciousness in humans.

24. **3** "observable evidence." The author cites "several legitimate plant scientists" and reliable, published research to support each illustration of the plant world's "impressive capabilities."

PART 2—Argument Response

Sample Essay Response

Elementary school is a pivotal time for the development of children. A child's brain, emotions, and skills are very rapidly developing. With all of the structure and classroom education forced into children at that age, a time to unwind and grow interpersonally is crucial. Recess is a very important part of child development and should be a time for free, unlimited expression—not structured play.

Anyone who watches children play freely can see that they are completely capable of creating games and physical activities on their own. Students have shown that during this free playing time, "intellectual and cognitive growth, emotional intelligence, and benefits social interactions" are all benefited and promoted (Text 2, lines 28–29). At a time when the brain is most delicate and moldable, these experiences are crucial. On the other hand, structured play forces a burden onto children who may not enjoy or feel comfortable in group sports and games. At one school practicing structured recess, the children would claim they, "were bored . . . had tired feet . . . were no good at running" (Text 4, line 8). In these programs, children are told they have "no choice" and are thus apt to develop negative attitudes toward physical activity and group play if they are forced to participate. Unstructured recess allows children a period of time to make their own choices and freely express themselves in a safe environment, while structured play takes away from this freedom and restricts the developing minds of young children.

Although structured recess shows potential benefits, there is contradictory and negative evidence. Supporters of structured recess claim that "significantly less bullying and exclusionary behavior" occurs during recess with structured play programs (Text 3 line 65). However, there is no shown reduction in more general aggressive behavior. The lower aggression levels solely during recess will remain only during that period of time. Children will still find a way to bully and hurt others. Therefore, a simple reduction in immediate bullying is not worth further taking away from the freedom and creative expression of children. Reducing child obesity is another objective on the minds of supporters. However, children in elementary school are already offered a physical education class, which they regularly attend. The option to pursue more physical activities should then be left up to the students, and not miserably forced upon them.

Structured recess is an unnecessary stressor on young children. This form of play takes away from children's creative expression and initial exposure to freedom. Children should be allowed freedom at recess time, and schools should not force structured play upon them.

Analysis

This is a good response to the task. The writer establishes a clear and thoughtful position in the opening paragraph: "Recess is a very important part of child development and should be a time for free, unlimited expression—not structured play." The argument is then briefly, but adequately, developed in the body of the essay and supported with relevant references to the texts. The argument is logical, coherent, and generally well written. The final sentence of the second paragraph is an especially strong assertion of the writer's argument: "Unstructured recess allows children a period of time to make their own choices and freely express themselves in a safe environment, while structured play takes away from this freedom and restricts the developing minds of young children."

An even stronger response to this part of the exam would offer a more extensive discussion, with additional examples and citations from the wide range of evidence in the texts. This response, however, reflects understanding of the main issue and offers a strong argument on one side of the issue. This response would merit a high score.

(See pages 79–80 for the scoring guidelines.)

PART 3—Text-Analysis Response

Sample Essay Response

   *The South Pole explorer develops an important and central theme through-
out this memoir, excerpted from his diary. The explorer conveys that the destruction of the Endurance, the ship that was more than just his "floating home," was
heartbreaking. The explorer states that it was in the ship that he had "centred
ambitions, hopes, and desires." At several points, the explorer declares that he
finds it difficult to put into words his true feelings about the demise of the
Endurance. He explains that even though he had planned for the possible disaster and that the end of the ship was "looming ahead for many months," he was
profoundly disturbed by the loss. The explorer recounts this devastating loss in
vivid language and images.*

   *The South Pole explorer, Edwin Shackleton, develops this central theme
through the use of figurative language, primarily personification. He gives the
ship human qualities to illustrate the importance of the Endurance in his life
and heart. The most vivid example of personification is, "Now straining and
groaning . . . her wounds gaping, she is slowly giving up her sentient life. . . ."
This personification shows how Shackleton feels the pain of his ship "dying." He
also personifies the cause of destruction, the floes in which the ship is breaking
up, "mortally hurt," as "the attack of the ice." The explorer also uses a simile in
describing the breaking up of the Endurance, which was "snapping with a noise
like heavy gunfire." For Shackleton, it was as if a loved one was being gunned
down. This South Pole explorer successfully conveys his profound loss to the
reader in beautiful and moving figurative language.*

Analysis

This writer recognizes the author's powerful use of figurative language to describe a central incident in this passage, an account that is otherwise composed in the language of factual detail and scientific observation. The first paragraph explains the significance of the event to the author and establishes the central idea of the response. In the second paragraph, this writer illustrates, with relevant quotes, how Shackleton conveys the heartbreak of the loss of his ship. The significance of the examples is presented clearly and convincingly, with skillful use of complex sentence structures. There are no significant errors in the conventions. This response would merit a high score.

(See pages 81–82 for the scoring guidelines.)

Regents ELA Examination August 2017
English Language Arts

PART 1—Reading Comprehension

Directions (1–24): Closely read each of the three passages below. After each passage, there are several multiple-choice questions. Select the best suggested answer to each question and write its number in the space provided. You may use the margins to take notes as you read.

Reading Comprehension Passage A

In this passage, Dora-Rouge, a Native American Indian elder, is traveling back to her homeland by canoe with a small group of women.

. . .As we traveled, we entered time and began to trouble it, to pester it apart or into some kind of change. On the short nights we sat by firelight and looked at the moon's long face on water. Dora-Rouge would lie on the beaver blankets and tell us what place we would pass on the next day. She'd
(5) look at the stars in the shortening night and say, "the Meeting Place," or "God Island." True to her word, the next day we reached those places. . . .
Now, looking back, I understand how easily we lost track of things. The time we'd been teasing apart, unraveled. And now it began to unravel us as we entered a kind of timelessness. Wednesday was the last day we called by
(10) name, and truly, we no longer needed time. We were lost from it, and lost in this way, I came alive. It was as if I'd slept for years, and was now awake. The others felt it, too. Cell by cell, all of us were taken in by water and by land, swallowed a little at a time. What we'd thought of as our lives and being on earth was gone, and now the world was made up of pathways of its own
(15) invention. We were only one of the many dreams of earth. And I knew we were just a small dream.

But there was a place inside the human that spoke with land, that entered dreaming, in the way that people in the north found direction in their dreams. They dreamed charts of land and currents of water. They dreamed
(20) where food animals lived. These dreams they called hunger maps and when they followed those maps, they found their prey. It was the language animals and humans had in common. People found their cures in the same way. . . .

For my own part in this dreaming, as soon as I left time, when Thursday and Friday slipped away, plants began to cross my restless sleep in
(25) abundance. A tendril reached through darkness, a first sharp leaf came up from the rich ground of my sleeping, opened upward from the place in my body that knew absolute truth. It wasn't a seed that had been planted there, not a cultivated growing, but a wild one, one that had been there all along, waiting. I saw vines creeping forward. Inside the thin lid of an eye, petals
(30) opened, and there was pollen at the center of each flower. Field, forest, swamp. I knew how they breathed at night, and that they were linked to us in that breath. It was the oldest bond of survival. I was devoted to woods the wind walked through, to mosses and lichens. Somewhere in my past, I had lost the knowing of this opening light of life, the taking up of minerals
(35) from dark ground, the magnitude of thickets and brush. Now I found it once again. Sleep changed me. I remembered things I'd forgotten, how a hundred years ago, leaves reached toward sunlight, plants bent into currents of water. Something persistent nudged me and it had morning rain on its leaves.
(40)   Maybe the roots of dreaming are in the soil of dailiness, or in the heart, or in another place without words, but when they come together and grow, they are like the seeds of hydrogen and the seeds of oxygen that together create ocean, lake, and ice. In this way, the plants and I joined each other. They entangled me in their stems and vines and it was a beautiful
(45) entanglement. . . .

Some mornings as we packed our things, set out across water, the world was the color of copper, a flood of sun arrived from the east, and a thick mist rose up from black earth. Other mornings, heating water over the fire, we'd see the world covered with fog, and the birdsongs sounded forlorn and far
(50) away. There were days when we traveled as many as thirty miles. Others we traveled no more than ten. There were times when I resented the work, and days I worked so hard even Agnes' liniment and aspirin would not relax my aching shoulders and I would crave ice, even a single chip of it, cold and

shining. On other days I felt a deep contentment as I poled[1] inside shallow
(55) currents or glided across a new wide lake.

We were in the hands of nature. In these places things turned about
and were other than what they seemed. In silence, I pulled through the
water and saw how a river appeared through rolling fog and emptied into
the lake. One day, a full-tailed fox moved inside the shadows of trees, then
(60) stepped into a cloud. New senses came to me. I was equal to the other
animals, hearing as they heard, moving as they moved, seeing as they saw.

One night we stayed on an island close to the decaying, moss-covered
pieces of a boat. Its remains looked like the ribs of a large animal. In the
morning, sun was a dim light reaching down through the branches of trees.
(65) Pollen floated across the dark water and gathered, yellow and lifegiving,
along the place where water met land. . . .

One evening it seemed cooler. The air had a different feel, rarefied,
clean, and thin. Wolves in the distance were singing and their voices made a
sound that seemed to lie upon the land, like a cloud covering the world from
(70) one edge of the horizon to the other. We sat around the fire and listened, the
light on our faces, our eyes soft. Agnes warmed her hands over the flames.

There was a shorter time of darkness every night, but how beautiful the
brief nights, with the stars and the wolves. . . .

Sometimes I felt there were eyes around us, peering through trees
(75) and fog. Maybe it was the eyes of land and creatures regarding us, taking
our measure. And listening to the night, I knew there was another horizon,
beyond the one we could see. And all of it was storied land, land where
deities[2] walked, where people traveled, desiring to be one with infinite
space.

(80) We were full and powerful, wearing the face of the world, floating
in silence. Dora-Rouge said, "Yes, I believe we've always been lost," as
we traveled through thick-grown rushes, marsh, and water so shallow our
paddles touched bottom.

The four of us became like one animal. We heard inside each other
(85) in a tribal way. I understood this at once and was easy with it. With my
grandmothers, there was no such thing as loneliness. Before, my life had
been without all its ears, eyes, without all its knowings. Now we, the four of
us, all had the same eyes, and when Dora-Rouge pointed a bony finger and
said, "This way," we instinctively followed that crooked finger.

---

[1]poled—propelled a boat with a pole
[2]deities—gods

(90)   I never felt lost. I felt newly found, opening, like the tiny eggs we found in a pond one day, fertile and transparent. I bent over them. The life was already moving inside them, like an eye or heartbeat. One day we passed alongside cliff walls that bore red, ancient drawings of moose and bear. These were said to have been painted not by humans, but by spirits. . . .

—Linda Hogan
excerpted from "Solar Storms," 1995
Scribner

1 In lines 3 through 6, the narrator portrays Dora-Rouge as

  (1) compassionate   (3) knowledgeable

  (2) detached   (4) misguided   1 _____

2 In lines 15 and 16, the narrator compares people's lives to dreams in order to illustrate the idea of

  (1) resourcefulness   (3) vulnerability

  (2) individuality   (4) insignificance   2 _____

3 Which phrase from the text best illustrates the meaning of "tendril" as used in line 25?

  (1) "I saw vines creeping forward" (line 29)

  (2) "there was pollen at the center" (line 30)

  (3) "Field, forest, swamp" (lines 30 and 31)

  (4) "woods the wind walked through" (line 35)   3 _____

4 The imagery in lines 29 through 33 can best be described as

  (1) amusing   (3) confusing

  (2) threatening   (4) enlightening   4 _____

5 The description in lines 56 through 61 creates a sense of

  (1) transformation   (3) division

  (2) isolation   (4) vindication   5 _____

6 The phrase, "We were full and powerful, wearing the face of the world," (line 80) suggests that the group

  (1) believed they were something they were not

  (2) developed a kinship with the environment

  (3) became outwardly proud and aggressive

  (4) adopted a casual attitude toward nature   6 _____

7 The language use in lines 90 through 94 serves to
 (1) link the past with the future
 (2) continue an ongoing struggle
 (3) present a cultural dilemma
 (4) clarify the need for cooperation　　　　　　　　7 _____

8 The passage is primarily developed through the use of
 (1) rhetorical questions
 (2) comparison and contrast
 (3) parallel structure
 (4) personal narrative　　　　　　　　　　　　　　8 _____

9 The passage as a whole supports the theme that with
 (1) approval of society comes cultural freedom
 (2) clarity of mind comes connection of spirit
 (3) support of others comes environmental change
 (4) passage of time comes acceptance of nature　　　9 _____

10 Which quotation best supports a central idea of the passage?
 (1) "Maybe the roots of dreaming are in the soil of dailiness"
 　　(line 40)
 (2) "On other days I felt a deep contentment as I poled inside shal-
 　　low currents or glided across a new wide lake" (lines 54 and 55)
 (3) "The air had a different feel, rarefied, clean, and thin" (lines 67
 　　and 68)
 (4) "And listening to the night, I knew there was another horizon,
 　　beyond the one we could see" (lines 76 and 77)　　　10 _____

Reading Comprehension Passage B

I Am Vertical ——

But I would rather be horizontal.
I am not a tree with my root in the soil
Sucking up minerals and motherly love
So that each March I may gleam into leaf,
(5) Nor am I the beauty of a garden bed
Attracting my share of Ahs and spectacularly painted,
Unknowing I must soon unpetal.
Compared with me, a tree is immortal
And a flower-head not tall, but more startling,
(10) And I want the one's longevity and the other's daring.

Tonight, in the infinitesimal[1] light of the stars,
The trees and flowers have been strewing their cool odors.
I walk among them, but none of them are noticing.
Sometimes I think that when I am sleeping
(15) I must most perfectly resemble them—
Thoughts gone dim.
It is more natural to me, lying down.
Then the sky and I are in open conversation,
And I shall be useful when I lie down finally:
(20) Then the trees may touch me for once, and the flowers
have time for me.

—Sylvia Plath
from *Uncollected Poems*, 1965
Turret Books

---

[1]infinitesimal—very small

11 The word "unpetal" in line 7 suggests

(1) inspiration   (3) isolation
(2) invisibility   (4) impermanence   11 ____

12 Lines 11 through 13 reveal the narrator's awareness of

(1) the limited time people exist on earth
(2) the unexpected changes that affect one's life
(3) her anxiety over the shifting of seasons
(4) her insignificance in the eyes of nature   12 ____

13 In lines 14 through 16, the narrator suggests that

(1) consciousness is a barrier to connecting with nature
(2) nature's ability to impress surpasses human's imagination
(3) the future depends on natural forces beyond human control
(4) nature's cruelty causes one to feel helpless   13 ____

14 Throughout the poem, the tone can best be described as

(1) envious   (3) skeptical
(2) hostile   (4) indignant   14 ____

Reading Comprehension Passage C

Jian Lin was 14 years old in 1973, when the Chinese government under Mao Zedong recruited him for a student science team called "the earthquake watchers." After a series of earthquakes that had killed thousands in northern China, the country's seismologists[1] thought that if they augmented[2] their
(5) own research by having observers keep an eye out for anomalies like snakes bolting early from their winter dens and erratic[3] well-water levels, they might be able to do what no scientific body had managed before: issue an earthquake warning that would save thousands of lives.

In the winter of 1974, the earthquake watchers were picking up some
(10) suspicious signals near the city of Haicheng. Panicked chickens were squalling and trying to escape their pens; water levels were falling in wells. Seismologists had also begun noticing a telltale pattern of small quakes. "They were like popcorn kernels," Lin tells me, "popping up all over the general area." Then, suddenly, the popping stopped, just as it had before a
(15) catastrophic earthquake in 1966 that killed more than 8,000. "Like 'the calm before the storm,' " Lin says. "We have that exact same phrase in Chinese." On the morning of February 4, 1975, the seismology bureau issued a warning: Haicheng should expect a big earthquake, and people should move outdoors.

(20) At 7:36 p.m., a magnitude 7.0 quake struck. The city was nearly leveled, but only about 2,000 people were killed. Without the warning, easily 150,000 would have died. "And so you finally had an earthquake forecast that did indeed save lives," Lin recalls. "People were excited. Or, you could say, uplifted. *Uplifted* is a great word for it." But uplift turned to heartbreak
(25) the very next year, when a 7.5 quake shattered the city of Tangshan without so much as a magnitude 4 to introduce it. When the quake hit the city of 1.6 million at 3:42 a.m., it killed nearly 250,000 people, most of whom were asleep. "If there was any moment in my life when I was scared of earthquakes, that was it," Lin says. "You think, what if it happened to you?
(30) And it could. I decided that if I could do anything—*anything*—to save lives lost to earthquakes, it would be worth the effort."

Lin is now a senior scientist of geophysics at Woods Hole Oceanographic Institution, in Massachusetts, where he spends his time studying not the scurrying of small animals and fluctuating electrical current between trees
(35) (another fabled warning sign), but seismometer readings, GPS coordinates,

---

[1]seismologists—people who study earthquakes   [2]augmented—added to   [3]erratic—unpredictable

and global earthquake-notification reports. He and his longtime collaborator, Ross Stein of the U.S. Geological Survey, are champions of a theory that could enable scientists to forecast earthquakes with more precision and speed.

(40)   Some established geophysicists[4] insist that all earthquakes are random, yet everyone agrees that aftershocks are not. Instead, they follow certain empirical laws. Stein, Lin, and their collaborators hypothesized that many earthquakes classified as main shocks are actually aftershocks, and they went looking for the forces that cause faults to fail.

(45)   Their work was in some ways heretical:[5] For a long time, earthquakes were thought to release only the stress immediately around them; an earthquake that happened in one place would decrease the possibility of another happening nearby. But that didn't explain earthquake sequences like the one that rumbled through the desert and mountains east of Los

(50) Angeles in 1992. The series began on April 23 with a 6.2 near the town of Joshua Tree; two months later, on June 28, a 7.3 struck less than 15 miles away in the desert town of Landers. Three and a half hours after that, a 6.5 hit the town of Big Bear, in the mountains overlooking the Mojave. The Big Bear quake was timed like an aftershock, except it was too far off the Landers

(55) earthquake's fault rupture. When Lin, Stein, and Geoffrey King of the Paris Geophysical Institute got together to analyze it, they decided to ignore the distance rule and treat it just as a different kind of aftershock. Their ensuing report, "Static Stress Changes and the Triggering of Earthquakes," became one of the decade's most-cited earthquake research papers.

(60)   Rocks can be subject to two kinds of stresses: the "clamping" stress that pushes them together, and the "shear" stress they undergo as they slide past each other. Together, these stresses are known as Coulomb stress, named for Charles-Augustin de Coulomb, an 18th-century French physicist. Coulomb calculations had been used for years in engineering, to find the failure points

(65) of various building materials, but they'd never been applied properly to faults. It turned out, though, that faults in the ground behave much like rocks in the laboratory: they come unglued when shear stress exceeds the friction and pressure (the clamping stress) holding them together. When Stein, Lin, and King applied the Coulomb model to the California sequence,

(70) they found that most of the earthquakes had occurred in areas where the shifting of the ground had caused increased stress.

---

[4]geophysicists—people who study the physics of the earth and its environment, including seismology
[5]heretical—against the opinion of authorities

In 1997, Stein and two other geologists using the model found that there was a 12 percent chance that a magnitude 7 or greater would hit near Izmit, Turkey, within 30 years; two years later, on August 17, 1999, a magnitude (75) 7.4 destroyed the city, which wasn't designed to withstand such a tremor. A Turkish geologist named Aykut Barka quickly wrote up a paper warning that Coulomb stress from the Izmit quake could trigger a similar rupture near Düzce, a town roughly 60 miles east. His work persuaded authorities there to close school buildings damaged during the Izmit shaking. On November (80) 12, a segment of the North Anatolian Fault gave way, in a magnitude 7.2. The empty school buildings collapsed.

Lin and Stein both admit that Coulomb stress doesn't explain all earthquakes. Indeed, some geophysicists, like Karen Felzer, of the U.S. Geological Survey, think their hypothesis gives short shrift[6] to the impact (85) that dynamic stress—the actual rattling of a quake in motion—has on neighboring faults.

In the aftermath of the disastrous March 11 Tohoku quake, both camps are looking at its well-monitored aftershocks (including several within 100 miles of Tokyo) for answers. Intriguingly, it was *preceded* by a flurry of (90) earthquakes, one as large as magnitude 7.2, that may have been foreshocks, although no one thought so at the time; the researchers are trying to determine what those early quakes meant.

When I ask Lin whether California, where I live, is next, he laughs. "I understand that the public now thinks that we've entered a global (90) earthquake cluster. Even my own mother in China thinks that. But there's no scientific evidence whatsoever to suggest that the earthquake in New Zealand triggered the earthquake in Japan, or Japan will trigger one in California." Still, Lin and his colleagues do wonder whether Tohoku has pushed neighboring faults closer to rupture. "I am particularly interested in (100) how this earthquake might have changed the potential of future earthquakes to the south, even closer to Tokyo," Lin tells me. "There, even a much smaller earthquake could be devastating."

—Judith Lewis Mernit
"Is San Francisco Next?"
The Atlantic, June 2011

---

[6]short shrift—little consideration

15 As used in line 5, the word "anomalies" most nearly means

    (1) seasonal changes
    (2) odd occurrences
    (3) dangerous incidents
    (4) scheduled events

    15 _____

16 The first paragraph contributes to a central idea in the text by

    (1) contributing historical facts
    (2) contrasting early theories
    (3) comparing two philosophies
    (4) challenging cultural beliefs

    16 _____

17 The figurative language in lines 13 and 14 conveys a sense of

    (1) disbelief
    (2) disappointment
    (3) apathy
    (4) urgency

    17 _____

18 The contrast drawn between the Haicheng and Tangshan earthquakes (lines 9 through 31) contributes to a central idea that earthquakes are

    (1) preceded by reliable signs
    (2) controlled by observable factors
    (3) not always predictable
    (4) not often studied

    18 _____

19 The purpose of lines 32 through 36 is to emphasize that Jian Lin

    (1) relied on his past experience to identify earthquakes
    (2) modified his methods of observing earthquakes
    (3) changed his understanding about the causes of earthquakes
    (4) disagreed with his co-researcher on the measurement of earthquakes

    19 _____

20 The word "champions" as used in line 37 most nearly means

    (1) advisers   (3) supporters

    (2) adaptors   (4) survivors   20 _____

21 Which statement reflects a long-held belief disproved by Lin, Stein, and King?

    (1) "many earthquakes classified as main shocks are actually aftershocks" (lines 42 and 43)

    (2) "an earthquake that happened in one place would decrease the possibility of another happening nearby" (lines 46 and 47)

    (3) "Rocks can be subject to two kinds of stresses" (line 60)

    (4) "faults in the ground behave much like rocks in the laboratory" (lines 66 and 67)   21 _____

22 According to lines 60 through 71, seismologists realized that the California sequence of earthquakes happened because

    (1) shear stress forced rocks to fuse together

    (2) clamping stress caused rocks to move apart

    (3) shear stress was greater than clamping stress

    (4) clamping stress balanced the shear stress   22 _____

23 Throughout the text, the author portrays Jian Lin as

    (1) satisfied   (3) superstitious

    (2) cautious   (4) dedicated   23 _____

24 Jian Lin's research regarding earthquakes can best be described as

    (1) flawed by inconsistent methodology

    (2) concurrent with prior theories

    (3) challenged by conflicting findings

    (4) important to future studies   24 _____

PART 2—Argument Response

Directions: Closely read each of the *four* texts on pages 213 through 221 and write a source-based argument on the topic below. You may use the margins to take notes as you read and scrap paper to plan your response. Write your argument on a separate sheet of paper.

Topic: Should self-driving cars replace human drivers?

Your Task: Carefully read each of the *four* texts provided. Then, using evidence from at least *three* of the texts, write a well-developed argument regarding whether or not self-driving cars should replace human drivers. Clearly establish your claim, distinguish your claim from alternate or opposing claims, and use specific, relevant, and sufficient evidence from at least *three* of the texts to develop your argument. Do *not* simply summarize each text.

  Guidelines:

   Be sure to
   - Establish your claim regarding whether or not self-driving cars should replace human drivers.
   - Distinguish your claim from alternate or opposing claims.
   - Use specific, relevant, and sufficient evidence from at least *three* of the texts to develop your argument.
   - Identify each source that you reference by text number and line number(s) or graphic (for example: Text 1, line 4 or Text 2, graphic).
   - Organize your ideas in a cohesive and coherent manner.
   - Maintain a formal style of writing.
   - Follow the conventions of standard written English.
  Texts:

   Text 1—How Google's Self-Driving Car Will Change Everything

   Text 2—Google's Driverless Cars Run Into Problem: Cars With Drivers

   Text 3—Autonomous Vehicles Will Replace Taxi Drivers, But That's Just the Beginning

   Text 4—Along for the Ride

Text 1

How Google's Self-Driving Car Will Change Everything

Imagine getting in your car, typing or speaking a location into your vehicle's interface, then letting it drive you to your destination while you read a book, surf the web or nap. Self-driving vehicles—the stuff of science fiction since the first roads were paved—are coming, and they're going to
(5) radically change what it's like to get from point A to point B.

Basic Technology Already In Use
. . .The first big leap to fully autonomous[1] vehicles is due in 2017, when Google Inc. (GOOG) said it would have an integrated system ready to market. Every major automotive manufacturer is likely to follow by the early 2020s, though their systems could wind up being more sensor-based, and rely less
(10) on networking and access to map information. Google probably wont [*sic*] manufacture cars. More likely, it'll license the software and systems.

A Drastic Change
As with the adoption of any new revolutionary technology, there will be problems for businesses that don't adjust fast enough. Futurists estimate that hundreds of billions of dollars (if not trillions) will be lost by automakers,
(15) suppliers, dealers, insurers, parking companies, and many other car-related enterprises. And think of the lost revenue for governments via licensing fees, taxes and tolls, and by personal injury lawyers and health insurers.
Who needs a car made with heavier-gauge steel and eight airbags (not to mention a body shop) if accidents are so rare? Who needs a parking spot
(20) close to work if your car can drive you there, park itself miles away, only to pick you up later? Who needs to buy a flight from Boston to Cleveland when you can leave in the evening, sleep much of the way, and arrive in the morning?
Indeed, Google's goal is to increase car utilization from 5–10% to 75%
(25) or more by facilitating sharing. That means fewer cars on the road. Fewer cars period, in fact. Who needs to own a car when you can just order a shared one and it'll drive up minutes later, ready to take you wherever you want? . . .

---

[1]autonomous—self-directed

Changing Oil Demand

(30)   If you're in the business of finding, extracting, refining and marketing hydrocarbons,[2] such as Exxon Mobil Corp. (EOX), Chevron Corp. (CVX) or BP plc (BP), you could see your business fluctuate as use changes.

      "These vehicles should practice very efficient eco-driving practices, which is typically about 20% better than the average driver," said [Robin] *Chase*[3] [*sic*]
(35) "On the other hand, if these cars are owned by individuals, I see a huge rise in the number of trips, and vehicle miles traveled. People will send out their car to run errands they would never do if they had to be in the car and waste their own time. If the autonomous cars are shared vehicles and people pay for each trip, I think this will reduce demand, and thus (vehicle miles traveled)."

Safety Dividend

      . . ."Over 90% of accidents today are caused by driver error," said
(40) Professor Robert W. Peterson of the Center for Insurance Law and Regulation at Santa Clara University School of Law. "There is every reason to believe that self-driving cars will reduce frequency and severity of accidents, so insurance costs should fall, perhaps dramatically."

      "Cars can still get flooded, damaged or stolen," notes Michael Barry,
(45) the v.p. [vice president] of media relations at the Insurance Information Institute. "But this technology will have a dramatic impact on underwriting[4]. A lot of traditional underwriting criteria will be upended."

      Barry said it's too early to quantify exactly how self-driving vehicles will affect rates, but added that injured parties in a crash involving a selfdriving
(50) car may choose to sue the vehicle's manufacturer, or the software company that designed the autonomous capability. . . .

Risks, Hurdles and the Unknown

      There are regulatory and legislative obstacles to widespread use of selfdriving cars, and substantial concerns about privacy (who will have access to any driving information these vehicles store?). There's also the question
(55) of security, as hackers could theoretically take control of these vehicles, and are not known for their restraint or civic-mindedness.

---

[2]hydrocarbons—organic compounds that are chief components of petroleum and natural gas
[3]Robin Chase—founder and CEO of Buzzcar
[4]underwriting—risk determination

The Bottom Line

    However it plays out, these vehicles are coming—and fast. Their full adoption will take decades, but their convenience, cost, safety and other factors will make them ubiquitous[5] and indispensable. Such as with any
(60) technological revolution, the companies that plan ahead, adjust the fastest and imagine the biggest will survive and thrive. And companies invested in old technology and practices will need to evolve or risk dying.

—Joseph A. Dallegro
excerpted and adapted from "How Google's
Self-Driving Car Will Change Everything"
www.investopedia.com, 2015

---

[5]ubiquitous—everywhere

Text 2

Google's Driverless Cars Run Into Problem: Cars With Drivers

Google, a leader in efforts to create driverless cars, has run into an odd safety conundrum:[1] humans.

Last month, as one of Google's self-driving cars approached a crosswalk, it did what it was supposed to do when it slowed to allow a pedes trian to
(5) cross, prompting its "safety driver" to apply the brakes. The pedestrian was fine, but not so much Google's car, which was hit from behind by a human-driven sedan.

Google's fleet of autonomous test cars is programmed to follow the letter of the law. But it can be tough to get around if you are a stickler for
(10) the rules. One Google car, in a test in 2009, couldn't get through a fourway stop because its sensors kept waiting for other (human) drivers to stop completely and let it go. The human drivers kept inching forward, looking for the advantage—paralyzing Google's robot.

It is not just a Google issue. Researchers in the fledgling[2] field of auton
(15) omous vehicles say that one of the biggest challenges facing automated cars is blending them into a world in which humans don't behave by the book. "The real problem is that the car is too safe," said Donald Norman, director of the Design Lab at the University of California, San Diego, who studies autonomous vehicles. . . .

(20) Traffic wrecks and deaths could well plummet in a world without any drivers, as some researchers predict. But wide use of self-driving cars is still many years away, and testers are still sorting out hypothetical risks—like hackers—and real world challenges, like what happens when an autonomous car breaks down on the highway.

(25) For now, there is the nearer-term problem of blending robots and humans. Already, cars from several automakers have technology that can warn or even take over for a driver, whether through advanced cruise control or brakes that apply themselves. Uber is working on the self-driving car technology, and Google expanded its tests in July to Austin, Tex[as].

(30) Google cars regularly take quick, evasive maneuvers or exercise caution in ways that are at once the most cautious approach, but also out of step with the other vehicles on the road. . . .

Since 2009, Google cars have been in 16 crashes, mostly fenderbenders, and in every single case, the company says, a human was at fault. This
(35) includes the rear-ender crash on Aug. 20, and reported Tuesday by Google.

---

[1]conundrum—difficult problem   [2]fledgling—new and inexperienced

The Google car slowed for a pedestrian, then the Google employee manually applied the brakes. The car was hit from behind, sending the employee to the emergency room for mild whiplash.

(40) Google's report on the incident adds another twist: While the safety driver did the right thing by applying the brakes, if the autonomous car had been left alone, it might have braked less hard and traveled closer to the crosswalk, giving the car behind a little more room to stop. Would that have prevented the collision? Google says it's impossible to say.

(45) There was a single case in which Google says the company was responsible for a crash. It happened in August 2011, when one of its Google cars collided with another moving vehicle. But, remarkably, the Google car was being piloted at the time by an employee. Another human at fault. . . .

On a recent outing with *New York Times* journalists, the Google driverless car took two evasive maneuvers that simultaneously displayed
(50) how the car errs on the cautious side, but also how jarring that experience can be. In one maneuver, it swerved sharply in a residential neighborhood to avoid a car that was poorly parked, so much so that the Google sensors couldn't tell if it might pull into traffic.

More jarring for human passengers was a maneuver that the Google
(55) car took as it approached a red light in moderate traffic. The laser system mounted on top of the driverless car sensed that a vehicle coming the other direction was approaching the red light at higher-than-safe speed. The Google car immediately jerked to the right in case it had to avoid a collision. In the end, the oncoming car was just doing what human drivers so often
(60) do: not approach a red light cautiously enough, though the driver did stop well in time.

Courtney Hohne, a spokeswoman for the Google project, said current testing was devoted to "smoothing out" the relationship between the car's software and humans. For instance, at four-way stops, the program lets the
(65) car inch forward, as the rest of us might, asserting its turn while looking for signs that it is being allowed to go.

The way humans often deal with these situations is that "they make eye contact. On the fly, they make agreements about who has the right of way," said John Lee, a professor of industrial and systems engineering and expert
(70) in driver safety and automation at the University of Wisconsin.

"Where are the eyes in an autonomous vehicle?" he added. . . .

—Matt Richtel and Conor Dougherty
excerpted and adapted from
"Google's Driverless Cars Run Into Problem: Cars With Drivers"
www.nytimes.com, Sept. 1, 2015

Text 3

Autonomous Vehicles Will Replace Taxi Drivers, But That's Just the Beginning

    . . .According to the Bureau of Labor Statistics [BLS] there are about 178,000 people employed as taxi drivers or chauffeurs in the United States. But once driverless technology advances to the point that vehicles can be fully autonomous—without the need for any human behind the wheel in case
(5) of emergencies—professional drivers will become a thing of the past. Bus drivers, whether they're for schools, cities, or long-distance travel, would be made obsolete. Once cars drive themselves, food deliveries will be a matter of restaurants filling a car with orders and sending it off, eliminating the need for a delivery driver. Each of these professions employ more people
(10) and are better paid than taxi drivers, as shown in the table below.

Occupation	Average annual wage	Number of jobs	Total annual wages
Taxi drivers & chauffeurs	$25,690	178,260	$4,579,499,400
Bus drivers – transit & intercity	$39,410	158,050	$6,228,750,500
Driver / sales workers (delivering food, newspapers)	$27,720	405,810	$11,249,053,200
Bus drivers – school or special client	$29,910	499,440	$14,938,250,400
Postal service mail carriers	$51,790	307,490	$15,924,907,100
Light truck or delivery services drivers (UPS, FedEx)	$33,870	797,010	$26,994,728,700
Heavy and tractor-trailer truck drivers	$41,930	1,625,290	$68,148,409,700
TOTAL	$35,760.00	3,971,350	$148,063,599,000.00

Source: Bureau of Labor Statistics

    Some of these may be a bit surprising, like postal carriers. But once fully autonomous vehicles are commonplace it would make sense for the Postal Service to make use of the technology to deliver mail, especially in areas where curbside mailboxes are standard and it would be rather simple
(15) for a mechanical arm to deposit and retrieve mail directly. Drivers of delivery trucks for companies like UPS and FedEx may also face extinction, if they're not replaced by Amazon's delivery drones first—or perhaps they'll

develop a combined system where self-driving trucks bring packages from the warehouse to their destination, and a drone delivers them the last few
(20) yards from curbside to doorstep.

     Despite their importance for the economy, each of these professions pale [*sic*] in comparison to heavy and tractor-trailer truck drivers. This field employs the most by far—nine times as many people work as truckers than as taxi drivers, and it's the most common job in a whopping 29 states—
(25) and is also better paid than most, with an average salary of about $42,000. When considering the total amount of wages paid to each of the seven occupations in the table above, truck drivers make up nearly half, while taxi drivers & chauffeurs only account for 3%. The development of self-driving tractor-trailers won't be far behind automated taxi cabs, with companies like
(30) Daimler already testing out partially-automated trucks in Nevada.

     While there may be other driving-focused jobs not included in these BLS statistics, there are certainly many more industries that will be impacted by the replacement of humans with self-driving vehicles. If this technology leads to a sharp decline in car ownership like many predict,
(35) insurance companies will have far fewer customers and may not need as many employees to service them. The same goes for mechanics and auto part manufacturers, who could face a massive drop in demand. Fewer human truckers on the road means fewer motel stays and rest stop visits, and cheaper trucking could take business away from freight trains or even
(40) oil pipelines. Vehicles programmed to obey traffic laws won't need nearly as much policing, which also means fewer traffic tickets and less revenue for municipalities. The full scale of these economic shifts will be impossible to understand until they're upon us, but the one thing we can know for sure is that they'll touch almost every aspect of society. . . .

—Sam Tracy
excerpted and adapted from "Autonomous Vehicles Will
Replace Taxi Drivers, But That's Just the Beginning"
www.huffingtonpost.com, June 11, 2015

Text 4

Along for the Ride

. . .Automotive designers have a good incentive to get human drivers out from behind the wheel: public safety. In 2012, according to the most recent figures from the National Highway Traffic Safety Administration (NHTSA), 33,561 people were killed in car crashes in the United States, and
(5) an estimated 2.36 million were injured. According to NHTSA, a number of major crash studies have found that human error caused more than 90 percent of those crashes. In a perfect world, technology would take driver error out of the equation. . . .

But before society can reap those benefits, experts caution there are
(10) important problems to solve. Namely, since people interact with technology in unexpected ways, how will each individual driver engage with an automated car?

For some people, automation might lead to complacency,[1] says Nicholas Ward, PhD, a human factors psychologist in the department of mechanical
(15) and industrial engineering at Montana State University. Drivers who put too much trust in automation may become overly reliant on it, overestimating what the system can do for them. . . .

Information overload may be another concern, says Neville Stanton, PhD, a psychologist at the University of Southampton in the United
(20) Kingdom, who studies human performance in technological systems. While automated systems are designed to take pressures off the driver, he's found that they may add complexity in some cases. In an automated system, drivers may feel compelled to monitor the behavior of the system as well as keep an eye on the driving environment. That extra pressure might increase stress
(25) and error. . . .

Given a nearly infinite combination of driver personalities, road conditions and vehicle technologies, the answer is anything but straightforward. In a study using a driving simulator, for example, Stanton found that adaptive cruise control—in which a car maintains a safe following distance
(30) from the vehicle ahead of it—can reduce a driver's mental workload and stress levels. However, that technology also caused a reduction in drivers' situational awareness. And while a lower mental workload may be a good thing in tricky traffic jams, it could cause problems if drivers totally tune out.

---

[1]complacency—a feeling of security, often while unaware of potential dangers

(35)   Indeed, driver disengagement is a serious concern for automated-car designers. Users in such vehicles are expected to tune out. After all, the appeal of such cars is that they can transport us to and fro without our having to do the hard work. But that presents a problem for our busy brains. . . .

    Detached from the activity of driving, most people soon begin to *(40)* experience "passive fatigue," says Gerald Matthews, PhD, a psychologist at the Applied Cognition and Training in Immersive Virtual Environments Lab at the University of Central Florida. That cognitive muddling can be a big problem, Matthews says, if the driver has to take back control of the vehicle (when leaving a highway "platoon" of automated cars to re-enter city streets, *(45)* for instance—or, in a worst-case scenario, if automated systems fail). . . .

    Like it or not, though, carmakers are pressing forward with automated systems, and psychologists can play a role in making them as safe as possible. One important issue, says Pradhan,[2] is how drivers of different ages, personalities, experience levels and cognitive abilities will deal with such *(50)* systems. "There is no average driver. The field is so new, we're still asking a lot of fundamental questions—and there are very few people looking at driver characteristics," he says. "Automation has to be designed for everybody." . . .

—Kirsten Weir
excerpted from "Along for the Ride"
www.apa.org, January 2015

---

[2]Anuj K. Pradhan, PhD—a research scientist who studies driver behavior and injury prevention at the University of Michigan Transportation Research Institute

PART 3—Text-Analysis Response

Your Task: Closely read the text on pages 223 through 225 and write a well-developed, text-based response of two to three paragraphs. In your response, identify a central idea in the text and analyze how the author's use of *one* writing strategy (literary element or literary technique or rhetorical device) develops this central idea. Use strong and thorough evidence from the text to support your analysis. Do *not* simply summarize the text. You may use the margins to take notes as you read and scrap paper to plan your response. Write your response on a separate sheet of paper.

   Guidelines:

   Be sure to

- Identify a central idea in the text.
- Analyze how the author's use of *one* writing strategy (literary element or literary technique or rhetorical device) develops this central idea. Examples include: characterization, conflict, denotation/connotation, metaphor, simile, irony, language use, point-of-view, setting, structure, symbolism, theme, tone, etc.
- Use strong and thorough evidence from the text to support your analysis.
- Organize your ideas in a cohesive and coherent manner.
- Maintain a formal style of writing.
- Follow the conventions of standard written English.

Text

The following excerpt is taken from a novel set in France during the World War II era.

Sixteen paces to the water fountain, sixteen back. Forty-two to the stairwell, forty-two back. Marie-Laure draws maps in her head, unreels a hundred yards of imaginary twine, and then turns and reels it back in. Botany smells like glue and blotter paper and pressed flowers. Paleontology
(5) smells like rock dust, bone dust. Biology smells like formalin and old fruit; it is loaded with heavy cool jars in which float things she has only had described for her: the pale coiled ropes of rattlesnakes, the severed hands of gorillas. Entomology smells like mothballs and oil: a preservative that, Dr. Geffard explains, is called naphthalene. Offices smell of carbon paper,
(10) or cigar smoke, or brandy, or perfume. Or all four.

She follows cables and pipes, railings and ropes, hedges and sidewalks. She startles people. She never knows if the lights are on.

The children she meets brim with questions: Does it hurt? Do you shut your eyes to sleep? How do you know what time it is?
(15) It doesn't hurt, she explains. And there is no darkness, not the kind they imagine. Everything is composed of webs and lattices and upheavals of sound and texture. She walks a circle around the Grand Gallery, navigating between squeaking floorboards; she hears feet tramp up and down museum staircases, a toddler squeal, the groan of a weary grandmother lowering
(20) herself onto a bench.

Color—that's another thing people don't expect. In her imagination, in her dreams, everything has color. The museum buildings are beige, chestnut, hazel. Its scientists are lilac and lemon yellow and fox brown. Piano chords loll in the speaker of the wireless in the guard station, projecting rich blacks
(25) and complicated blues down the hall toward the key pound.[1] Church bells send arcs of bronze careening off the windows. Bees are silver; pigeons are ginger and auburn and occasionally golden. The huge cypress trees she and her father pass on their morning walk are shimmering kaleidoscopes, each needle a polygon of light.
(30) She has no memories of her mother but imagines her as white, a soundless brilliance. Her father radiates a thousand colors, opal, strawberry red, deep russet, wild green; a smell like oil and metal, the feel of a lock tumbler sliding home, the sound of his key rings chiming as he walks. He is

---

[1]key pound—the office of her father, the museum locksmith

an olive green when he talks to a department head, an escalating series of
(35) oranges when he speaks to Mademoiselle Fleury from the greenhouses, a
bright red when he tries to cook. He glows sapphire when he sits over his
workbench in the evenings, humming almost inaudibly as he works, the tip
of his cigarette gleaming a prismatic blue.

She gets lost. Secretaries or botanists, and once the director's assistant,
(40) bring her back to the key pound. She is curious; she wants to know the
difference between an alga and a lichen, a *Diplodon charruanus* and a
Diplodon delodontus. Famous men take her by the elbow and escort her
through the gardens or guide her up stairwells. "I have a daughter too,"
they'll say. Or "I found her among the hummingbirds."
(45)   "*Toutes mes excuses*,"[2] her father says. He lights a cigarette; he plucks
key after key out of her pockets. "What," he whispers, "am I going to do with
you?"

On her ninth birthday, when she wakes, she finds two gifts. The first is
a wooden box with no opening she can detect. She turns it this way and that.
(50) It takes her a little while to realize one side is spring-loaded; she presses it
and the box flips open. Inside waits a single cube of creamy Camembert that
she pops directly into in [*sic*] her mouth.

"Too easy!" her father says, laughing.

The second gift is heavy, wrapped in paper and twine. Inside is a massive
(55) spiral-bound book. In Braille.

"They said it's for boys. Or very adventurous girls." She can hear him
smiling.

She slides her fingertips across the embossed[3] title page. *Around. The.
World. In. Eighty. Days.* "Papa, it's too expensive."
(60)   "That's for me to worry about."

That morning Marie-Laure crawls beneath the counter of the key
pound and lies on her stomach and sets all ten fingertips in a line on a page.
The French feels old-fashioned, the dots printed much closer together than
she is used to. But after a week, it becomes easy. She finds the ribbon she
(65) uses as a bookmark, opens the book, and the museum falls away.

Mysterious Mr. Fogg lives his life like a machine. Jean Passepartout
becomes his obedient valet. When, after two months, she reaches the novel's
last line, she flips back to the first page and starts again. At night she runs
her fingertips over her father's model: the bell tower, the display windows.
(70) She imagines Jules Verne's characters walking along the streets, chatting in

---

[2]*toutes mes excuses*—my apologies   [3]*embossed*—a stamped, molded or carved design

shops; a half-inch-tall baker slides speck-sized loaves in and out of his ovens; three minuscule burglars hatch plans as they drive slowly past the jeweler's; little grumbling cars throng the rue[4] de Mirbel, wipers sliding back and forth. Behind a fourth-floor window on the rue des Patriarches, a miniature (75) version of her father sits at a miniature workbench in their miniature apartment, just as he does in real life, sanding away at some infinitesimal[5] piece of wood; across the room is a miniature girl, skinny, quick-witted, an open book in her lap; inside her chest pulses something huge, something full of longing, something unafraid.

—Anthony Doerr
excerpted from *All the Light We Cannot See*, 2014
Scribner

---

[4]rue—street   [5]infinitesimal—very small

Regents ELA Answers August 2017

English Language Arts

Answer Key

PART 1

1. 3	9. 2	17. 4
2. 4	10. 4	18. 3
3. 1	11. 4	19. 2
4. 4	12. 4	20. 2
5. 1	13. 1	21. 2
6. 2	14. 1	22. 3
7. 1	15. 2	23. 4
8. 4	16. 1	24. 4

PART 2   *See Answers and Explanations*

PART 3   *See Answers and Explanations*

Regents Examination in English Language Arts—August 2017

Chart for Converting Total Weighted Raw Scores to Final Exam Scores (Scale Scores) (Use for the August 2017 examination only.)

Weighted Raw Score*	Scale Score	Performance Level		Weighted Raw Score*	Scale Score	Performance Level
56	100	5		27	52	1
55	99	5		26	48	1
54	99	5		25	45	1
53	99	5		24	41	1
52	99	5		23	38	1
51	98	5		22	34	1
50	98	5		21	31	1
49	97	5		20	27	1
48	96	5		19	24	1
47	94	5		18	21	1
46	92	5		17	17	1
45	91	5		16	14	1
44	89	5		15	12	1
43	88	5		14	10	1
42	87	5		13	8	1
41	85	5		12	8	1
40	84	4		11	7	1
39	82	4		10	6	1
38	80	4		9	5	1
37	79	4		8	4	1
36	76	3		7	4	1
35	74	3		6	3	1
34	72	3		5	2	1
33	69	3		4	2	1
32	67	3		3	1	1
31	65	3		2	1	1
30	61	2		1	1	1
29	58	2		0	0	1
28	55	2				

The conversion table is determined independently for each administration of the exam.

Answers and Explanations

PART 1—Reading Comprehension

Multiple-Choice Questions

Passage A

1. **3** "knowledgeable." In this introductory scene, the character of Dora-Rouge would look at the stars and, ". . . tell us what place we would pass on the next day." The narrator tells us that the next day they did reach those places.

2. **4** "insignificance." In this passage, the narrator illustrates how the characters enter a sense of timelessness and leave behind their lives on earth; they become, ". . . just a small dream among the . . . many dreams of earth." "Insignificance" best describes these feelings.

3. **1** "I saw vines creeping forward." A tendril is a vine or stem. The meaning of the word is revealed in the images of a leaf and flowers reaching up through darkness to reveal a truth, ". . . that had been there all along . . . ." None of the other choices expresses the feeling in these images.

4. **4** "enlightening." In this passage, the narrator describes how she recovers a lost knowledge, "the oldest bond of survival . . . this opening light of life . . . ." This passage does not suggest feelings of confusion, amusement, or threat.

5. **1** "transformation." Here the narrator tells us that, "New senses came to me." In becoming equal to other animals (transformed), she moves, ". . . as they moved, seeing as they saw."

6. **2** "developed a kinship with the environment." For the women in this story, the experience of their journey is one of recovering an ancestral relationship with the natural world. Among the choices, this answer best expresses the meaning of their experience.

7. **1** "link the past with the future." Toward the end of the passage, the narrator tells us that she, ". . . felt newly found . . . ." Before recovering a lost relationship with nature and her ancestral past, she felt her life had been, ". . . without all its knowings." Looking forward, she says, "Now we, the four of us, all had the same eyes, ..."

8. **4** "personal narrative." This passage, from a novel, is a vivid example of a first-person narrative of a significant experience.

9. **2** "[with] clarity of mind comes connection of spirit." This statement best describes the spiritual journey of the narrator and her companions. The other choices express themes that might reliably fit other contexts but are not central to this passage.

10. **4** "And listening to the night, I knew there was another horizon, beyond the one we could see." This quote best supports the central idea of rediscovery and spiritual enlightenment in the passage. It recalls both the experience of the journey and suggests its meaning for the women in the future.

Passage B

11. **4** "impermanence." The poet creates her own verb to describe what happens as flowers wither and die: they lose their petals. None of the other choices is suggested in this stanza.

12. **4** "her insignificance in the eyes of nature." In these lines, the poet remarks that, ". . . none of [The trees and flowers] are noticing [her]" as she walks among them. This best describes what the narrator is feeling in these lines.

13. **1** "consciousness is a barrier to connecting with nature." The narrator expresses the feeling that she, ". . . most perfectly resembles" the trees and flowers, ". . . when I am sleeping . . . ." The poet and the sky are, ". . . in open conversation," only with, "Thoughts gone dim." None of the other choices expresses these ideas in this poem.

14. **1** "envious." In the first stanza, the narrator tells us that she does not, "gleam into leaf . . ." like a tree, or dazzle with beauty like a flower. She wishes she had (envies) the tree's longevity and the flower's daring.

Passage C

15. **2** "odd occurrences." The meaning of "anomalies" is clarified in the examples that follow: snakes that leave their winter dens early and erratic (unpredictable) well-water levels are best described as odd occurrences.

16. **1** "contributing historical facts." The article begins with a reference to a decision by the Chinese government, after a series of devastating earthquakes in 1973, to recruit young students to be "earthquake watchers." The article is developed and uses historical and scientific facts throughout.

17. **4** "urgency." The sense of urgency is felt when, suddenly, ". . . the popping stopped, just as it had before a catastrophic earthquake in 1966 that killed more than 8,000."

18. **3** "not always predictable." The contrast between the two earthquakes in this passage are (1) the warnings were effective and saved many lives, and (2) the quake hit without warning and ". . . killed nearly 250,000 people, most of whom were asleep." None of the other choices is an accurate statement about earthquakes.

19. **2** "modified his methods of observing earthquakes." This paragraph reports on how as a scientist Jian Lin no longer observes odd behavior in snakes but, instead, uses sophisticated scientific methods to observe earthquakes. This section of the article focuses on how his methods of study changed.

20. **2** "supporters." The meaning of "champions" as supporters and advocates is clarified in the context of the sentence and in the subsequent information about how the scientists presented their theories to other scientists.

21. **2** "an earthquake that happened in one place would decrease the possibility of another happening nearby." This long-held belief about earthquakes failed to explain a sequence of quakes in Los Angeles in 1992; further analysis by Lin, Stein and King ignored this belief and showed them to be a series of aftershocks. Their work became "one of the decade's most-cited earthquake research papers." Review of the text will show that each of the other choices is reported as reliable.

22. **3** "shear stress was greater than clamping stress." Determining the answer to this question requires careful reading of the paragraph to understand the two kinds of stress and how they account for earthquakes. The seismologists determined that, ". . . most of the earthquakes [in the Los Angeles series] had occurred in areas where the shifting of the ground had caused increased stress." None of the other choices is consistent with the information in the passage.

23. **4** "dedicated." As a young man, Jian Lin experienced a devastating earthquake in China: ". . . I was scared of earthquakes . . . . I decided that if I could do anything—*anything*—to save lives lost to earthquakes, it would be worth the effort." None of the other choices adequately describes his character and determination.

24. **4** "important to future studies." Throughout the article, there are references to the ways in which Lin's work has supported further research. At the end, we understand that Lin and other seismologists continue their research to find ways to reliably predict earthquakes and to save lives.

PART 2—Argument Response

Sample Essay Response

   As technology advances, innovations are introduced to society on a regular basis. One of these innovations, which humans may see in the near future, is a self-driving car. Although this idea may seem promising, many disadvantages come along with it. Self-driving cars should not replace human drivers, despite how beneficial they sound.

   A primary reason to oppose self-driving cars is that many people would lose their jobs. At present, autonomous cars usually have a person in the driver's seat in case of a problem. However, once the cars can function safely without human intervention, professional drivers will no longer be needed. Heavy truck and tractor-trailer drivers have "the most common job in a whopping 29 states." (Text 3, line 24) In addition to the 1,625,290 heavy and tractor-trailer drivers who would lose their jobs, other workers, such as taxi drivers, bus drivers, and mail carriers, might face unemployment. (Text 3, graphic)

   Another concern about self-driving cars is the risk of confusion that can occur between drivers and robots. This is not a good idea, "blending [self-driving cars] into a world in which humans don't behave by the book." (Text 2, line 16) One example of this confusion is when a Google car, "sensed that a vehicle coming the other direction was approaching the red light at a higher-than-safe speed." (Text 2, lines 56–57) In response, the Google car immediately veered to the side in anticipation of a crash; however, the driver of the other car stopped in plenty of time. Although challenging driving situations may occur on a regular basis, "the way humans often deal with these situations is that, "they make eye contact." (Text 2, lines 67–68) This interaction is not possible between a self-driving car and a human. An automated reaction could result in otherwise avoidable crashes.

   A third issue with self-driven cars is privacy. Just as home computers and other technology can be hacked, the same applies for the software in a self-driving car. For example, "who will have access to any driving information these vehicles store?" (Text 1, lines 53 and 54) If the vehicle stores a person's payment information or a record of places the person usually goes, a hacker might have access to significant personal and financial information of someone who rides in a self-driving car.

   Supporters of self-driving cars argue that self-driving cars are safer. They explain that, "Over 90% of accidents today are caused by driver error." (Text 1, line 39) However, that does not prove that self-driving cars will be safer. Humans make errors, but technology can malfunction. Errors and accidents can still occur, whether they are caused by a human or by a computer.

The idea of self-driving cars is exciting, but the truth is that technology is never 100% reliable. Self-driving cars, once they become part of everyday life, could bring about a loss of jobs, confusion between human and automated drivers, and concerns about privacy. Although the immediate attraction is that self-driving cars are safer than human drivers, the reality is this world is not ideal or perfect. These two worlds—realistic and idealistic—will never mesh. Too many risks are at stake here, with little to no benefits.

Analysis

This argument represents a good response to the task. The first paragraph identifies the context and establishes a claim that is distinguished from opposing claims. The argument is clearly organized, and each section begins with an appropriate transition: "A primary reason . . . Another concern . . . A third issue . . . ." The writer's claim is supported by relevant evidence in the texts. Development is adequate, but the argument would be stronger if the fifth paragraph, refuting the claim that self-driving cars are safer, were more fully developed with evidence from Text 4. The conclusion appropriately acknowledges the appeal of self-driving cars but forcefully urges the need for caution. The writing is clear and free of significant errors in the conventions. This response would merit a high score.

(See pages 79–80 for the scoring guidelines.)

PART 3—Text-Analysis Response

Sample Essay Response

The story centers around a young girl who, after losing her sense of sight, compensates for it by heightening the strength of her imagination and other senses. Through the vivid, colorful things that she imagines on a morning walk, such as the image of "huge cypress trees" that "are shimmering kaleidoscopes, with each needle a polygon of light," the character, Marie-Laure, is able to construct her own vision of the world without letting her blindness cripple her. The author intends to express to the reader that there are no limitations to what a human can do. A person with a disability such as Marie-Laure's can function nearly as well as anyone, and can even go beyond seeing and feeling what people normally can. For their loss of a sense, these people develop a creativity that cannot be mimicked and is entirely unique to themselves.

The author uses imagery to convey the point of the story. He answers questions such as, "How does Marie-Laure feel being blind?" and, "How exactly is she able to live in the world without sight?" We understand that Marie-Laure must have had vision at one time: "In her imagination, in her dreams, everything has color." When other children are curious and ask her what it is like, she assures them that it does not hurt, and it is not all darkness. She says, ". . . everything is composed of webs and lattices and upheavals of sound and texture."

The author chose to use images to create a visual in the reader's mind, where Marie has color in her imagination, where "museum buildings are beige, chestnut, hazel," and its scientists are "lilac and lemon yellow and fox brown." She describes bees as silver and "pigeons are ginger and auburn and occasionally gold." The author's use of vivid imagery gives the reader a clear sense of the girl's experiences and her imaginative way of seeing her world.

Analysis

This response (edited for clarity) is especially good in the way the central idea is expressed as answers to a series of questions: "How does Marie-Laure feel being blind?" and, "How exactly is she able to live in the world without sight?" The analysis is supported through extensive use of relevant quotes and skillful use of the language of vision, seeing, and imagery. The response is brief but clearly organized in two paragraphs. The writing is appropriately formal and demonstrates control of complex sentence structures and the conventions. This response would merit a high score.

(See pages 81–82 for the scoring guidelines.)

Regents ELA Examination June 2018

English Language Arts

PART 1—Reading Comprehension

Directions (1–24): Closely read each of the three passages below. After each passage, there are several multiple-choice questions. Select the best suggested answer to each question and write its number in the space provided. You may use the margins to take notes as you read.

Reading Comprehension Passage A

     "That woman's art-jargon[1] tires me," said Clovis to his journalist friend. "She's so fond of talking of certain pictures as 'growing on one,' as though they were a sort of fungus."

     "That reminds me," said the journalist, "of the story of Henri Deplis.
(5) Have I ever told it [to] you?"

     Clovis shook his head.

     "Henri Deplis was by birth a native of the Grand Duchy of Luxemburg. On maturer reflection he became a commercial traveller. His business activities frequently took him beyond the limits of the Grand Duchy, and
(10) he was stopping in a small town of Northern Italy when news reached him from home that a legacy[2] from a distant and deceased relative had fallen to his share.

     "It was not a large legacy, even from the modest standpoint of Henri Deplis, but it impelled him towards some seemingly harmless extravagances.
(15) In particular it led him to patronise local art as represented by the tattoo-

[1]art-jargon—language specific to the art world
[2]legacy—inheritance

needles of Signor Andreas Pincini. Signor Pincini was, perhaps, the most brilliant master of tattoo craft that Italy had ever known, but his circumstances were decidedly impoverished, and for the sum of six hundred francs he gladly undertook to cover his client's back, from the collarbone down to the
(20) waistline, with a glowing representation of the Fall of Icarus.[3] The design, when finally developed, was a slight disappointment to Monsieur Deplis, who had suspected Icarus of being a fortress taken by Wallenstein in the Thirty Years' War, but he was more than satisfied with the execution of the work, which was acclaimed by all who had the privilege of seeing it as
(25) Pincini's masterpiece.

"It was his greatest effort, and his last. Without even waiting to be paid, the illustrious craftsman departed this life, and was buried under an ornate tombstone, whose winged cherubs would have afforded singularly little scope[4] for the exercise of his favourite art. There remained, however, the
(30) widow Pincini, to whom the six hundred francs were due. And thereupon arose the great crisis in the life of Henri Deplis, traveller of commerce. The legacy, under the stress of numerous little calls on its substance,[5] had dwindled to very insignificant proportions, and when a pressing wine bill and sundry[6] other current accounts had been paid, there remained
(35) little more than 430 francs to offer to the widow. The lady was properly indignant, not wholly, as she volubly explained, on account of the suggested writing-off of 170 francs, but also at the attempt to depreciate the value of her late husband's acknowledged masterpiece. In a week's time Deplis was obliged to reduce his offer to 405 francs, which circum stance fanned
(40) the widow's indignation into a fury. She cancelled the sale of the work of art, and a few days later Deplis learned with a sense of consternation[7] that she had presented it to the municipality of Bergamo, which had gratefully accepted it. He left the neighbourhood as unobtrusively as possible, and was genuinely relieved when his business commands took him to Rome, where
(45) he hoped his identity and that of the famous picture might be lost sight of.

"But he bore on his back the burden of the dead man's genius. On presenting himself one day in the steaming corridor of a vapour bath, he was at once hustled back into his clothes by the proprietor, who was a

---

[3]Fall of Icarus—In Greek mythology Icarus wore wings made of wax and feathers so he could fly. However, because of his excessive pride and carelessness he flew too close to the sun. His wings melted and he plunged to his death in the sea.
[4]scope—opportunity
[5]little calls on its substance—withdrawals from the inheritance
[6]sundry—various
[7]consternation—alarmed amazement

North Italian, and who emphatically refused to allow the celebrated Fall
(50) of Icarus to be publicly on view without the permission of the municipality
of Bergamo. Public interest and official vigilance increased as the matter
became more widely known, and Deplis was unable to take a simple dip
in the sea or river on the hottest afternoon unless clothed up to the collarbone in a substantial bathing garment. Later on the authorities of Bergamo
(55) conceived the idea that salt water might be injurious to the masterpiece, and
a perpetual injunction[8] was obtained which debarred[9] the muchly harassed
commercial traveller from sea bathing under any circumstances. Altogether,
he was fervently thankful when his firm of employers found him a new range
of activities in the neighbourhood of Bordeaux. His thankfulness, however,
(60) ceased abruptly at the Franco-Italian frontier. An imposing array of official
force barred his departure, and he was sternly reminded of the stringent
law, which forbids the exportation of Italian works of art.

"A diplomatic parley ensued between the Luxemburgian and Italian
Governments, and at one time the European situation became overcast
(65) with the possibilities of trouble. But the Italian Government stood firm; it
declined to concern itself in the least with the fortunes or even the existence
of Henri Deplis, commercial traveller, but was immovable in its decision
that the Fall of Icarus (by the late Pincini, Andreas) at present the property
of the municipality of Bergamo, should not leave the country. . . .

(70)   "Meanwhile, the unhappy human background fared no better than
before, and it was not surprising that he drifted into the ranks of Italian
anarchists. Four times at least he was escorted to the frontier as a dangerous
and undesirable foreigner, but he was always brought back as the Fall of
Icarus (attributed to Pincini, Andreas, early Twentieth Century). And then
(75) one day, at an anarchist congress at Genoa, a fellow-worker, in the heat of
debate, broke a phial full of corrosive liquid over his back. The red shirt that
he was wearing mitigated[10] the effects, but the Icarus was ruined beyond
recognition. His assailant was severely reprimanded for assaulting a fellow-
anarchist and received seven years' imprisonment for defacing a national art
(80) treasure. As soon as he was able to leave the hospital Henri Deplis was put
across the frontier as an undesirable alien.

---

[8]injunction—restraint
[9]debarred—prevented
[10]mitigated—lessened

"In the quieter streets of Paris, especially in the neighbourhood of the Ministry of Fine Arts, you may sometimes meet a depressed, anxious-looking man, who, if you pass him the time of day, will answer you with a slight (85) Luxemburgian accent. He nurses the illusion that he is one of the lost arms of the Venus de Milo,[11] and hopes that the French Government may be persuaded to buy him. On all other subjects I believe he is tolerably sane."

—H.H. Munro ("Saki")
excerpted and adapted from "The Background"
The Chronicles of Clovis, 1912
John Lane, The Bodley Head

---

[11]Venus de Milo—a famous statue of the goddess Venus

1 Lines 13 through 16 and lines 29 through 35 reveal that Henri Deplis

   (1) invests wisely
   (2) behaves impulsively
   (3) avoids confrontation
   (4) resists change   1 _____

2 The municipality of Bergamo owns the artwork on Henri Deplis's back as a result of

   (1) a harmless misunderstanding
   (2) widow Pincini's vengeance
   (3) a fair exchange
   (4) Henri Deplis's pride   2 _____

3 As used in line 43, the word "unobtrusively" most nearly means

   (1) reluctantly
   (2) indecisively
   (3) rebelliously
   (4) inconspicuously   3 _____

4 The figurative language in line 46 implies that Henri Deplis feels

   (1) the tattoo is a curse to him
   (2) responsible for the artist's death
   (3) the tattoo is a thing of beauty
   (4) obligated to display the artwork   4 _____

5 Lines 59 through 62 indicate that Henri Deplis's situation causes him to become

   (1) successful
   (2) powerless
   (3) manipulative
   (4) respected   5 _____

6 It can be inferred that Henri Deplis joins the "Italian anarchists" (lines 71 and 72) because he

   (1) is afraid for his future
   (2) desires wealthy friends
   (3) is unconcerned with international politics
   (4) seeks gainful employment   6 _____

7 Lines 78 through 81 support a central idea that

   (1) people can achieve their personal goals
   (2) governments often choose stability over change
   (3) societies often value objects above individuals
   (4) governments can develop reasonable regulations   7 _____

8 The phrase "nurses the illusion" (line 85) reveals that Henri Deplis is

   (1) fulfilling his ambitious dream
   (2) searching for anonymity
   (3) struggling with reality
   (4) enjoying his freedom   8 _____

9 The subject of Henri Deplis's tattoo implies a parallel to his

   (1) social ignorance
   (2) economic worth
   (3) sense of humility
   (4) loss of control   9 _____

Reading Comprehension Passage B

Carmel Point

The extraordinary patience of things!
This beautiful place defaced with a crop of surburban houses —
How beautiful when we first beheld it,
Unbroken field of poppy and lupin[1] walled with clean cliffs;
(5) No intrusion but two or three horses pasturing,
Or a few milch[2] cows rubbing their flanks on the outcrop[3] rock-heads —
Now the spoiler has come: does it care?
Not faintly. It has all time. It knows the people are a tide
That swells and in time will ebb, and all
(10) Their works dissolve. Meanwhile the image of the pristine[4] beauty
Lives in the very grain of the granite,
Safe as the endless ocean that climbs our cliff. — As for us:
We must uncenter our minds from ourselves;
We must unhumanize our views a little, and become confident
(15) As the rock and ocean that we were made from.

—Robinson Jeffers
The Collected Poetry of Robinson Jeffers, Volume Three, 1991
Stanford University Press

---

[1]poppy and lupin—brightly colored wildflowers
[2]milch—milk
[3]outcrop—protruding
[4]pristine—pure, unspoiled

10 The word "defaced" (line 2) suggests that the narrator is

    (1) suspicious   (3) worried

    (2) confused   (4) critical   10 _____

11 The description in lines 3 through 6 creates a mood of

    (1) despair   (3) tranquility

    (2) amusement   (4) negativity   11 _____

12 The metaphor in lines 8 through 10 suggests that

    (1) humanity's impact is beneficial

    (2) nature's power is limited

    (3) humanity's influence is temporary

    (4) nature's significance is exaggerated   12 _____

13 The words "uncenter" (line 13) and "unhumanize" (line 14) suggest that people should

    (1) become more tolerant

    (2) recognize their superiority

    (3) uphold their values

    (4) become less egocentric   13 _____

14 The narrator implies that humans are

    (1) protective of their environment

    (2) unaware of their insignificance

    (3) perplexed by their surroundings

    (4) satisfied with their indifference   14 _____

Reading Comprehension Passage C

Learning to Love Volatility[1]

    Several years before the financial crisis descended on us, I put forward the concept of "black swans": large events that are both unexpected and highly consequential. We never see black swans coming, but when they do arrive, they profoundly shape our world: Think of World War I, 9/11, the
(5) Internet, the rise of Google.
    In economic life and history more generally, just about everything of consequence comes from black swans; ordinary events have paltry[2] effects in the long term. Still, through some mental bias, people think in hindsight that they "sort of" considered the possibility of such events; this gives
(10) them confidence in continuing to formulate predictions. But our tools for forecasting and risk measurement cannot begin to capture black swans. Indeed, our faith in these tools make it more likely that we will continue to take dangerous, uninformed risks.
    Some made the mistake of thinking that I hoped to see us develop
(15) better methods for predicting black swans. Others asked if we should just give up and throw our hands in the air: If we could not measure the risks of potential blowups, what were we to do? The answer is simple: We should try to create institutions that won't fall apart when we encounter black swans— or that might even gain from these unexpected events.
(20)   Fragility is the quality of things that are vulnerable to volatility. Take the coffee cup on your desk: It wants peace and quiet because it incurs more harm than benefit from random events. The opposite of fragile, therefore, isn't robust or sturdy or resilient—things with these qualities are simply difficult to break.
(25)   To deal with black swans, we instead need things that gain from volatility, variability, stress and disorder. My (admittedly inelegant) term for this crucial quality is "antifragile." The only existing expression remotely close to the concept of antifragility is what we derivatives traders[3] call "long gamma," to describe financial packages that benefit from market volatility.
(30) Crucially, both fragility and antifragility are measurable.
    As a practical matter, emphasizing antifragility means that our private and public sectors should be able to thrive and improve in the face of disorder. By grasping the mechanisms of antifragility, we can make better

---

[1]volatility—the amount of uncertainty or risk about the size of changes in investment values
[2]paltry—insignificant
[3]derivative traders—financial professionals who work buying and selling stock options, futures, and other contracts

decisions without the illusion of being able to predict the next big thing.
(35) We can navigate situations in which the unknown predominates[4] and our
understanding is limited.

　　　Herewith are five policy rules that can help us to establish antifragility
as a principle of our socioeconomic life.

Rule 1: Think of the economy as being more like a cat than a washing machine.

　　　We are victims of the post-Enlightenment view that the world functions
(40) like a sophisticated machine, to be understood like a textbook engineering
problem and run by wonks.[5] In other words, like a home appliance, not
like the human body. If this were so, our institutions would have no self-
healing properties and would need someone to run and micromanage them,
to protect their safety, because they cannot survive on their own.

(45)　　　By contrast, natural or organic systems are antifragile: They need some
dose of disorder in order to develop. Deprive your bones of stress and they
become brittle. This denial of the antifragility of living or complex systems
is the costliest mistake that we have made in modern times. Stifling natural
fluctuations masks real problems, causing the explosions to be both delayed
(50) and more intense when they do take place. As with the flammable material
accumulating on the forest floor in the absence of forest fires, problems hide
in the absence of stressors, and the resulting cumulative harm can take on
tragic proportions. . . .

Rule 2: Favor businesses that benefit from their own mistakes, not those whose mistakes percolate into the system.

　　　Some businesses and political systems respond to stress better than
(55) others. The airline industry is set up in such a way as to make travel safer
after every plane crash. A tragedy leads to the thorough examination and
elimination of the cause of the problem. The same thing happens in the
restaurant industry, where the quality of your next meal depends on the
failure rate in the business—what kills some makes others stronger. Without
(60) the high failure rate in the restaurant business, you would be eating Soviet-
style cafeteria food for your next meal out.

　　　These industries are antifragile: The collective enterprise benefits from
the fragility of the individual components, so nothing fails in vain. These

---

[4]predominates—exerts control or influence
[5]wonks—experts

businesses have properties similar to evolution in the natural world, with
(65) a well-functioning mechanism to benefit from evolutionary pressures, one
error at a time. . . .

Rule 3: Small is beautiful, but it is also efficient.

Experts in business and government are always talking about economies
of scale. They say that increasing the size of projects and institutions brings
cost savings. But the "efficient," when too large, isn't so efficient. Size
(70) produces visible benefits but also hidden risks; it increases exposure to the
probability of large losses. Projects of $100 million seem rational, but they
tend to have much higher percentage overruns than projects of, say, $10
million. Great size in itself, when it exceeds a certain threshold, produces
fragility and can eradicate all the gains from economies of scale. To see how
(75) large things can be fragile, consider the difference between an elephant
and a mouse: The former breaks a leg at the slightest fall, while the latter
is unharmed by a drop several multiples of its height. This explains why we
have so many more mice than elephants. . . .

Rule 4: Trial and error beats academic knowledge.

Things that are antifragile love randomness and uncertainty, which also
(80) means—crucially—that they can learn from errors. Tinkering by trial and
error has traditionally played a larger role than directed science in Western
invention and innovation. Indeed, advances in theoretical science have most
often emerged from technological development, which is closely tied to
entrepreneurship.[6] Just think of the number of famous college dropouts in
(85) the computer industry.

But I don't mean just any version of trial and error. There is a crucial
requirement to achieve antifragility: The potential cost of errors needs
to remain small; the potential gain should be large. It is the asymmetry
between upside and downside that allows antifragile tinkering to benefit
(90) from disorder and uncertainty. . . .

America has emulated this earlier model, in the invention of everything
from cybernetics[7] to the pricing formulas for derivatives. They were
developed by practitioners in trial-and-error mode, drawing continuous
feedback from reality. To promote antifragility, we must recognize that there
(95) is an inverse relationship between the amount of formal education that a
culture supports and its volume of trial-and-error by tinkering. Innovation
doesn't require theoretical instruction, what I like to compare to "lecturing
birds on how to fly."

---

[6]entrepreneurship—new business development and ownership
[7]cybernetics—related to computer networks

Rule 5: Decision makers must have skin in the game.

At no time in the history of humankind have more positions of power
(100) been assigned to people who don't take personal risks. But the idea of
incentive in capitalism demands some comparable form of disincentive.
In the business world, the solution is simple: Bonuses that go to managers
whose firms subsequently fail should be clawed back, and there should be
additional financial penalties for those who hide risks under the rug. This
(105) has an excellent precedent[8] in the practices of the ancients. The Romans
forced engineers to sleep under a bridge once it was completed.

Because our current system is so complex, it lacks elementary clarity:
No regulator will know more about the hidden risks of an enterprise than the
engineer who can hide exposures to rare events and be unharmed by their
(110) consequences. This rule would have saved us from the banking crisis, when
bankers who loaded their balance sheets with exposures to small probability
events collected bonuses during the quiet years and then transferred the
harm to the taxpayer, keeping their own compensation.

In these five rules, I have sketched out only a few of the more obvious
(115) policy conclusions that we might draw from a proper appreciation of
antifragility. But the significance of antifragility runs deeper. It is not just a
useful heuristic[9] for socioeconomic matters but a crucial property of life in
general. Things that are antifragile only grow and improve under adversity.
This dynamic can be seen not just in economic life but in the evolution of all
(120) things, from cuisine, urbanization and legal systems to our own existence as
a species on this planet. . . .

—Nassim Nicholas Taleb
excerpted from "Learning to Love Volatility"
The Wall Street Journal, November 16, 2012

---

[8]precedent—established example
[9]heuristic—formula

15 The author believes that "black swans" (line 2) are

(1) used to anticipate failures
(2) unimportant setbacks
(3) unpredictable occurrences
(4) used to guarantee benefits　　　　　　　　　　15 _____

16 What is the tone of lines 17 through 19?

(1) insistent　　　　　　　　　(3) reverent
(2) sarcastic　　　　　　　　　(4) pessimistic　　　　16 _____

17 The reference to "long gamma" (lines 28 and 29) serves to

(1) introduce a political theory
(2) provide a relevant example
(3) oppose a previous argument
(4) support a scientific proposal　　　　　　　　　17 _____

18 It can be inferred from lines 45 through 53 that stressors

(1) should be seen as signals of faulty systems
(2) can be expected to occur in predictable cycles
(3) must be carefully managed to avoid instability
(4) should be viewed as opportunities to improve performance　　18 _____

19 Lines 54 through 61 contribute to a central idea by emphasizing the

(1) role of government in quality management
(2) dismissal of progressive practices
(3) importance of setbacks to industry success
(4) consequences of ignoring standards　　　　　　19 _____

20 Rule 3 suggests the most "efficient" way to manage projects is to

(1) have an economic plan
(2) resist unnecessary growth
(3) encourage fragile economics
(4) revise corporate regulation　　　　　　　　　20 _____

21 As used in line 91, the word "emulated" most nearly means

(1) imitated   (3) accelerated

(2) discredited   (4) ignored   21 _____

22 The comparison drawn in lines 96 through 98 illustrates that innovation

(1) can be instinctive

(2) relies on education

(3) can be rigid

(4) depends on technology   22 _____

23 The phrase "clawed back" (line 103) implies that some managers

(1) are intolerant of traditional rules

(2) should be open to constructive criticism

(3) are wary of unconventional ideas

(4) should be accountable for careless decisions   23 _____

24 Which statement best reflects a central idea about disorder?

(1) "Things that are antifragile love randomness and uncertainty, which also means—crucially—that they can learn from errors" (lines 79 and 80)

(2) "There is a crucial requirement to achieve antifragility: The potential cost of errors needs to remain small; the potential gain should be large" (lines 86 through 88)

(3) "At no time in the history of humankind have more positions of power been assigned to people who don't take personal risks" (lines 99 and 100)

(4) "No regulator will know more about the hidden risks of an enterprise than the engineer who can hide exposures to rare events" (lines 108 through 110)   24 _____

PART 2—Argument Response

Directions: Closely read each of the *four* texts on pages 250 through 259 and write a source-based argument on the topic below. You may use the margins to take notes as you read and scrap paper to plan your response. Write your argument on a separate sheet of paper.

Topic: Is graffiti vandalism?

Your Task: Carefully read each of the *four* texts provided. Then, using evidence from at least *three* of the texts, write a well-developed argument regarding whether or not graffiti is vandalism. Clearly establish your claim, distinguish your claim from alternate or opposing claims, and use specific, relevant, and sufficient evidence from at least *three* of the texts to develop your argument. Do *not* simply summarize each text.

Guidelines:

Be sure to

- Establish your claim regarding whether or not graffiti is vandalism.
- Distinguish your claim from alternate or opposing claims.
- Use specific, relevant, and sufficient evidence from at least *three* of the texts to develop your argument.
- Identify each source that you reference by text number and line number(s) or graphic (for example: Text 1, line 4 or Text 2, graphic).
- Organize your ideas in a cohesive and coherent manner.
- Maintain a formal style of writing.
- Follow the conventions of standard written English.

Texts:

Text 1—What Is Street Art? Vandalism, Graffiti or Public Art—Part I

Text 2—Graffiti Vandals Cost Public Millions

Text 3—Is Urban Graffiti a Force for Good or Evil?

Text 4—Art or Vandalism: Banksy, 5Pointz and the Fight for Artistic Expression

Text 1

What Is Street Art? Vandalism, Graffiti or Public Art—Part I

What is Street Art?

There is as yet no simple definition of street art. It is an amorphous[1] beast encompassing art which is found in or inspired by the urban environment. With anti-capitalist and rebellious undertones, it is a democratic form of popular public art probably best understood by seeing it in situ.[2] It is not
(5) limited to the gallery nor easily collected or possessed by those who may turn art into a trophy.

Considered by some a nuisance, for others street art is a tool for communicating views of dissent,[3] asking difficult questions and expressing political concerns.
(10)   Its definition and uses are changing: originally a tool to mark territorial boundaries of urban youth today it is even seen in some cases as a means of urban beautification and regeneration.

Whether it is regarded as vandalism or public art, street art has caught the interest of the art world and its lovers of beauty.

Is street art vandalism?

(15)   In an interview with the Queens Tribune, New York City's Queens Museum of Art Executive Director Tom Finkelpearl said public art "is the best way for people to express themselves in this city." Finkelpearl, who helps organize socially conscious art exhibitions, added, "Art gets dialogue going. That's very good." However, he doesn't find graffiti to be art, and
(20) says, "I can't condone vandalism. . . . It's really upsetting to me that people would need to write their names over and over again in public space. It's this culture of fame. I really think it's regrettable that they think that's the only way to become famous."

Is street art illegal?

The legal distinction between permanent graffiti and art is permission,
(25) but the topic becomes even more complex regarding impermanent, nondestructive forms of graffiti (yarn bombing, video projection, and street installation).

---

[1]amorphous—hard to define
[2]in situ—in its original place
[3]dissent—differing opinion

With permission, traditional painted graffiti is technically considered public art. Without permission, painters of public and private property (30) are committing vandalism and are, by definition, criminals. However, it still stands that most street art is unsanctioned, and many artists who have painted without permission, (Banksy, Shepard Fairey) have been glorified as legitimate and socially conscious artists. . . .

Broken Window Theory: Vandalism vs. Street Art

Vandalism is inexcusable destruction of property, and has been shown (35) to have negative repercussions on its setting. It has also been observed by criminologists to have a 'snowball effect' of generating more negativity within its vicinity. Dr. James Q. Wilson and Dr. George Kelling studied the effects of disorder (in this case, a broken window) in an urban setting, and found that one instance of neglect increases the likelihood of more broken (40) windows and graffiti will appear. Then, there is an observable increase in actual violent crime. The researchers concluded there is a direct link between vandalism, street violence, and the general decline of a society.

Their theory, named the Broken Window Theory and first published in 1982, argues that crime is the inevitable result of disorder, and that if neglect (45) is present in a place, whether it is disrepair or thoughtless graffiti, people walking by will think no one cares about that place, and the unfavorable damage is therefore acceptable.

Street Art and Gentrification[4]

Thoughtful and attractive street art, however, has been suggested to have regenerative effects on a neighborhood. In fact, the popular street artist (50) Banksy, who has catapulted his guerilla[5] street art pastime into a profitable career as an auctionable contemporary artist, has come under criticism for his art contributing to the gentrification of neighborhoods. Appropriate Media claims that:

> "Banksy. . . sells his lazy polemics[6] to Hollywood movie stars
> (55)   for big bucks. . . Graffiti artists are the performing spraycan
>   monkeys for gentrification. In collusion with property developers,
>   they paint deprived areas bright colours to indicate the latest

---

[4]gentrification—the process of renovation and revival of deteriorated urban neighborhoods that results in the displacement of lower income residents by higher income residents
[5]guerilla—combative
[6]polemics—criticisms

funky inner city area ripe for regeneration. Pushing out low income families in their wake, to be replaced by middle class
(60)   *metrosexuals with their urban art collections." [Times Online] . . .*

Video Projection

Digitally projecting a computer-manipulated image onto a surface via a light and projection system.

Street Installation

Street installations are a growing trend within the 'street art' movement. Whereas conventional street art and graffiti is done on surfaces or walls, (65) 'street installations' use 3-D objects and space to interfere with the urban environment. Like graffiti, it is non-permission based and once the object or sculpture is installed it is left there by the artist. . . .

Yarn Bombing

Yarn Bombing is a type of street art that employs colourful displays of knitted or crocheted cloth rather than paint or chalk. The practice is (70) believed to have originated in the U.S. with Texas knitters trying to find a creative way to use their leftover and unfinished knitting projects, but has since spread worldwide. While other forms of graffiti may be expressive, decorative, territorial, socio-political commentary, advertising or vandalism, yarn bombing is almost exclusively about beautification and creativity.

—Erin Wooters Yip
excerpted from "What Is Street Art? Vandalism,
Graffiti or Public Art—Part I"
http://artradarjournal.com, January 21, 2010

Text 2

Graffiti Vandals Cost Public Millions

There is a certain rhythm to Michael Parks' job. He paints, they tag, he paints, they tag. . . .

It's a silent tango between those who scrawl graffiti and those who are paid to remove it. The dance pauses briefly when one side gives up. Maybe a
(5) tagger gets bored—or caught. Maybe a painter moves on to something else.

For now, that won't be Parks. He shows up as a "graffiti ranger" for Seattle Public Utilities (SPU) every day, just as he has for the past six years, in a white uniform and orange vest. He and a partner roam Seattle neighborhoods in a city-owned truck, their solvent cans, brushes and paint
(10) drums clanging in the back.

They stop at stairwells, bridges, trash cans, postal boxes, retaining walls. Graffiti disappears. And it all comes back the next week. . . .

In Seattle, rangers are only one faction. The parks department, Seattle's Department of Transportation, King County Metro Transit and Sound
(15) Transit all pay workers to erase the mess. For years, Seattle police even had a "graffiti detective," but he retired in 2007 and the position never was filled.

The effort is expensive. Seattle Public Utilities spent about $1 million last year for graffiti enforcement, removal, education and outreach, while King County Metro Transit spent $734,000 last year to rid buses, tunnels,
(20) park and rides and bus shelters of graffiti.

Add it all up and, overall, city and county agencies are spending millions in tax dollars a year trying to combat the ubiquitous[1] squiggles, tags, gang symbols and drawings that mar public property.

Its persistence creates headaches for private-property owners required to
(25) get rid of it, and anxiety from residents worried about neighborhood blight. . . .

No centralized front

It's hard for officials to talk with any certainty about graffiti trends. Because so many city agencies deal with it, no one keeps a centralized database of complaints.

And there are a lot.

(30) Seattle Public Utilities has averaged about 7,300 a year since 2008, said Linda Jones, manager of the graffiti-rangers team. Some are divvied up among the six rangers. The rest are handed off to other city agencies, she said.

---

[1]ubiquitous—found everywhere

The rangers erased or painted out 445,000 square feet of graffiti in 2009. That's almost eight football fields.

(35)   Hate messages take first priority; those have to be gone in 24 hours. Everything else is tackled within six to 10 days, Jones said. . . .

Certainly, graffiti seems to tattoo all urban landscapes. Look around Seattle and you'll find it everywhere: billboards, construction sites, businesses and homes.

(40)   Overhead highway signs and train cars hold particular appeal, evidence of the adrenaline rush—and grudging respect of other taggers—that go along with the crime, officials say.

In some cities, such as Los Angeles, these signs are wrapped with barbed wire to prevent vandalism. But that's not the case in Washington, said Jamie
(45) Holter, spokeswoman for the Washington state Department of Transportation.

To clean a freeway sign, workers have to shut down a lane at night, get in a truck and raise a boom.[2] . . .

Last year, a 28-year-old Miami man made national news after he fell to his death while tagging a sign on the Palmetto Expressway. In 1997, one
(50) prolific Seattle tagger severed a foot while tagging a train in Golden Gardens. But that didn't stop him. Records show he pleaded guilty for tagging again in 1999 and 2000. . . .

Hard to catch . . .

Arrest numbers fluctuate wildly year to year. For instance, Seattle police made 234 graffiti-related arrests in 2008. That number fell to 41 last year.
(55)   "Usually [taggers] are on foot, so they can just drop the stuff and run," police spokesman Mark Jamieson said.

And property owners are left to clean it up.

Under the city's Graffiti Nuisance Ordinance, if private businesses or homes get tagged and owners don't act promptly, SPU sends a letter asking
(60) them to remove it within 10 days. Ignore the notice, and property owners could face fines of $100 per day with a maximum of $5,000.

SPU sent 1,392 first-time warnings to property owners last year. About 75 percent complied, Jones said. After a second warning, nearly all got rid of the graffiti, she said. . . .

—Sonia Krishnan
excerpted from "Graffiti Vandals Cost Public Millions"
www.seattletimes.com, April 25, 2010

---

[2]boom—a maneuverable arm of a truck used to lift workers for aerial work

Text 3

Is Urban Graffiti a Force for Good or Evil?

Ban it, legalise it, put it behind glass . . . no matter what city councils do, graffiti remains the scapegoat for all manner of urban ills, from burglary on one extreme to gentrification on the other. But it may have another effect on cities entirely.

(5)   In the spring of 2008, the Tate Modern opened the world's first major public museum display of graffiti and street art, inviting six international artists to decorate its facade[1] with enormous, eye-catching murals.

Meanwhile, just down the riverbank at Southwark crown court, eight members of London's well-known DPM crew[2] were tried for an estimated
(10) £1m[3] in graffiti-related damages across the country, and sentenced to a total of 11 years in prison—the biggest prosecution for graffiti that the UK [United Kingdom] has ever seen. . . .

Since its contemporary birth in 1960s Philadelphia, city leaders have tended to condemn graffiti as mindless vandalism. Policing later began
(15) leaning towards the "broken window" theory, which argues that if petty crime like graffiti is visibly ignored, suggesting general neglect, it could inspire more serious offences. The UK spends £1bn[4] on graffiti removal each year.

But as cities seek to "clean up", could graffiti's ephemeral[5] role within the urban environment actually be good for cities?
(20)   For Ben Eine, a graffiti artist whose work was gifted to Barack Obama by David Cameron,[6] graffiti leads not to drug deals and robberies, as the broken windows theory suggests, but to something very different. "If they [councils] stopped painting over them, they would get tagged and then they'd do silver stuff over it. And then eventually, people would do nice
(25) paintings over it . . . The natural evolution of graffiti is that it will just turn out looking nice," he told the recent Graffiti Sessions academic conference. . . .

Embracing graffiti's cultural value can do wonders for a city's tourism industry, too. In Bristol, the 2012 See No Evil festival saw 50,000 people flock to the streets; in Stavanger, Norway, the city walls are transformed into a canvas for
(30) the highly successful annual NuArt festival. Even without a dedicated event, for every painted wall in a city there is most likely a tour to go with it. A three-hour

---

[1]facade—front of a building
[2]DPM crew—graffiti gang
[3]£1m—one million British pounds
[4]£1bn—one billion British pounds
[5]ephemeral—short-lived
[6]David Cameron—British Prime Minister 2010–2016

graffiti walk around the streets of Shoreditch could set you back £20, and in colourful Buenos Aires a tour of the decorated walls can cost $25 (£16).

(35) Buenos Aires is a particularly fascinating example of a city where the walls talk, telling tales of a turbulent past. Here, graffiti has been continuously harnessed as a tool of political communication, resistance and activism by citizens caught up in a cycle of military dictatorship, restored democracy and economic collapse. Although there are laws prohibiting graffiti, the city has gained worldwide recognition for its urban art. Now a new bill proposes

(40) to assign a registry of graffiti artists to designated spots in Buenos Aires, with the aim of decreasing undesirable markings elsewhere.

A similar approach has been adopted in Toronto, where a Graffiti Management Plan sees that "graffiti vandalism" is removed by city staff, while "graffiti art and other street art that adds vibrancy" may remain if

(45) commissioned by the building's owner. Toronto council has even assigned an official panel of specialists to judge the value of graffiti, deciding whose markings are artistically worthy to grace the city's bricks. . . .

Legal or not, as graffiti seeps into the fabric of neighbourhoods, it becomes a natural fact of everyday life in the city, a cultural practice appreciated and

(50) legitimised by young urban dwellers. Simultaneously, it is harnessed by local authorities and property owners as a method of cultural branding, to create the sort of "poor but sexy" neighbourhoods that work so well for cities like Berlin. Active curation[7] of street art really got into full swing in pre-Olympic London when the work of a local crew was scrubbed from the walls of the

(55) River Lea Navigation to make way for street art by several international artists, specially commissioned by the Olympic legacy's public art body. . . .

From its roots as a means of visual communication for disenfranchised[8] youth to both hide and be seen, graffiti has developed into a bona fide art form, a legitimate force for economic, cultural and social good—and, as we

(60) continue to shift towards increasingly sanitised urban environments, one of the few remaining ways we have to respond to our surroundings in an expressive, public way. "Good" v "bad" graffiti might continue to be disputed between fervid councillors,[9] but Eine says the public have moved on. "The whole world is covered in graffiti. No one cares. It's just part of urban noise."

—Athlyn Cathcart-Keays
excerpted and adapted from "Is Urban Graffiti a Force for Good or Evil?"
www.theguardian.com, January 7, 2015

---

[7]curation—to organize for presentation
[8]disenfranchised—marginalized or powerless
[9]fervid councillors—passionate community representatives

Text 4

Art or Vandalism: Banksy, 5Pointz
and the Fight for Artistic Expression

In 1974, Norman Mailer wrote, *The Faith of Graffiti*, one of the first literary works that looked at the origins and importance of graffiti in modern urban culture. Mailer's belief was not widespread with many opponents looking at graffiti as no more than vandalism. The battle between those two
(5)   camps[1] has waged ever since, although the graffiti artists, (now given the more politically correct name of street artist), have slowly begun to win the battle.

Artists like Banksy and Mr. Brainwash have actually made the public salivate with anticipation as they await their next creative exploits. While
(10) often unsanctioned, street art allows the artist to bypass the confines of the formal art world where only the elite can participate. Communicating directly with the public allows street artists to present socially relevant content while at the same time beautifying the bleak sprawl of urban decay.

Whether graffiti is art or crime has an implication in protecting the
(15) integrity of a street artist's work. If considered art, the creative works might be shielded under the Visual Arts Rights Act (VARA). VARA protects the work of visual art, from intentional distortion, mutilation or other modification. As a crime, these works can be washed away without further consideration, as has been the fate of many.

(20)   *"It's a very frustrated feeling you get when the only people*
with good photos of your work are the police department."

—*Banksy*

Street artists across the country have been fighting back using the VARA argument. 5Pointz, an outdoor art exhibit space in Long Island City, New
(25) York, is considered to be the world's premiere "graffiti Mecca." Since 1993, with the property owner's permission, artists have been creating unique artistic works on numerous walls of a 200,000-square-foot factory. 5Pointz has now become a tourist attraction, with hundreds visiting each week. Now, the building is supposed to be razed to make way for a luxury apartment
(30) complex. Sixteen artists have sued to preserve the space citing VARA. They are currently seeking a temporary injunction.[2]

---

[1]camps—groups
[2]injunction—a judicial order that restrains a person from beginning or continuing an action that threatens the legal rights of another

Los Angeles, often on the forefront of intellectual property issues, recently passed a new murals ordinance making street art legal if you pay for a permit, get permission from the location, and publicly post your
(35) intentions. Shepard Fairey, best known for his Obama Hope poster and his Obey campaign, has teamed up with renowned graffiti artist, Risk to create a major piece in Skid Row. Another work will be painted in the Arts District by culture-jamming contemporary artist, Ron English.

Other artists thrive on the illegality of their work. Banksy recently
(40) hit New York City, creating 17 works throughout various neighborhoods. Despite their aesthetic value, the NYPD's Vandal Squad want to question him in connection with the vandalism, and if they catch him, he will be charged. The vandal squad is currently combing through hours of surveillance footage looking for clues to Banksy's whereabouts. Mayor Bloomberg said that any
(45) Banksy works on public property will be removed. . . .

So, while the battle rages on, it at least seems for the time being that street artists are gaining public support and it may only be a matter of time before laws like the one in L.A. are the norm.

—Steve Schlackman
excerpted from "Art or Vandalism: Banksy, 5Pointz
and the Fight for Artistic Expression"
http://artlawjournal.com, October 26, 2013

PART 3—Text-Analysis Response

Your Task: Closely read the text on pages 261 through 263 and write a well-developed, text-based response of two to three paragraphs. In your response, identify a central idea in the text and analyze how the author's use of *one* writing strategy (literary element or literary technique or rhetorical device) develops this central idea. Use strong and thorough evidence from the text to support your analysis. Do *not* simply summarize the text. You may use the margins to take notes as you read and scrap paper to plan your response. Write your response on a separate sheet of paper.

Guidelines:

Be sure to

- Identify a central idea in the text.
- Analyze how the author's use of *one* writing strategy (literary element or literary technique or rhetorical device) develops this central idea. Examples include: characterization, conflict, denotation/connotation, metaphor, simile, irony, language use, point-of-view, setting, structure, symbolism, theme, tone, etc.
- Use strong and thorough evidence from the text to support your analysis.
- Organize your ideas in a cohesive and coherent manner.
- Maintain a formal style of writing.
- Follow the conventions of standard written English.

Text

He always feels hot, I always feel cold. In the summer when it really is hot he does nothing but complain about how hot he feels. He is irritated if he sees me put a jumper[1] on in the evening.

He speaks several languages well; I do not speak any well. He manages—
(5) in his own way—to speak even the languages that he doesn't know.

He has an excellent sense of direction, I have none at all. After one day in a foreign city he can move about in it as thoughtlessly as a butterfly. I get lost in my own city; I have to ask directions so that I can get back home again. He hates asking directions; when we go by car to a town we don't
(10) know he doesn't want to ask directions and tells me to look at the map. I don't know how to read maps and I get confused by all the little red circles and he loses his temper.

He loves the theatre, painting, music, especially music. I do not understand music at all, painting doesn't mean much to me and I get bored
(15) at the theatre. I love and understand one thing in the world and that is poetry.

He loves museums, and I will go if I am forced to but with an unpleasant sense of effort and duty. He loves libraries and I hate them.

He loves travelling, unfamiliar foreign cities, restaurants. I would like
(20) to stay at home all the time and never move. . . .

He tells me I have no curiosity, but this is not true. I am curious about a few, a very few, things. And when I have got to know them I retain scattered impressions of them, or the cadence[2] of phrase, or a word. But my world, in which these completely unrelated (unless in some secret fashion unbeknown
(25) to me) impressions and cadences rise to the surface, is a sad, barren place. His world, on the other hand, is green and populous and richly cultivated; it is a fertile, well-watered countryside in which woods, meadows, orchards and villages flourish.

Everything I do is done laboriously, with great difficulty and uncertainty.
(30) I am very lazy, and if I want to finish anything it is absolutely essential that I spend hours stretched out on the sofa. He is never idle, and is always doing something; when he goes to lie down in the afternoons he takes proofs to correct or a book full of notes; he wants us to go to the cinema, then to a reception, then to the theatre—all on the same day. In one day he succeeds
(35) in doing, and in making me do, a mass of different things, and in meeting extremely diverse kinds of people. If I am alone and try to act as he does I

---

[1]jumper—sweater
[2]cadence—rhythm

get nothing at all done, because I get stuck all afternoon somewhere I had meant to stay for half an hour, or because I get lost and cannot find the right street, or because the most boring person and the one I least wanted to meet
(40) drags me off to the place I least wanted to go to. . . .

I don't know how to dance and he does.

I don't know how to type and he does.

I don't know how to drive. If I suggest that I should get a licence too he disagrees. He says I would never manage it. I think he likes me to be
(45) dependent on him for some things. . . .

And so—more than ever—I feel I do everything inadequately or mistakenly. But if I once find out that he has made a mistake I tell him so over and over again until he is exasperated. I can be very annoying at times. . . .
(50)   When he was a young man he was slim, handsome and finely built; he did not have a beard but long, soft moustaches instead, and he looked like the [British] actor Robert Donat. He was like that about twenty years ago when I first knew him, and I remember that he used to wear an elegant kind of Scottish flannel shirt. I remember that one evening he walked me
(55) back to the *pensione*[3] where I was living; we walked together along the *Via Nazionale*.[4] I already felt that I was very old and had been through a great deal and had made many mistakes, and he seemed a boy to me, light years away from me. I don't remember what we talked about on that evening walking along the *Via Nazionale*; nothing important, I suppose, and the
(60) idea that we would become husband and wife was light years away from me. Then we lost sight of each other, and when we met again he no longer looked like Robert Donat, but more like Balzac [French writer]. When we met again he still wore his Scottish shirts but on him now they looked like garments for a polar expedition; now he had his beard and on his head he
(65) wore his ridiculous crumpled woollen hat; everything about him put you in mind of an imminent[5] departure for the North Pole. Because, although he always feels hot, he has the habit of dressing as if he were surrounded by snow, ice and polar bears; or he dresses like a Brazilian coffee-planter, but he always dresses differently from everyone else.
(70)   If I remind him of that walk along the *Via Nazionale* he says he remembers it, but I know he is lying and that he remembers nothing; and I sometimes ask myself if it was us, these two people, almost twenty years ago

---

[3]pensione—boarding house
[4]Via Nazionale—a grand boulevard
[5]imminent—upcoming or about to occur

on the *Via Nazionale*; two people who conversed so politely, so urbanely,[6] as the sun was setting; who chatted a little about everything perhaps and (75) about nothing; two friends talking, two young intellectuals out for a walk; so young, so educated, so uninvolved, so ready to judge one another with kind impartiality; so ready to say goodbye to one another for ever, as the sun set, at the corner of the street.

—Natalia Ginzburg
excerpted and adapted from "He and I"
The Little Virtues, 1962 Arcade Publishing

---

[6]urbanely—elegantly

Regents ELA Answers June 2018

English Language Arts

Answer Key

PART 1

1. 2	9. 4	17. 2
2. 2	10. 4	18. 4
3. 4	11. 3	19. 3
4. 1	12. 3	20. 2
5. 2	13. 4	21. 1
6. 1	14. 2	22. 1
7. 3	15. 3	23. 4
8. 3	16. 1	24. 1

PART 2 *See Answers and Explanations*

PART 3 *See Answers and Explanations*

Regents Examination in English Language Arts—June 2018

Chart for Converting Total Weighted Raw Scores to Final Exam Scores (Scale Scores) (Use for the June 2018 examination only.)

Weighted Raw Score*	Scale Score	Performance Level	Weighted Raw Score*	Scale Score	Performance Level
56	100	5	27	52	2
55	99	5	26	48	1
54	99	5	25	45	1
53	99	5	24	42	1
52	99	5	23	38	1
51	98	5	22	35	1
50	97	5	21	32	1
49	96	5	20	29	1
48	94	5	19	25	1
47	92	5	18	22	1
46	91	5	17	19	1
45	89	5	16	16	1
44	88	5	15	13	1
43	87	5	14	11	1
42	86	5	13	9	1
41	85	5	12	8	1
40	83	5	11	7	1
39	81	4	10	6	1
38	80	4	9	6	1
37	79	4	8	54	1
36	76	4	7	4	1
35	73	3	6	3	1
34	71	3	5	3	1
33	69	3	4	2	1
32	66	3	3	2	1
31	65	3	2	1	1
30	60	3	1	1	1
29	57	2	0	0	1
28	55	2			

The conversion table is determined independently for each administration of the exam.

Answers Explained

PART 1—Reading Comprehension

Multiple-Choice Questions

Passage A

1. **2** "behaves impulsively." The narrator tells us that Deplis "was impelled" to spend nearly all of his small inheritance (his modest legacy) on having a local tattoo master, Signor Andreas Pincini, cover his back with the representation of a painting.

2. **2** "widow Pincini's vengeance." The narrator reports that following the sudden death of her husband and Deplis's failure to pay her what was owed, the widow Pincini canceled the sale and presented the art work (the tattoo) as a gift to the municipality.

3. **4** "inconspicuously." Here, both terms mean "unnoticeably, discreetly, and quietly." In other words, Deplis left Bergamo without drawing attention to himself. Deplis was hoping that "his identity and that of the famous picture might be lost sight of."

4. **1** "the tattoo is a curse to him." The details in the paragraph that contains lines 47–64 reveals situations in which the tattooed painting on his back prevents Deplis from taking a "simple dip in the sea" or from traveling outside of Italy. None of the other choices suggests the feeling of a burden or a curse that Deplis comes to experience.

5. **2** "powerless." These lines illustrate how "official force . . . [and] stringent law" deny Deplis the opportunity to take on "a new range of activities" in Bordeaux (France). The passage reveals the ways in which Deplis has become powerless to change or improve his life. None of the other choices expresses Deplis's increasingly unhappy condition.

6. **1** "is afraid for his future." Joining up with Italian anarchists suggests that Deplis becomes desperate about how his life will continue. None of the other choices is supported by the text.

7. **3** "societies often value objects above individuals." Following the incident in which Deplis is attacked by a fellow anarchist, we are told that "his assailant was severely reprimanded [criticized, scolded] for attacking a fellow-anarchist" and sentenced to seven years in prison for defacing the (tattooed) painting, "a national art treasure." Now that the tattoo was no longer a pristine work of art, "Henri Deplis was put across the frontier as an undesirable alien."

8. **3** "struggling with reality." The end of the story reveals that Deplis inhabits the streets of Paris near the Ministry of Fine Arts, telling passersby that he is actually "one of the lost arms" of a famous ancient Greek statue. He hopes the French government will buy him! None of the other choices accurately describes Deplis's state of mind.

9. **4** "loss of control." Footnote 3 (at line 20) reminds the reader of the story of Icarus: the young man who, in pride and recklessness, flies too close to the sun and plunges to his death. Deplis's choice of the painting of Icarus as the subject of his tattoo is an ironic parallel to the consequences of Deplis's own impulsiveness.

Passage B

10. **4** "critical." *To deface* means "to mar, ruin, or disfigure." The critical tone in the speaker's voice, however, becomes evident only in the poem as a whole. This question reveals the importance of understanding an entire passage before determining the meaning of many specific details.

11. **3** "tranquility." The images in these lines evoke feelings of quiet and calm beauty; there is "no intrusion" of noise or human disruption. None of the other choices suggests the tone of this passage.

12. **3** "humanity's influence is temporary." The beautiful place the poet is addressing, "Knows the people are a tide . . . and [that] all/Their works dissolve." The central idea of the poem is that nature, in its pristine beauty, is patient and will endure in "rock and ocean." The "spoiler" of human activity will come and go as do the tides.

13. **4** "become less egocentric." Line 13 offers a clear and vivid definition of what it means to be "egocentric." To "unhumanize" our views means to think beyond human concerns, to recognize the ageless source of life in "rock and ocean."

14. **2** "unaware of their insignificance." The poet is urging us to "uncenter our minds" and to "unhumanize our views" because we fail to understand that humans are only a small part of the natural world.

Passage C

15. **3** "unpredictable occurrences." The author defines the term *black swans* as "large events that are both unexpected [unpredictable] and highly consequential [very important]." None of the other choices accurately explains what the author means.

16. **1** "insistent." This word best describes the author's tone in answering the rhetorical question "what were we to do?" The author insists that "we should try to create institutions that won't fall apart." The tone is positive, assertive, and practical; it is not sarcastic, reverent, or pessimistic.

17. **2** "provide a relevant example." The term "long gamma" is offered as an example of what the author means by "antifragility."

18. **4** "should be viewed as opportunities to improve performance." In lines 46–54, the author develops further the concept of "antifragility," leading to the central idea established in item 19 below.

19. **3** "importance of setbacks to industry success." Note that Rule 2 argues that "businesses . . . benefit from evolutionary pressures, one error at a time. . . ."

20. **2** "resist unnecessary growth." Rule 3 explains both that small is efficient and that unnecessarily large businesses or political systems become fragile and fail to gain from "economies of scale." None of the other choices supports the author's views on efficient ways to manage projects.

21. **1** "imitated." The sentence that starts in line 91 says that in the invention of cybernetics and pricing formulas, America has used, copied, or adopted an "earlier model" of trial and error. This question is an example of understanding vocabulary in context.

22. **1** "can be instinctive." In Rule 4, the author argues that formal education and theoretical instruction actually work against, or have an inverse relationship to, trial-and-error tinkering. Trying things and seeing what works or doesn't is, in the author's view, central to Western invention and innovation. Innovation may use technology, but the author would not say that innovation depends on technology.

23. **4** "should be accountable for careless decisions." The author says very forcefully that managers of failed companies should give back any bonuses they received and should even pay additional penalties. None of the other choices conveys the meaning of the expression "clawed back."

24. **1** "Things that are antifragile love randomness and uncertainty, which also means—crucially—that they can learn from errors (lines 79 and 80)." Among the choices, this best expresses the author's central idea about disorder, namely that, "things that are antifragile only grow and improve under adversity" (line 118).

PART 2—Argument Response

Sample Essay Response

Graffiti on public or private urban buildings has been a problem for decades. In recent years, many have jumped to the defense of graffiti artists by passing legislation and using the softer label "street artists." Nevertheless, graffiti is still nothing more than brightly colored vandalism.

Graffiti is, by its nature, selfish. Most graffiti is just covering others' buildings with the so-called artist's name in eye-catching fonts (Text 1, line 21). Many are doing it for attention, and they do it at the expense of property owners and taxpayers. In one year, for example, the city of Seattle spent $1 million getting rid of graffiti on public buildings and vehicles, catching and punishing perpetrators, and attempting to prevent future crimes (Text 2, lines 17–20). In the UK, the figure is about £1 billion on graffiti removal a year (Text 3, line 17). This does not include the burden put on private property owners, who have to remove their unwanted graffiti under risk of fines (Text 2, lines 60–61). Graffiti artists who don't bother to get permission from the city or from building owners are just creating a financial burden on taxpayers and property owners.

Another major problem of graffiti is described by the broken window theory. If the public sees crime go unpunished, such as a broken window left in full view or graffiti not removed or covered, there is an increased likelihood that more crimes of similar natures will be committed (Text 1, lines 37–42). This can escalate. For example, graffiti of a person's name left out in the open can encourage graffiti of profanity, hate messages, and symbols and, finally, more active violent forms of vandalism. Unpunished graffiti encourages more crime.

Legislation has been passed to protect the so-called street art, but it is misguided. The Visual Arts Rights Act (VARA) protects public art as long as it is done with permission (Text 4, lines 15 and 16). However, VARA has also been used to protest the renovation of a building in New York. Several graffiti artists decorated a private factory's exterior with permission; the factory has since been sold and the new owner wants to change the exterior. Although the new owners can do whatever they please with their building, 16 artists are seeking an injunction to prevent destruction of their work. Legislation such as VARA will only reinforce graffiti artists' notion that they have the right to vandalize their cities. In the end, no matter how attractive the art is, property rights should come first.

Graffiti art is always vandalism unless done with explicit permission of the building's owner, which is rarely the case. Efforts to excuse or protect graffiti will only further harm the victims of the crime.

Analysis

This is a clear and forcefully developed argument that demonstrates understanding of a complex subject. This writer accepts the proposition that all graffiti is vandalism and supports that view with appropriate citations from all four texts. The argument is also strengthened by granting, briefly, the distinction between so-called street art and vandalism. The former is acceptable if done with permission. The latter is a violation of property rights and often creates a financial burden.

This essay is well organized. Each paragraph concludes with a strong assertion of the main idea. "Graffiti is still nothing more than brightly colored vandalism." "Graffiti artists who don't bother to get permission . . . are just creating a financial burden on taxpayers and property owners." "Unpunished graffiti encourages more crime." "In the end, no matter how attractive the art is, property rights should come first." Each is an example of a "precise and insightful claim."

This writer demonstrates skill in varying sentence structures and shows command of the conventions. (Minor errors in punctuation or usage have been edited.) This essay would merit a high score.

(See pages 79–80 for the scoring guidelines.)

PART 3—Text-Analysis Response

Sample Essay Response

From the first line of the text, the author is already shaping the two characters through the use of juxtaposition. By using simple comparisons at first, like hot and cold, the author gradually develops the comparisons to be much more insightful. For example, she compares her world as a sad, empty wasteland to his world, which is lavish, abundant, and beautiful. Through these comparisons, the author is able to characterize herself and her husband as two completely different people. Placing these contrasting characteristics right next to each other actually further pushes the two figures to opposite ends of the spectrum, dramatically developing the idea that people grow and evolve over time.

Although one might interpret these opposing qualities to mean that the narrator and her husband balance out each other, this is clearly not the central idea she is trying to get across. At the end of the passage, the author offers an anecdote about how she and her husband walked along the Via Nazionale when they first met twenty years before. She likens their earlier selves to those of friends and intellectuals, similar in their likes and interests. This part of the passage, juxtaposed with the stark contrasts in the characters they have become, shows how significantly they have evolved as people and as a couple over the years. Once similar, their personalities not only oppose now but also clash. In the larger context, these images of opposition and evolution over time illustrate important ideas about marriage and other human relationships.

Analysis

This text is developed as a series of dramatic, unsentimental assertions about the differences in the lives and personalities of the author and her husband. Many writers focused on the author's effective use of parallel construction and repetition; some commented on the use of a first person point of view. This essay successfully demonstrates how the juxtaposition of ideas and details serves the author's purpose.

The essay is brief, insightful, and generally well written. The first sentence reveals the writer's understanding of how Ginzburg's method and subject are complementary, "From the first line of the text, the author is already shaping the two characters through the use of juxtaposition." The essay is further developed to show how the method of juxtaposition not only tells us about the characters but also dramatizes the larger theme of how people change and how marriages evolve over time. The writer demonstrates command of sentence variety and of the conventions. This essay would merit a high score.

(See pages 81–82 for the scoring guidelines.)

Regents ELA Examination August 2018

English Language Arts

PART 1—Reading Comprehension

Directions (1–24): Closely read each of the three passages below. After each passage, there are several multiple-choice questions. Select the best suggested answer to each question and write its number in the space provided. You may use the margins to take notes as you read.

Reading Comprehension Passage A

When my mother found out that the large mirror in the living room was inhabited, we all gradually went from disbelief to astonishment, and from this to a state of contemplation, ending up by accepting it as an everyday thing.

(5)   The fact that the old, spotted mirror reflected the dear departed in the family was not enough to upset our life style. Following the old saying of "let the house burn as long as no one sees the smoke," we kept the secret to ourselves since, after all, it was nobody else's business.

At any rate, some time went by before each one of us would feel
(10) absolutely comfortable about sitting down in our favorite chair and learning that, in the mirror, that same chair was occupied by somebody else. For example, it could be Aurelia, my grandmother's sister (1939), and even if cousin Natalie would be on my side of the room, across from her would be the almost forgotten Uncle Nicholas (1927). As could have been expected,
(15) our departed reflected in the mirror presented the image of a family gathering almost identical to our own, since nothing, absolutely nothing in the living-room—the furniture and its arrangement, the light, etc.—was changed in the mirror. The only difference was that on the other side it was them instead of us.

(20)   I don't know about the others, but I sometimes felt that, more than a vision in the mirror, I was watching an old worn-out movie, already clouded. The deceased's efforts to copy our gestures were slower, restrained, as if the mirror were not truly showing a direct image but the reflection of some other reflection.

(25)   From the very beginning I knew that everything would get more complicated as soon as my cousin Clara got back from vacation. Because of her boldness and determination, Clara had long given me the impression that she had blundered into our family by mistake. This suspicion had been somewhat bolstered by her being one of the first women dentists in the *(30)* country. However, the idea that she might have been with us by mistake went away as soon as my cousin hung up her diploma and started to embroider sheets beside my grandmother, aunts and other cousins, waiting for a suitor who actually did show up but was found lacking in one respect or another— nobody ever really found out why.

(35)   Once she graduated, Clara became the family oracle,[1] even though she never practiced her profession. She would prescribe painkillers and was the arbiter[2] of fashion; she would choose the theater shows and rule on whether the punch had the right amount of liquor at each social gathering. In view of all this, it was fitting that she take one month off every year to go to the *(40)* beach. . . .

Naturally, the idea of moving the mirror to the dining-room was hers. And so was its sequel: to bring the mirror near the big table, so we could all sit together for meals.

In spite of my mother's fears that the mirror people would run away *(45)* or get annoyed because of the fuss, everything went fine. I must admit it was comforting to sit every day at the table and see so many familiar faces, although some of those from the other side were distant relatives, and others, due to their lengthy—although unintentional—absence, were almost strangers. There were about twenty of us sitting at the table every *(50)* day, and even if their gestures and movements seemed more remote than ours and their meals a little washed-out, we generally gave the impression of being a large family that got along well. . . .

For a while we ate all together, without further incidents or problems. We mustn't forget Clara, however, whom we had allowed to sit at the *(55)* frontier between the two tables, the equator separating what was from what was not. Although we paid no attention to the situation, we should have.

---

[1] oracle—a person who gives wise or authoritative opinions
[2] arbiter—judge

Compounding our regrettable oversight was the fact that lethargic[3] Eulalia
sat across from her so that one night, with the same cordiality with which she
had addressed Gus [a family member], Clara asked Eulalia to pass the salad.
(60) Eulalia affected the haughty disdain[4] of offended royalty as she passed the
spectral[5] salad bowl, filled with dull lettuce and grayish semi-transparent
tomatoes which Clara gobbled up, smiling mischievously at the novelty
of it all. She watched us with the same defiance in her eyes that she had
on the day she enrolled in a man's subject. There was no time to act. We
(65) just watched her grow pale, then her smile faded away until finally Clara
collapsed against the mirror.

Once the funeral business was over and we sat back down at the table
again, we saw that Clara had taken a place on the other side. She was between
cousin Baltazar (1940) and a great-uncle whom we simply called "Ito."
(70)   This *faux pas*[6] dampened our conviviality[7] somewhat. In a way, we felt
betrayed; we felt that they had grievously abused our hospitality. However,
we ended up divided over the question of who was really whose guest. It
was also plain that our carelessness and Clara's irrepressible inquisitiveness
had contributed to the mishap. In fact, a short time later we realized that
(75) there wasn't a great deal of difference between what Clara did before and
what she was doing now, and so we decided to overlook the incident and get
on with things. Nevertheless, each day we became less and less sure about
which side was life and which its reflection, and as one bad step leads to
another, I ended up taking Clara's empty place.
(80)   I am now much closer to them. I can almost hear the distant rustle
of the folding and unfolding of napkins, the slight clinking of glasses and
cutlery, the movement of chairs. The fact is that I can't tell if these sounds
come from them or from us. I'm obviously not worried about clearing that
up. What really troubles me, though, is that Clara doesn't seem to behave
(85) properly, with either the solemnity or with the opacity owed to her new
position; I don't know how to put it. Even worse, the problem is that I—
more than anybody else in the family—may become the target of Clara's
machinations,[8] since we were always joined by a very special affection,
perhaps because we were the same age and had shared the same children's
(90) games and the first anxieties of adolescence. . .

---

[3] lethargic—sluggish
[4] disdain—contempt
[5] spectral—ghostly
[6] *faux pas*—social mistake
[7] conviviality—liveliness
[8] machinations—schemes

As it happens, she is doing her best to get my attention, and ever since last Monday she has been waiting for me to slip up so she can pass me a pineapple this big, admittedly a little bleached-out, but just right for making juice and also a bit sour, just as she knows I like it.

—María Elena Llano
excerpted and adapted from "In the Family"
Short Stories by Latin American Women: The Magic and the Real, 1990
translated by Beatriz Teleki
Arte Público Press

1 Lines 1 through 8 introduce the family's

    (1) tendency to gossip   (3) process of adaptation

    (2) experience with loss   (4) attempt to socialize   1 _____

2 The description in lines 9 through 19 reinforces the

    (1) isolation of the deceased relatives

    (2) strangeness of the family's situation

    (3) fearfulness of the insecure relatives

    (4) tension of the family's interaction   2 _____

3 The statement, "The only difference was that on the other side it was them instead of us" (lines 18 and 19) emphasizes a central idea of the

    (1) rivalry among different generations

    (2) continuity between life and death

    (3) conflict between tradition and change

    (4) respect among distant relatives   3 _____

4 The use of the word "However" (line 30) signals a change in

    (1) the narrator's perception of Clara's place in the family

    (2) Clara's understanding of the narrator's submission to the family

    (3) the narrator's resentment of Clara's profession

    (4) Clara's rejection of the family's eccentricities   4 _____

5 Clara's title of "family oracle" (line 35) is most likely a result of her

    (1) assertive personality   (3) warm demeanor

    (2) disciplined character   (4) generous spirit   5 _____

6 Lines 44 through 49 suggest that the mirror people are

    (1) an inconvenience to the living family

    (2) curious about the living family

    (3) welcomed by the living family

    (4) disturbed by the living family   6 _____

7 The phrases "regrettable oversight" (line 57) and "funeral business" (line 67) imply that the narrator's reaction to her cousin's
death can best be described as

(1) indifferent
(3) impulsive
(2) irritated
(4) irrational   7 _____

8 Lines 91 through 94 suggest that the narrator

(1) loses her identity
(3) distrusts her cousin
(2) dislikes intrusions
(4) resents routines   8 _____

9 Which detail best reveals Clara's character?

(1) "been with us by mistake" (line 30)
(2) "waiting for a suitor" (line 32)
(3) "gobbled up, smiling mischievously" (line 62)
(4) "collapsed against the mirror" (line 66)   9 _____

10 Which quotation best reflects a central idea in the text?

(1) "the idea of moving the mirror to the
dining-room was hers" (line 41)
(2) "There were about twenty of us sitting at the table every day"
(lines 49 and 50)
(3) "We just watched her grow pale, then her smile faded away"
(lines 64 and 65)
(4) "we became less and less sure about which side
was life and which its reflection" (lines 77 and 78)   10 _____

Reading Comprehension Passage B

Pears, Unstolen

I was stopped on the sidewalk by pears
glowing on their tree like antique ornaments
with flaking paint, a green metallic shimmer,
hinting at yellow, mottled with a few flecks of red.

(5) As light flickered over them, they seemed
to flutter like candles in the leaves.
But no—they were pears, and probably hard,
I told myself, probably inedible and holding

their juices tight, if they had juices at all.
(10) Besides, something was pitting[1] them like brass,
splotching, as if trying to spoil. Still, I wanted them.
I wanted that September light fingering each fruit,

so it seemed lit from without and within,
a fleshy tallow. I wanted the season's clock
(15) stopped before the next strike, stopped
in this amber afternoon, my walk halfway,

the shiny leaves just starting to curl,
but still far from falling, and the pears
half hidden among them like birds singing
(20) so sweetly you step closer, peer in,

careful, careful, wanting to touch that song,
but not spoil it. I stood there wanting
to hoard time, a thief trying to steal
a song I couldn't hear, a fool believing

(25) there's something sweet that won't disappoint,
that pears in the hand could be anything
like pears dreamed in the mind, or a moment
stopped could be kept from rotting.

---

[1] pitting—scarring

But what's so bad, a thief will ask: How is
(30) plucking a piece of fruit worse than worms
tunneling in, or bees sating themselves
on that honeyed light, or mold blotching it?

Surely a saint has an answer to that,
something about how too much sweetness spoils,
(35) or there's another sweetness that grows within.
For weeks I went back and forth, stopping

at the tree, watching first one pear let go
of its limb, then many begin to fall,
flickering briefly like coals in the grass
(40) before they shrivel, letting their seeds slip out.

"That's the way it goes," mutters the thief.
"As scripture says they must," muses the saint,
while a few last pears glow on their brittle stems,
and the wind-strummed boughs bend toward earth.

—Betsy Sholl
from *www.imagejournal.org*, Issue 66

11 The description of the pears in lines 1 through 11 helps to illustrate the

(1) balance between stability and change
(2) difficulty of recognizing imperfection
(3) difference between perception and reality
(4) importance of overcoming obstacles   11 _____

12 The word "sating" as used in line 31 is closest in meaning to

(1) indulging   (3) sunning
(2) blinding   (4) endangering   12 _____

13 The narrator's conflict in lines 36 through 42 is resolved through

(1) understanding the nature of humans
(2) posing philosophical arguments
(3) accepting the cycle of the seasons
(4) questioning religious beliefs   13 _____

14 The narrator in the poem can best be described as

(1) hopeful and excited
(2) dejected and alienated
(3) impulsive and carefree
(4) reflective and resigned   14 _____

Reading Comprehension Passage C

I had a farm in Africa, at the foot of the Ngong Hills. The Equator runs across these highlands, a hundred miles to the North, and the farm lay at an altitude of over six thousand feet. In the day-time you felt that you had got high up, near to the sun, but the early mornings and evenings were limpid[1] and
(5) restful, and the nights were cold. . . .

We grew coffee on my farm. The land was in itself a little too high for coffee, and it was hard work to keep it going; we were never rich on the farm. But a coffee-plantation is a thing that gets hold of you and does not let you go, and there is always something to do on it: you are generally just a
(10) little behind with your work. . . .

Coffee-growing is a long job. It does not all come out as you imagine, when, yourself young and hopeful, in the streaming rain, you carry the boxes of your shining young coffee-plants from the nurseries, and, with the whole number of farm-hands in the field, watch the plants set in the regular rows
(15) of holes in the wet ground where they are to grow, and then have them thickly shaded against the sun, with branches broken from the bush, since obscurity is the privilege of young things. It is four or five years till the trees come into bearing, and in the meantime you will get drought on the land, or diseases, and the bold native weeds will grow up thick in the fields,—
(20) the black-jack, which has long scabrous[2] seed-vessels that hang on to your clothes and stockings. Some of the trees have been badly planted with their tap-roots bent; they will die just as they begin to flower. You plant a little over six hundred trees to the acre, and I had six hundred acres of land with coffee; my oxen dragged the cultivators up and down the fields, between
(25) the rows of trees, many thousand miles, patiently, awaiting coming bounties.

There are times of great beauty on a coffee-farm. When the plantation flowered in the beginning of the rains, it was a radiant sight, like a cloud of chalk, in the mist and the drizzling rain, over six hundred acres of land. The coffee-blossom has a delicate slightly bitter scent, like the black-thorn
(30) blossom. When the field reddened with the ripe berries, all the women and the children, whom they call the Totos, were called out to pick the coffee off the trees, together with the men; then the waggons and carts brought it down to the factory near the river. Our machinery was never quite what it should have been, but we had planned and built the factory ourselves
(35) and thought highly of it. Once the whole factory burned down and had to

---

[1] limpid—clear
[2] scabrous—rough

be built up again. The big coffee-dryer turned and turned, rumbling the coffee in its iron belly with a sound like pebbles that are washed about on the sea-shore. Sometimes the coffee would be dry, and ready to take out of the dryer, in the middle of the night. That was a picturesque moment, with
(40) many hurricane lamps in the huge dark room of the factory, that was hung everywhere with cobwebs and coffee-husks, and with eager glowing dark faces, in the light of the lamps, round the dryer; the factory, you felt, hung in the great African night like a bright jewel in an Ethiope's ear. Later on the coffee was hulled, graded, and sorted by hand, and packed in sacks sewn up
(45) with a saddler's needle. . . .

My farm was a little too high up for growing coffee. It happened in the cold months that we would get frost on the lower land and in the morning the shoots of the coffee-trees, and the young coffee-berries on them, would be all brown and withered. The wind blew in from the plains, and even in
(50) good years we never got the same yield of coffee to the acre as the people in the lower districts of Thika and Kiambu, on four thousand feet.

We were short of rain, as well, in the Ngong country, and three times we had a year of real drought, which brought us very low down. In a year in which we had fifty inches of rain, we picked eighty tons of coffee, and in a
(55) year of fifty-five inches, nearly ninety tons; but there were two bad years in which we had only twenty-five and twenty inches of rain, and picked only sixteen and fifteen tons of coffee, and those years were disastrous to the farm.

At the same time coffee-prices fell: where we had got a hundred pounds
(60) a ton we now got sixty or seventy. Times grew hard on the farm. We could not pay our debts, and we had no money for the running of the plantation. My people at home, who had shares in the farm, wrote out to me and told me that I would have to sell. . . .

Our real trouble was that we were short of capital, for it had all been
(65) spent in the old days before I took over the running of the farm. We could not carry through any radical improvements, but had to live from hand to mouth,—and this, in the last years, became our normal mode of living on the farm. . . .

When I had no more money, and could not make things pay, I had to
(70) sell the farm. A big Company in Nairobi bought it. They thought that the place was too high up for coffee, and they were not going in for farming. But they meant to take up all the coffee-trees, to divide up the land and lay out roads, and in time, when Nairobi should be growing out to the West, they meant to sell the land for building-plots. That was towards the end of
(75) the year.

Even as it was then, I do not think that I should have found it in me to give up the farm if it had not been for one thing. The coffee-crop that was still unripe upon the trees belonged to the old owners of the farm, or to the Bank which was holding a first mortgage in it. This coffee would not
(80) be picked, handled in the factory and sent off, till May or later. For such a period I was to remain on the farm, in charge of it, and things were to go on, unaltered to the view. And during this time, I thought, something would happen to change it all back, since the world, after all, was not a regular or calculable place. . . .

—Karen Blixen
excerpted from *Out of Africa*, 1948
Putnam

15 The second paragraph introduces a central idea of

    (1) security in the farm's abundance
    (2) perseverance in spite of obstacles
    (3) trust in the crop's profitability
    (4) success in spite of inexperience   15 _____

16 The language in lines 11 through 17 suggests that new coffee plants require

    (1) isolation   (3) irrigation
    (2) fertilization   (4) protection   16 _____

17 The words "black-jack" (line 20) and "tap-roots" (line 22) provide evidence of the

    (1) narrator's knowledge
    (2) workers' responsibility
    (3) farm's prosperity
    (4) trees' hardiness   17 _____

18 The imagery in lines 26 through 30 highlights the farm's

    (1) diversity   (3) appeal
    (2) routine   (4) history   18 _____

19 The figurative language in lines 36 through 38 reinforces the

    (1) power of the ocean   (3) heat of the dryer
    (2) rattle of the machine   (4) noise of the night   19 _____

20 The purpose of lines 46 through 51 is to explain the

    (1) impact of the farm's elevation
    (2) benefits of the farm's size
    (3) fragility of the immature berries
    (4) success of the annual harvests   20 _____

21 The details in lines 52 through 58 demonstrate that the

    (1) growing conditions are beneficial
    (2) natural events are unpredictable
    (3) excessive rain lowers coffee prices
    (4) careful records improve crop yields   21 _____

22 The phrase "hand to mouth" (lines 66 to 67) most likely means

    (1) using unusual resources
    (2) enjoying occasional luxuries
    (3) covering basic necessities
    (4) ignoring financial problems   22 _____

23 The statement in lines 82 through 84 reflects the narrator's

    (1) sympathy   (3) ignorance
    (2) indifference   (4) optimism   23 _____

24 Which statement best represents a central idea of the text?

    (1) "Our machinery was never quite what it should
        have been, but we had planned and built the
        factory ourselves" (lines 33 and 34)
    (2) "That was a picturesque moment, with many hurricane lamps
        in the huge dark room of the factory" (lines 39 and 40)
    (3) "But they meant to take up all the coffee-trees, to divide up the
        land and lay out roads" (lines 72 and 73)
    (4) "Even as it was then, I do not think that I should have
        found it in me to give up the farm" (lines 76 and 77)   24 _____

PART 2—Argument Response

Directions: Closely read each of the *four* texts provided on pages 289 through 297 and write a source-based argument on the topic below. You may use the margins to take notes as you read and scrap paper to plan your response. Write your argument on a separate sheet of paper.

Topic: Should shark netting be used on coastal beaches?

Your Task: Carefully read each of the *four* texts provided. Then, using evidence from at least *three* of the texts, write a well-developed argument regarding whether or not shark netting should be used on coastal beaches. Clearly establish your claim, distinguish your claim from alternate or opposing claims, and use specific, relevant, and sufficient evidence from at least *three* of the texts to develop your argument. Do *not* simply summarize each text.

Guidelines:

Be sure to:
- Establish your claim regarding whether or not shark netting should be used on coastal beaches.
- Distinguish your claim from alternate or opposing claims.
- Use specific, relevant, and sufficient evidence from at least *three* of the texts to develop your argument.
- Identify each source that you reference by text number and line number(s) or graphic (for example: Text 1, line 4 or Text 2, graphic).
- Organize your ideas in a cohesive and coherent manner.
- Maintain a formal style of writing.
- Follow the conventions of standard written English.

Texts:

Text 1 – Shark Nets

Text 2 – Shark Nets: A Tangled Web of Destruction

Text 3 – Nick Carroll on: Beyond the Panic, the Facts about Shark Nets

Text 4 – Sharing the Sea with Sharks

Text 1

Shark Nets

. . . For over 70 years, shark nets have been protecting Australian swimmers from a death almost too awful to contemplate. Since their introduction in 1936, not one fatal shark attack has been recorded at beaches where nets have been installed.

(5)   But a growing body of scientific evidence suggests that shark nets remove more than just big-fanged predators from our beaches.

Protected species such as whales, dolphins and manta rays also get trapped in these nets. Ironically, another protected species, the majestic but terrifying Great White Shark is regularly caught in shark nets in significant numbers. No (10) one really knows what removing such a high level predator from the marine food chain will do. . . .

Shark nets are used on open ocean beaches, and are simply a straight, rectangular piece of net suspended in the water column between buoys. The mesh holes are 50 cm wide, small enough to entangle sharks and other (15) large marine species, while leaving smaller fish alone.

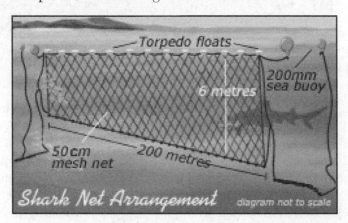

Most shark nets stretch about 200 metres along the beach and down to a depth of six metres. Lines of torpedo floats at the top and sinkers at the bottom keep the net upright in the water. They are anchored at either end, usually about 200 metres from shore in roughly 10 metres of water. The nets (20) are not intended to form a complete barrier, and sharks can still get through. The Queensland Shark Control Program uses another technique in addition to nets: hooks baited with fresh fish suspended from buoys to catch the sharks. In a typical 20 km stretch of coastal surf beach, a strip of net will be set up every couple of kilometres along the beach.

(25)   Shark enclosures, on the other hand, are more rigid constructions used on harbour beaches, and offer an unbroken barrier against incoming predators. The mesh in enclosures is much smaller than shark nets, and doesn't usually entangle any living creatures. These enclosures can't be easily built on open ocean beaches because experience has shown that the
(30) energy of the waves will eventually tear them to pieces. And like all beach constructions, they can also cause major sand erosion. When, for example, a temporary volleyball stadium was built on Bondi Beach for the Sydney Olympics a new surfing wave was created, dubbed the 'Olympic Lefts' by local surfers.

(35)   Now certain sections of the public and conservation groups such as the WWF (World Wide Fund for Nature) are calling for shark nets (the ones used at ocean beaches) to be completely removed. Not only do nets kill protected marine species, they argue, they don't guarantee protection for swimmers either. But how much more risk would we face without the nets?
(40) What if they were removed, would governments face big liability claims if a shark attack were to then occur on a previously protected beach? . . .

To net or not to net?

Weighing the benefits of the reduced risk of shark attack against the relatively unknown environmental impact of shark meshing is complicated by several highly emotive[1] issues. The impact on the marine ecology of removing large
(45) predatory sharks is not completely known, and protected species such as

----

[1] emotive—emotional

dolphins, turtles, and whales can also fall victim to the nets. For instance, in May 2001, a humpback whale calf became entangled in the nets off the Gold Coast[2] and died while its 20 plus tonne mother looked on. As a result of this and other incidents, there is increasing pressure on the NSW [New South Wales]

(50) and Queensland governments, which administer nets, to cease the practice.

Our fear of sharks

. . .It is true that shark meshing was introduced as a response to a perceived public demand almost seventy years ago. But a report submitted by the government appointed 'Shark Menace Advisory Committee' in 1935 is remarkably rational for its time. The document shows that the media's

(55) obsession with sharks probably dates back to well before the film 'Jaws', which has received much of the blame for sparking widespread white shark killings. In the absence of fatal attacks since meshing began, it is difficult to know whether the public reaction would be significantly different today if the nets were removed and fatalities returned. . . .

—Ruben Meerman
excerpted and adapted from "Shark Nets"
www.abc.net.au, January 16, 2009

---

[2] Gold Coast—an Eastern coastal area of Australia, between the states of New South Wales and Queensland

Text 2

Shark Nets: A Tangled Web of Destruction

... Throughout the world, people get into the water without shark deterrents; the extremely slim chance of even encountering a shark—much less being bitten—does not weigh heavily in their decision-making. Nor does it merit unnecessarily killing a threatened or harmless animal. In the last 100 years,
(5) there were over 4 times more shark bites in the United States than in Natal [South Africa]. And, there have never been nets in the U.S., including in the "shark bite capital" of the world, Volusia County, Florida. Even there, the risk of shark bite is so low that many more stitches are administered as the result of shell and glass lacerations than shark bites. ...

(10)   True, if one takes the nets at face value, there are far more destructive practices occurring worldwide. The nets are currently responsible for the deaths of between 500–700 sharks yearly, a very small percentage of the total number of sharks killed worldwide—or even in Southern Africa. Over one hundred million sharks will be killed this year. That's 11,432 every hour.
(15) With some regional populations down 90%, we could witness the extinction of [shark] species during our lifetimes.

However, it is the mere existence of the nets that is the most damaging due to their impact on our collective psyches.[1] Their installation reinforces our misguided and irrational fears of sharks, providing a very real example
(20) that our concerns are valid. This in turn fuels the biggest issue faced in shark conservation: the public's apathy or even loathing towards sharks. The media-created and shark-net reinforced image of sharks makes it difficult for many people to understand why sharks are worth saving—let alone take measures to do so.

(25)   The frightening reality is, like them or not, we need sharks on this planet. Remove the apex predators from the oceans, and we are tampering with elements essential to our survival and the livelihoods of the 400 million that rely on the oceans for their income. Sharks are a critical component in an ecosystem that controls our planet's temperature and weather,
(30) provides 1/3 of the world with food, and generates more oxygen than all the rainforests combined. Recent studies indicate that regional elimination of sharks caused disastrous effects including the collapse of fisheries and the death of coral reefs.

---

[1] collective psyches—shared understanding

Fortunately, there are many other options to the archaic practice
(35) of killing sharks with nets and drumlines,[2] many of which have been
implemented successfully in other locations—including the other coast
of South Africa. Other methods of harmless deterrents such as electrical
current, alloys, and chemicals are also being developed. If we can put a
man on the moon, we certainly can determine a method to ensure sharks
(40) and humans can peacefully coexist in the shark's domain. Programs like the
Shark Spotters in the Western Cape prove that there are viable alternatives
to shark nets and also, that education and awareness go far. . . .

The days of killing animals out of fear are over. And one only need
to look at Yellowstone Park, in the U.S., as a prime example[3] as to the far-
(45) reaching impacts of these short-sighted acts. South Africa—a country whose
environmental policies, fueled by booming eco-tourism, should be setting
precedence for the world. At a time when we are racing through our natural
resources at unsustainable rates, destroying wild animals simply because we
can, or because of irrational fears fueled by a lack of knowledge, is no longer
(50) acceptable. . . .

—Shark Angels
excerpted and adapted from "Shark Nets:
A Tangled Web of Destruction"
http://sharkangels.org, 2011

---

[2] drumlines—hooks baited with fresh fish, suspended from buoys
[3] prime example—Yellowstone's wolf-elimination program drastically altered the park's ecosystem by allowing elk to
flourish and overgraze on vital flora. Since the wolves were reintroduced in 1995 there has been a steady rebuilding
of balance in the ecosystem.

Text 3

Nick Carroll on: Beyond the Panic, the Facts about Shark Nets

Last week, after two shark attacks in ten days off Ballina's [Australia] beaches, NSW [New South Wales] Premier Mike Baird announced a six-month trial of meshing this suddenly very dangerous piece of coastline.

(5) The announcement came on top of other measures, "smart" drumlines,[1] tagging,[2] and sonar buoys,[3] in a further attempt to reduce a dramatic increase in attacks on local surfers and swimmers.

It inspired relief among many of Ballina's surfers and businesspeople, who've been dreading the news of another fatal attack and its potential effect on the town—yet it also raised angst[4] among green-thinking people,
(10) who dislike the idea of sharks and other sea life dying in human-laid traps.

Indeed, the whole idea of "shark nets" seems to press some serious buttons for everyone.

But beyond the relief and the angst: what *is* meshing? What does it do? What are its effects on marine life, and on human encounters with big
(15) sharks? . . .

Both NSW and Queensland's programs are a lot more sophisticated than they used to be. Queensland's program is a lot bigger, and more expensive: 83 beaches are meshed compared with NSW's current 51, and Queensland also employs numerous drumlines, from the Snapper Rocks area all the way
(20) up to Cairns. As a result, Queensland's shark catch is way bigger—in 2015 alone, for instance, it captured 297 tiger sharks, mostly in northern waters, and mostly on drumlines, which are considered more effective in catching large sharks than meshing. (Meshing is pretty effective against bull sharks in turbid[5] water, which might help a bit at Lighthouse.) . . .

(25) What does seem obvious is when it comes to separating humans and large sharks, meshing works. In the years from 1900 to 1937, 13 people were killed off NSW surf beaches by sharks; over the next 72 years, the death rate fell to eight, only one of which was at a meshed beach. This in a period when the NSW human population rose from 1.4 million to seven million—and
(30) way more people began going to the beach.

---

[1] drumlines—hooks baited with fresh fish, suspended from buoys
[2] tagging—attachment of identification tags for monitoring sharks
[3] sonar buoys—buoys with sound receivers and radio transmitters
[4] angst—anxiety
[5] turbid—cloudy

Similar figures can be seen elsewhere. In Dunedin, New Zealand, between 1964 and 1968, three fatal great white shark attacks occurred off a series of local beaches. Local authorities took a look at the NSW meshing program, and nets were laid off those beaches; nobody has since been (35) attacked in the area while the nets were set. . . .

Then there is the emotionally loaded, and occasionally very visible, issue of bycatch.[6] It's one reason why the authorities have been so cautious about meshing Ballina's beaches—the idea that the nets kill a lot more than just sharks.

(40) The records make it clear they do—but perhaps not nearly as much as you'd suspect. Meshing is supported by pingers[7] designed to alert marine mammals to their existence, and by and large they seem to work. In NSW, the meshing averages one humpback whale every two years; the whale is almost always released alive. In Queensland in 2015, the bycatch included (45) one bottlenose and seven common dolphins (one released alive), 11 catfish, eight cow-nose rays, nine eagle rays, 13 loggerhead turtles, five manta rays (all but one survived), eight shovelnose rays, three toadfish, four tuna, and a white spotted eagle, which was safely released. . . .

Oh and here's something else the records make clear. If you're worried (50) about sharks' survival, or sea-life bycatch in general, you're way better off looking offshore. Australia's commercial shark fishing industry is taking over 1200 tonne of shark out of our various fisheries each year: everything from gummy shark to mako, and very likely a few white sharks as well. The NSW prawn trawling[8] industry alone results in 64 tonne of shark as bycatch each (55) year. Six percent of what's caught in the tuna longline fisheries in northern Australia is shark. . . .

Next to that action, as the figures show, surf zone protective meshing is a minnow in a very big pond.

—Nick Carroll
excerpted and adapted from "Nick Carroll on:
Beyond the Panic, the Facts about Shark Nets"
www.coastalwatch.com, October 21, 2016

---

[6] bycatch—the capture of non-target species
[7] pingers—devices that transmit short, high-pitched signals
[8] trawling—a method of fishing that drags nets behind a boat

Text 4

Sharing the Sea with Sharks

. . . In 1937, when the first shark nets were installed off Sydney beaches, on Australia's east coast, sea-bathing was still a relatively new pastime—prior to 1903, daylight ocean bathing had been banned as improper. At the time the nets were introduced, the state's beaches were experiencing, on average, one
(5) fatal shark bite every year. The government felt that it needed to be seen as proactive, and nets were one of the least hawkish measures proposed; suggestions made during a 1935 public-submissions process included mounting machine guns on headlands and setting explosives. From the outset, the purpose of the nets was to catch and kill sharks.
(10)   Almost eighty years later, the nets are still installed off the New South Wales coast. They go in at the start of September, the beginning of the warm-weather season, and are removed at the end of April. At each of the fifty-one participating beaches, nets are installed for fourteen days of the month. They do not act as a total barrier: they are generally only a hundred and fifty
(15) metres long and six metres wide, and are set beneath the surface in ten to twelve metres of water, five hundred metres out from the shore. They're anchored to the sea floor, but there is significant space above and below them. (A study of a similar shark-net program in South Africa found that thirty-five percent of the catch was "on the shoreward side of the nets"—in
(20) other words, sharks are often caught on their way out to sea.) . . .
     The most controversial aspect of shark-net programs is whether it has been scientifically proven that shark nets reduce shark bites. Some researchers who have worked for government shark-meshing programs over a long period wholeheartedly believe that they do. Since the start of the
(25) KwaZulu-Natal Sharks Board netting program[1]—which uses much larger nets, for a longer period, than the New South Wales program—there have been "only two attacks, both non-fatal . . . at protected beaches . . . over the past three decades." And the New South Wales government reports that since "the NSW shark meshing program was put in place in Sydney in 1937,
(30) there has only been one fatal attack on a meshed beach." . . .

---

[1] KwaZulu-Natal Sharks Board netting program—South African program

Either way, nets and drumlines[2] are increasingly painted as crude, antiquated[3] shark-culling[4] tools. Shark scientists and entrepreneurs are now starting to direct their energies toward finding a technological solution that could keep both humans and sharks safe. The KwaZulu–Natal Sharks Board,

(35) in response to growing opposition to shark nets, aims to come up with a "non-lethal alternative." It has been researching electronic shark-deterrent technologies since the nineteen-nineties, based on findings that a shark's electroreception system—clusters of nerve fibres in gel-filled canals, visible as dark pores on a shark's head—may be sensitive to changes in electrical

(40) fields. The board recently began testing a hundred-metre cable that emits a low-frequency pulsed electronic signal designed to repel sharks. . . .

Most of the shark scientists I spoke to believe public education is still the best method of protecting oceangoers and marine animals, especially while a technological solution is still years off. Many cite Cape Town's [South

(45) Africa] Shark Spotters program as a gold standard because of its emphasis on observation and education: community members on beachside cliffs use flags and alerts to keep the public informed of shark sightings. "As an effective approach, education is number one," [Robert] Hueter, the Florida-based shark expert, said. "Most people here have embraced the idea that this is the sharks'

(50) home, their natural habitat, we're going into their space. . . . People respond to a shark-bite incident differently now. It's a tragedy, yes, but it's accepted as something out of our control, like being struck by lightning." . . .

—Ceridwen Dovey
excerpted and adapted from "Sharing the Sea with Sharks"
www.newyorker.com, April 26, 2015

---

[2] drumlines—hooks baited with fresh fish, suspended from buoys
[3] antiquated—outdated
[4] culling—killing

PART 3—Text-Analysis Response

Your Task: Closely read the text provided on pages 299 through 301 and write a well-developed, text-based response of two to three paragraphs. In your response, identify a central idea in the text and analyze how the author's use of *one* writing strategy (literary element or literary technique or rhetorical device) develops this central idea. Use strong and thorough evidence from the text to support your analysis. Do *not* simply summarize the text. You may use the margins to take notes as you read and scrap paper to plan your response. Write your response on a separate sheet of paper.

Guidelines:

Be sure to:
- Identify a central idea in the text.
- Analyze how the author's use of *one* writing strategy (literary element or literary technique or rhetorical device) develops this central idea. Examples include: characterization, conflict, denotation/connotation, metaphor, simile, irony, language use, point of view, setting, structure, symbolism, theme, tone, etc.
- Use strong and thorough evidence from the text to support your analysis.
- Organize your ideas in a cohesive and coherent manner.
- Maintain a formal style of writing.
- Follow the conventions of standard written English.

Text

The following excerpt is from the 2013 Duke University commencement address, given by Melinda Gates, co-founder of the Bill & Melinda Gates Foundation.

. . .The people who say technology has disconnected you from others are wrong. So are the people who say technology automatically connects you to others. Technology is just a tool. It's a powerful tool, but it's just a tool. Deep human connection is very different. It's not a tool. It's not a means to
(5) an end. It is the end—the purpose and the result of a meaningful life—and it will inspire the most amazing acts of love, generosity, and humanity.

In his famous speech "Remaining Awake Through a Great Revolution," Martin Luther King Jr. said, "Through our scientific and technological genius, we have made of this world a neighborhood and yet we have not had
(10) the ethical commitment to make of it a brotherhood.". . .

What does it mean to make of this world a brotherhood and a sisterhood? That probably sounds like a lot to ask of you as individuals, or even as a graduating class. I'm pretty sure none of you will respond to the annoying question "What are you going to do after graduation?" by saying "I plan to
(15) have the ethical commitment to make of this world a brotherhood."

But you can change the way you think about other people. You can choose to see their humanity first—the one big thing that makes them the same as you, instead of the many things that make them different from you. . . .
(20)   Paul Farmer, the Duke graduate I admire most, is a testament to the deep human connection I'm talking about. As many of you know, Paul, who's here today, is a doctor and global health innovator. For years, he travelled back and forth from Boston, where he is a professor of medicine, to Haiti, where he ran a health clinic giving the highest quality care to the poorest
(25) people in the world. Now, he lives mostly in Rwanda, where he's working on changing the country's entire health care system.

I first met Paul in 2003, when I went to see him in Haiti. It took us forever to walk the 100 yards from our vehicle to the clinic because he introduced me to every single person we met along the way. I am not
(30) exaggerating. Every single person.

As we moved along, he introduced each person to me by first and last name, wished their families well, and asked for an update about their lives. He hugged people when he greeted them and looked them in the eyes throughout each conversation. If you believe love plays a role in healing,
(35) there was healing happening at every step of that journey. . . .

Of course, not everybody is Paul Farmer. Not everybody is going to dedicate their whole life to connecting with the poorest people in the world. But just because you don't qualify for sainthood doesn't mean you can't form deep human connections—or that your connections can't make a difference (40) in the world.

That's where technology comes in. If you make the moral choice to connect deeply to others, then your computer, your phone, and your tablet make it so much easier to do.

Today, there are 700 million cell phone subscribers in Africa. I (45) travelled to Kenya recently and spent a day in Kibera, which many people consider the largest slum in Africa. One image that sticks with me is all the cell phones piled up in a small kiosk where locals paid to recharge their batteries. Most people in Kibera don't have electricity—even the cell phone charging businesses steal it from the city's power grid—but everywhere (50) I looked young people were on their phones. And guess what they were doing? Exactly what you do. . . they were texting.

You and they can share your stories directly with each other, with literally billions of people, because you're all using the same technology. . . .

When my husband Bill [Gates] and I started our foundation, we didn't (55) know much about global health at all. I read the academic literature and talked to experts in the field. But most of what I learned was expressed in morbidity[1] and mortality rates, not in flesh and blood. So in 2001, I took my first foundation learning trip, to India and Thailand, to meet with people and find out what their lives were really like behind the veil of statistics. . . .

(60) Late in the afternoon, one of the women who'd been showing me around invited me into her home. We went inside and she produced two lawn chairs that were hanging from a nail in her kitchen. They were the aluminum folding kind with the itchy fabric seat you've sat on a million times, quite possibly when you were tenting in Krzyzewskiville.[2] When I (65) was growing up in Dallas, we had the same chairs. On Sunday nights in the summer, my parents and my siblings and I used to set them up on our back patio and gaze up into the sky together as a family.

It turned out my host wanted to show me her stunning view of the Himalayas, and as we sat and contemplated the planet's highest peaks, we (70) talked about our children and the future. Our aspirations were basically the same. We wanted our children to fulfill their potential. We wanted the love

---

[1] morbidity—the rate at which an illness occurs
[2] Krzyzewskiville—the annual tent city that is erected in celebration of the Duke versus UNC basketball game

and respect of family and friends. We wanted meaningful work. The biggest difference between us was not what we dreamt about, but how hard it was for her to make her dreams come true.

(75)   Some people assume that Bill and I are too rich to make a connection with someone who's poor, even if our intentions are good. But adjectives like rich and poor don't define who any of us truly are as human beings. And they don't make any one individual less human than the next. The universe is like computer code in that way. Binary. There is life, and there is everything

(80) else. Zeroes and ones. I'm a one. You're a one. My friend in the Himalayas is a one.

Martin Luther King was not a computer programmer, so he called this concept a brotherhood. His hope was that college students could bring a brotherhood into being. Dr. King thought the world had shrunk as much as

(85) it was going to shrink—in his words, we'd "dwarfed distance and placed time in chains." So the fact that people still didn't treat each other like brothers and sisters was, to him, an ethical failure.

I take a slightly different view. I believe we are finally creating the scientific and technological tools to turn the world into a neighborhood. And

(90) that gives you an amazing ethical opportunity no one has ever had before.

You can light up a network of 7 billion people with long-lasting and highly motivating human connections. . . .

I hope you will use the tool of technology to do what you already had it in your heart to do. . . To connect. . . To make of this world a brotherhood.

(95) . . and a sisterhood. . .

I can't wait to see what it looks like when you do. . . .

—Melinda Gates
excerpted and adapted from "Melinda Gates:
Duke Commencement 2013"
www.gatesfoundation.org, 2013

Regents ELA Answers August 2018
English Language Arts

Answer Key

PART 1

1. 3	9. 3	17. 1
2. 2	10. 4	18. 3
3. 2	11. 3	19. 2
4. 1	12. 1	20. 1
5. 1	13. 3	21. 2
6. 3	14. 4	22. 3
7. 1	15. 2	23. 4
8. 3	16. 4	24. 4

PART 2   *See Answers and Explanations*

PART 3   *See Answers and Explanations*

Regents Examination in English Language Arts—August 2018
Chart for Converting Total Weighted Raw Scores to Final Examination Scores (Scaled Scores)

Weighted Raw Score	Scale Score	Performance Level	Weighted Raw Score	Scale Score	Performance Level
56	100	5	27	49	1
55	99	5	26	45	1
54	99	5	25	42	1
53	99	5	24	39	1
52	98	5	23	36	1
51	97	5	22	32	1
50	96	5	21	29	1
49	95	5	20	26	1
48	94	5	19	23	1
47	93	5	18	20	1
46	92	5	17	17	1
45	90	5	16	14	1
44	89	5	15	12	1
43	87	5	14	10	1
42	86	5	13	9	1
41	85	5	12	8	1
40	83	4	11	7	1
39	81	4	10	6	1
38	79	4	9	5	1
37	77	3	8	5	1
36	75	3	7	4	1
35	72	3	6	3	1
34	70	3	5	3	1
33	67	3	4	2	1
32	65	3	3	2	1
31	61	2	2	1	1
30	58	2	1	1	1
29	55	2	0	0	1
28	52	1			

Answers Explained

PART 1—Reading Comprehension

Passage A

1. **3** "process of adaptation" The narrator outlines the family's gradual movement from disbelief that the mirror was inhabited to "accepting it as an everyday thing." She goes on to say that this was "not enough to upset our life style."

2. **2** "strangeness of the family's situation" The narrator remarks that it took a while for the family to feel "absolutely comfortable" with the arrangement, for example, in learning that the chair one sat in was occupied by someone else "on the other side." The feeling of strangeness is the best among the choices to describe the tone of this paragraph.

3. **2** "continuity between life and death" The narrator explains that the image of the departed in the mirror was "almost identical to our own [family gathering]." Nothing else "was changed in the mirror." This passage does not suggest feelings of rivalry or conflict, nor does it suggest the idea of respect among distant relatives.

4. **1** "the narrator's perception of Clara's place in the family" The narrator reveals that her first impression of Clara was that "she had blundered into our family by mistake." At lines 30 to 31, the idea that Clara was in the family by mistake "went away as soon as my cousin hung up her diploma." The narrator's perception is completely changed when Clara takes up traditional tasks with the other women in the family, in preparation for a suitable marriage. The narrator doesn't claim understanding of what has happened, she just observes it; and there is no sense of rejection or resentment in what the narrator describes.

5. **1** "assertive personality" Among the choices, this phrase best captures the effect Clara has on the family: it is Clara who prescribes medications and who dictates choices in fashion, entertainment, and hospitality for the family; and it is Clara, of course, whose idea it is to move the mirror to the dining room.

6. **3** "welcomed by the living family" This section of the story begins with the narrator telling us that, despite her mother's fears, "everything went fine" as the living family and the mirror people began to share meals. It was "comforting. . . and gave the impression of being a large family that got along well." The narrator does not suggest they felt disturbed or inconvenienced, nor does she mention that they felt especially curious.

7. **1** "indifferent" This is the best option among the answer choices, given the description of Clara's death and the family's reaction to it. The narrator tells us they just weren't paying attention when Clara was "allowed to sit at the frontier between the two tables. . . separating what was from what was not." The living family "just watched" as Clara was pulled into the world of the mirror people. There is a feeling of indifference in the way the narrator reports that "once the funeral business was over" the family "sat back down at the table again." The narrator does not say that the family acted irritated or irrational; Clara's actions may have been impulsive and led to her own death, but the tone in the narrator's reaction is almost without feeling.

8. **3** "distrusts her cousin" The narrator says that Clara has been trying to get her attention and is waiting for her to "slip up." Remember that what happened to Clara was the consequence of a "regrettable oversight" on the part of the family and Clara's own defiant curiosity. The narrator senses that Clara wants to pull her into the other side by tempting her to make juice from a pineapple that is "a little bleached-out." None of the other choices is supported by the story.

9. **3** "gobbled up, smiling mischievously" This phrase best describes the Clara we see at the table, eagerly sharing the salad passed from the other side, and the Clara we see at the end, mischievously trying to get the narrator to accept the pineapple she offers.

10. **4** "we became less and less sure about which side was life and which its reflection" Among the choices, this is the only statement that suggests a theme. As the story progresses, the narrator reports that Clara's behavior in the mirror is no different from her behavior before; she also reports that the family became "divided over the question of who was really whose guest." The narrator comes to feel closer to the mirror people than to the living people, and by the end of the story she is trying to resist becoming part of the mirror people as Clara has.

Passage B

11. **3** "difference between perception and reality" In the first two stanzas, the narrator describes in *simile* what she sees (her perception): the pears are "like antique ornaments. . .they seemed/to flutter like candles in the leaves." Then she sees that they are pears.

12. **1** "indulging" The images of worms and bees feeding on the fruit best support this answer among the choices.

13. **3** "accepting the cycle of the seasons" These lines describe the experience of the narrator as she walks by the tree over a period of weeks and observes how "first one pear let go/of its limb, then many begin to fall." The images in these lines are of the end of summer (September) as the pears gradually fall, shrivel, and let "their seeds slip out." The image in the final line of the poem anticipates the coming of winter.

14. **4** "reflective and resigned" This answer best describes how the narrator's feelings develop over weeks on her walks: she is resigned to the fact that she cannot stop the season's clock, that she cannot "hoard time" or prevent the fruit from rotting. She is reflective when she considers what a thief would say and what a saint might answer.

Passage C

15. **2** "perseverance in spite of obstacles" This is the best answer among the choices. The narrator explains that, even though "the land was. . .a little too high for coffee" and "it was hard work to keep it going," the coffee plantation "gets hold of you. . .and there is always something to do." The narrator's voice does not suggest feelings of security, profitability, or guaranteed success in these lines.

16. **4** "protection" The work described here is of farm-hands carefully planting and shading the young coffee plants, which need to mature over several years before they bear fruit.

17. **1** "narrator's knowledge" This entire paragraph offers the narrator's detailed description of both the plants themselves and the care they require over several years before harvesting. Informative throughout, the passage also details various risks and hazards, such as drought, disease, and weeds, which can threaten the plantation's success.

18. **3** "appeal" The images of "great beauty" in these lines offer vivid contrast in the narrator's description of the hard work and many challenges of running a coffee farm.

19. **2** "rattle of the machine" In these lines, the narrator is describing the noise of the beans in the coffee-dryer: "rumbling. . .with a sound like pebbles that are washed about on the sea-shore." This is the most precise answer among the choices.

20. **1** "impact of the farm's elevation" The first sentence establishes the topic of this paragraph: "My farm was a little too high up for growing coffee." The narrator then offers examples of the effects of higher elevation on the crop. There is reference to the effects of cold on the immature berries (choice 3), but the main idea is that the narrator's farm "never got the same yield" as farms at lower elevations would.

21. **2** "natural events are unpredictable" In this brief paragraph, the narrator shows how lack of adequate rain affected the crop yield; the range, from drought to years in which there was adequate rain, illustrates how vulnerable farmers are to unpredictable weather patterns.

22. **3** "covering basic necessities" To live from hand to mouth is a common expression used to describe how those who are poor, or have no money other than what is in their pockets, live from day to day. The narrator tells us that "our real trouble was that we were short of capital." In other words, there was no saved money available to make repairs or to cover expenses in the years when the farm had a small yield or when coffee prices fell.

23. **4** "optimism" This is the best among the choices. Despite years of struggle against natural and economic forces and the fact that the farm itself had been mortgaged, the narrator thought "something would happen to change it all back."

24. **4** "Even as it was then, I do not think that I should have found it in me to give up the farm" This expresses the narrator's central idea: her love for this farm is a hold that will not let her go. This theme is established at the beginning of the passage in lines 7–12.

PART 2—Argument Response

Sample Essay Response

Since the appearance of shark netting in the 1930s, its use has been widely debated. The world has developed a near universal fear of shark attacks, and many feel that the most effective preventive action is the installation of shark netting around coastal beaches. While netting may reduce shark attacks significantly, it comes with great literal and figurative costs. I believe officials at costal beaches should refrain from utilizing shark netting, because it has the potential to capture other sea life and to disrupt the food chain; overall, there are better and safer options.

While netting prevented numerous attacks in Australia during the 1900s, it removed more than just sharks from the water. For example, "Protected species such as whales, dolphins and manta rays also get trapped in these nets...the majestic but terrifying Great White Shark is regularly caught in shark nets in significant numbers. No one really knows what removing such a high level predator from the marine food chain will do." (Text 1, lines 7–11) Not only does shark netting create a high risk for the loss of important creatures such as great white sharks, which regulate the food chain, smaller creatures such as whales, dolphins and turtles often face the dangers of the nets as well. Ultimately, even though shark netting seems to be the best answer to widespread panic over shark attacks, shark netting poses great danger to other sea life as their "homes" are invaded.

The effectiveness of shark netting is debatable. As stated in an article titled "Sharing the Sea with Sharks": "The most controversial aspect of shark-net programs is whether it has been scientifically proven that shark nets reduce shark bites." (Text 4, lines 21–22) There are researchers who truly believe that nets are effective, while others do not. However, according to a KwaZulu-Natal Sharks Board program, the nets prevented all but two non-fatal attacks to occur in three decades. (Text 4, lines 25–28) This proves Nick Carroll somewhat wrong; he stated that "what does seem obvious is when it comes to separating humans and large sharks, meshing works." (Text 3, lines 25–26) If nets were truly as effective as Carroll and other researchers claim, then attacks would be all but impossible in netted areas.

There are, however, several more promising options for preventing shark attacks. Since the installation of nets only validates the world's collective fear of sharks, it is important that other preventive measures be taken. (Text 2, lines 17–20) One other possible method for preventing shark bites is the use of "harmless deterrents such as electrical current, alloys, and chemicals." (Text 2, lines 37–38) These methods can help keep sharks far away while protecting their safety. Yet another method is simply educating the world. Many scientists believe public education is the best method for protecting humans and sharks alike. (Text 4, lines 42–44) By educating humans, sharks can easily be protected and also avoided at almost no cost at all.

Ultimately, shark attacks can be prevented in a variety of ways. Though many argue that netting is, in fact, the most effective, the benefits do not outweigh the negative effects. By using shark netting, habitats are invaded and food chains are harmed. Other safe options are rejected, and other sea life is harmed.

Analysis

This is a good response because it presents a reasoned argument to support the writer's position on the use of shark netting. The opening paragraph effectively states the issue and acknowledges why it is controversial. The paragraph closes with a clear and forceful statement of the writer's central idea. Supported with multiple references to three of the four texts, the argument is developed clearly and coherently. The first sentence of each paragraph both signals the topic and clarifies the development of the overall argument: "While netting prevented numerous attacks. . ."; "The effectiveness. . .is debatable"; "There are. . .more promising options"; "Ultimately, shark attacks can be prevented in a variety of ways."

The writing is clear and appropriately formal, with no significant errors in diction or usage. This essay would merit a high score. (See the Scoring Rubric.)

(See pages 79–80 for the scoring guidelines.)

PART 3—Text-Analysis Response

Note: Many successful responses for this part emphasized effective use of point of view, personal anecdote, or optimistic tone. Some developed the concept that the speech is structured around the central theme of a famous speech by MLK cited at the beginning and then recalled toward the end. The response below is a good example of how point of view supports the author's central idea.

Sample Essay Response

Authors use different writing strategies to develop the central idea of their texts. The author of this text, who happens to be Bill Gates's wife, uses her personal experiences to show how technology connects people all around the world. In this text, which was a university commencement speech, she tells these stories in a first-person point of view to connect with her audience on a more personal level.

In one example, the author describes her visit to Kibera, a large slum in Kenya. To her surprise, there were young people on their phones everywhere, texting just like we do. She connects this personal story with her main point that technology allows us to communicate and connect with people all over. She tells her listeners, "You and they can share your stories directly with each other, with literally billions of people, because you're all using the same technology."

The author also shares a story about her trip to the Himalayas. While she was there, she met a family and went to their home. On this visit, they did not share any technology; they learned about each other's lives just by talking. She understands from her travels that people everywhere share many of the same hopes and desires for the future. The connections she makes around the world show her and the audience that people, rich or poor, are still people, and that technology allows us to reach out and make bonds with these people.

The author shares personal experiences to emphasize how important human connections are and how technology can improve these connections. She shares these experiences using first-person point of view to make her stories feel real to the audience, allowing her to connect with them on a personal level.

Analysis

Point of view is a logical choice of topic for this text, a commencement speech, and the writer of this response clearly establishes the central idea in the first paragraph: "she tells these stories in a first-person point of view to connect with her audience on a more personal level." The essay is adequately developed with two examples of the author's experiences, and the final two sentences are especially effective in expressing both the central theme of the speech and the effective use of first-person point of view to support that central theme.

The organization in four brief paragraphs is logical; the writing is clear and free of any significant errors in usage. This response would merit a high score. (See the Scoring Rubric.)

(See pages 81–82 for the scoring guidelines.)

Regents ELA Examination June 2019

English Language Arts

PART 1—Reading Comprehension

Directions (1–24): Closely read each of the three passages below. After each passage, there are several multiple-choice questions. Select the best suggested answer to each question and write its number in the space provided. You may use the margins to take notes as you read.

Reading Comprehension Passage A

When Marvin was ten years old, his father took him through the long, echoing corridors that led up through Administration and Power, until at last they came to the uppermost levels of all and were among the swiftly growing vegetation of the Farmlands. Marvin liked it here: it was fun
(5) watching the great, slender plants creeping with almost visible eagerness towards the sunlight as it filtered down through the plastic domes to meet them. The smell of life was everywhere, awakening inexpressible longings in his heart: no longer was he breathing the dry, cool air of the residential levels, purged of all smells but the faint tang of ozone. He wished he
(10) could stay here for a little while, but Father would not let him. They went onwards until they had reached the entrance to the Observatory, which he had never visited: but they did not stop, and Marvin knew with a sense of rising excitement that there could be only one goal left. For the first time in his life, he was going Outside.[1]
(15) There were a dozen of the surface vehicles, with their wide balloon tyres [tires] and pressurized cabins, in the great servicing chamber. His father must have been expected, for they were led at once to the little scout

---

[1]Outside—the part of the Moon outside of Marvin's space habitat

car waiting by the huge circular door of the airlock. Tense with expectancy,
Marvin settled himself down in the cramped cabin while his father started
(20) the motor and checked the controls. The inner door of the lock slid open
and then closed behind them: he heard the roar of the great air-pumps fade
slowly away as the pressure dropped to zero. Then the 'Vacuum' sign flashed
on, the outer door parted, and before Marvin lay the land which he had
never yet entered.

(25)   He had seen it in photographs, of course: he had watched it imaged
on television screens a hundred times. But now it was lying all around him,
burning beneath the fierce sun that crawled so slowly across the jet-black sky.
He stared into the west, away from the blinding splendour of the sun—and
there were the stars, as he had been told but had never quite believed. He
(30) gazed at them for a long time, marvelling that anything could be so bright
and yet so tiny. They were intense unscintillating[2] points, and suddenly he
remembered a rhyme he had once read in one of his father's books:
     Twinkle, twinkle, little star,
     How I wonder what you are.
(35)   Well, he knew what the stars were. Whoever asked that question must
have been very stupid. And what did they mean by 'twinkle'? You could see
at a glance that all the stars shone with the same steady, unwavering light. He
abandoned the puzzle and turned his attention to the landscape around him.
     They were racing across a level plain at almost a hundred miles an hour,
(40) the great balloon tyres sending up little spurts of dust behind them. There
was no sign of the Colony: in the few minutes while he had been gazing at
the stars, its domes and radio towers had fallen below the horizon. Yet there
were other indications of man's presence, for about a mile ahead Marvin
could see the curiously shaped structures clustering round the head of a
(45) mine. Now and then a puff of vapour would emerge from a squat smoke-
stack and would instantly disperse.
     They were past the mine in a moment: Father was driving with a
reckless and exhilarating skill as if—it was a strange thought to come into
a child's mind—he was trying to escape from something. In a few minutes
(50) they had reached the edge of the plateau on which the Colony had been
built. The ground fell sharply away beneath them in a dizzying slope whose
lower stretches were lost in shadow. Ahead, as far as the eye could reach, was
a jumbled wasteland of craters, mountain ranges, and ravines. The crests of
the mountains, catching the low sun, burned like islands of fire in a sea of
(55) darkness: and above them the stars still shone as steadfastly as ever. . . .

---

[2]unscintillating—not sparkling

And now on the right was a wrinkled, dusty plain, and on the left, its ramparts and terraces rising mile after mile into the sky, was a wall of mountains that marched into the distance until its peaks sank from sight below the rim of the world. There was no sign that men had ever explored
(60) this land, but once they passed the skeleton of a crashed rocket, and beside it a stone cairn[3] surmounted by a metal cross. . . .

The sun was now low behind the hills on the right: the valley before them should be in total darkness. Yet it was awash with a cold white radiance that came spilling over the crags beneath which they were driving. Then,
(65) suddenly, they were out in the open plain, and the source of the light lay before them in all its glory.

It was very quiet in the little cabin now that the motors had stopped. The only sound was the faint whisper of the oxygen feed and an occasional metallic crepitation[4] as the outer walls of the vehicle radiated away their
(70) heat. For no warmth at all came from the great silver crescent that floated low above the far horizon and flooded all this land with pearly light. It was so brilliant that minutes passed before Marvin could accept its challenge and look steadfastly into its glare, but at last he could discern the outlines of continents, the hazy border of the atmosphere, and the white islands of
(75) cloud. And even at this distance, he could see the glitter of sunlight on the polar ice.

It was beautiful, and it called to his heart across the abyss of space. There in that shining crescent were all the wonders that he had never known—the hues of sunset skies, the moaning of the sea on pebbled shores, the patter
(80) of falling rain, the unhurried benison[5] of snow. These and a thousand others should have been his rightful heritage, but he knew them only from the books and ancient records, and the thought filled him with the anguish of exile.

Why could they not return? It seemed so peaceful beneath those
(85) lines of marching cloud. Then Marvin, his eyes no longer blinded by the glare, saw that the portion of the disk that should have been in darkness was gleaming faintly with an evil phosphorescence: and he remembered. He was looking upon the funeral pyre[6] of a world—upon the radioactive aftermath of Armageddon.[7] Across a quarter of a million miles of space, the
(90) glow of dying atoms was still visible, a perennial reminder of the ruined past.

---

[3]cairn—memorial
[4]crepitation—crackling sound
[5]benison—blessing
[6]pyre—bonfire
[7]Armageddon—a catastrophic battle

It would be centuries yet before that deadly glow died from the rocks and life could return again to fill that silent, empty world. . . .

So, at last, Marvin understood the purpose of this pilgrimage. He [his father] would never walk beside the rivers of that lost and legendary world,
(95) or listen to the thunder raging above its softly rounded hills. Yet one day— how far ahead?—his children's children would return to claim their heritage. The winds and the rains would scour the poisons from the burning lands and carry them to the sea, and in the depths of the sea they would waste their venom until they could harm no living things. Then the great ships that were
(100) still waiting here on the silent, dusty plains could lift once more into space, along the road that led to home. . . .

—Arthur C. Clarke
excerpted and adapted from "If I Forget Thee, Oh Earth. . ."
Expedition to Earth, 1999
Orbit

1 The images in the first paragraph serve to

  (1) create a sense of solitude
  (2) illustrate the randomness of nature
  (3) create a feeling of anticipation
  (4) illustrate the importance of family   1 _____

2 Lines 15 through 24 establish

  (1) Marvin's misgivings about going Outside
  (2) the inhospitable conditions of Outside
  (3) Father's fears about traveling Outside
  (4) the unpleasant sensations of Outside   2 _____

3 The statement "it was a strange thought to come into a child's mind" (lines 48 and 49) signals

  (1) a change in Marvin's understanding
  (2) Marvin's growing embrace of the unknown
  (3) Marvin's objection to his father's behavior
  (4) a chance for Marvin's rescue   3 _____

4 The phrase "jumbled wasteland of craters, mountain ranges, and ravines" (line 53) reveals the

  (1) futility of the Colony
  (2) desolation of the Outside
  (3) uncertainty of Marvin's future
  (4) loneliness of Marvin's past   4 _____

5 The "glare" described in lines 73 and 86 represents Marvin's

  (1) romantic vision of the Earth
  (2) obsession with the Earth's past
  (3) vague memory of the Earth
  (4) faith in the Earth's restoration   5 _____

6 Lines 80 through 83 emphasize Marvin's

    (1) sense of deprivation
    (2) appreciation of his situation
    (3) fear of destruction
    (4) recollection of his childhood   6 _____

7 The details in lines 85 to 89 confirm the Earth has been damaged by

    (1) climate change
    (2) cosmic instability
    (3) human actions
    (4) natural occurences   7 _____

8 The images in lines 97 through 99 convey feelings of

    (1) fear and disappointment
    (2) cleansing and renewal
    (3) preservation and protection
    (4) confusion and impatience   8 _____

9 Which lines best capture Marvin's understanding of his father's perspective?

    (1) "Tense with expectancy, Marvin settled himself down in the cramped cabin while his father started the motor and checked the controls" (lines 18 through 20)
    (2) "They were intense unscintillating points, and suddenly he remembered a rhyme he had once read in one of his father's books" (lines 31 and 32)
    (3) "In a few minutes they had reached the edge of the plateau on which the Colony had been built" (lines 49 through 51)
    (4) "He [his father] would never walk beside the rivers of that lost and legendary world, or listen to the thunder raging above its softly rounded hills" (lines 93 through 95)   9 _____

Reading Comprehension Passage B

This Life

My grandmother told me there'd be good days
to counter the dark ones,
with blue skies in the heart as far
as the soul could see. She said
(5) you could measure a life in as many ways
as there were to bake a pound cake,
but you still needed real butter and eggs
for a good one—pound cake, that is,
but I knew what she meant. She was always
(10) talking around corners like that;
she knew words carried their treasures
like a grape clusters around its own juice.
She loved words; she thought a book
was a monument to the glory of creation
(15) and a library . . . well, sometimes
just trying to describe Jubilation
will get you a bit tongue, so let's
leave it at that. But my grandmother
was nobody's fool, and she'd tell anybody
(20) smart enough to listen. Don't let a little pain
stop you; try as hard as you can
every minute you're given or else
sit down and shut-up—though in her opinion,
keeping quiet in noisy times was a sin
(25) against everything God and democracy
intended us for. I know she'd like
where I'm standing right now. She'd say
a man who could measure his life in deeds
was larger inside than the vessel that carried him;
(30) she'd say he was a cluster of grapes.
My grandmother was only four feet ten
but when she entered a room, even the books
came to attention. Giants come in all sizes:

Sometimes a moment is a monument;
(35) sometimes an institution breathes—
like a library. Like this halcyon[1] day.

—Rita Dove
from *The Poets Laureate Anthology*, 2010
W. W. Norton & Company, Inc.

---

[1]halcyon—peaceful

10 Lines 1 through 4 establish the grandmother's

   (1) questioning nature
   (2) vivid imagination
   (3) cautious attitude
   (4) optimistic outlook

10 _____

11 The figurative language in lines 9 and 10 highlights the grandmother's

   (1) desire to avoid conflicts
   (2) tendency to keep secrets
   (3) strategy to impart wisdom
   (4) ability to create humor

11 _____

12 Which phrase from the poem clarifies the narrator's statement in line 30?

   (1) "there'd be good days" (line 1)
   (2) "smart enough to listen" (line 20)
   (3) "measure his life in deeds" (line 28)
   (4) "sometimes an institution breathes" (line 35)

12 _____

13 The personification in lines 32 and 33 emphasizes the grandmother's

   (1) small size
   (2) commanding presence
   (3) family history
   (4) successful career

13 _____

14 The overall tone of the poem can best be described as

   (1) objective
   (2) skeptical
   (3) respectful
   (4) critical

14 _____

Reading Comprehension Passage C

Texting isn't the first new technology blamed for ruining communication and common courtesy.

Is text-messaging driving us apart? These days, we talk to each other a lot with our thumbs—mashing out over six billion text messages a day in the United States, and likely a few billion more on services like WhatsApp and Facebook Messenger.

(5)   But some worry that so much messaging leads, paradoxically, to less communication. When Sherry Turkle, the MIT clinical psychologist and author, interviewed college students, they said texting was causing friction in their face-to-face interactions. While hanging out with friends they'd be texting surreptitiously at the same time, pretending to maintain eye contact
(10) but mentally somewhere else. The new form of communication was fun, sure, but it was colliding with—and eroding—the old one.

"Our texts are fine," as one student said. "It's what texting does to our conversations when we are together that's the problem." . . .

New technologies often unsettle the way we relate to one another,
(15) of course. But social ruptures caused by texting have a strong echo in the arguments we had a hundred years ago. That's when a newfangled appliance gave us a strange new way to contact one another en masse:[1] the telephone. . . .

At first, the telephone was marketed mainly as a tool for business.
(20) Physicians and drugstores bought them to process orders, and business owners installed them at home so they could be quickly reached. The phone, proclaimed early ad copy, gave business leaders an ESP-like "sixth sense"[2] of their far-flung operations. . . .

Nonetheless, the telephone quickly gave birth to curious new forms of
(25) socializing. Callers arranged regular weekly "visiting" calls, dialing remote family to catch up on news. "Distance rolls away and for a few minutes every Thursday night the familiar voices tell the little family gossip that both are so eager to hear," a Bell ad cooed in 1921.

Phone companies even boasted that the phone was an improvement
(30) over that stodgy, low-fi communication, the letter. "Correspondence will help for a time, but friendships do not flourish for long on letters alone," a 1931 Bell sales manual noted. "When you can't visit in person,

---

[1]en masse—in a group at the same time
[2]ESP-like "sixth sense"—heightened intuition

telephone periodically. Telephone calls will keep up the whole intimacy remarkably well."

(35)   Soon, though, social critics began to wonder: Was all this phone chatter good for us? Was it somehow a lesser form of communication than what had come before? "Does the telephone make men more active or more lazy?" wondered the Knights of Columbus in a 1926 meeting. "Does the telephone break up home life and the old practice of visiting

(40) friends?"

Others worried that the inverse would occur—that it would be so easy to talk that we'd never leave each other alone. "Thanks to the telephone, motor-car and such-like inventions, our neighbors have it in their power to turn our leisure into a series of interruptions," complained an American

(45) professor in 1929. And surely it couldn't be healthy to talk to each other so much. Wouldn't it create Too Much Information [TMI]?

"We shall soon be nothing but transparent heaps of jelly to each other," a London writer moaned in 1897. Others fretted that the telephone sped up life, demanding instant reactions. "The use of the telephone

(50) gives little room for reflection," wrote a British newspaper in 1899. "It does not improve the temper, and it engenders a feverishness in the ordinary concerns of life which does not make for domestic happiness and comfort." Perhaps the strangest thing was being in the room while a friend talked to someone else—someone outside the room. In 1880,

(55) Mark Twain wrote "A Telephonic Conversation," transcribing the half-a-conversation as he listened to his wife on the phone. To the observer, as the skit pointed out, a telephone call sounded like disjointed nonsense. Even phone companies worried about whether the device created new forms of rude behavior; a 1910 Bell ad warned about "Dr. Jekyll and

(60) Mr. Hyde at the Telephone." . . .

Indeed, some believed the phone improved our social behavior, because it forced a listener to pay closer attention to a speaker. Devoid of visual signals, we must be "all ears and memory," a pundit[3] wrote in 1915: "The mind cannot wander." Plus, by eradicating distance, wouldn't the phone

(65) reduce misunderstanding? War, even? "Someday we will build up a world telephone system making necessary to all peoples the use of a common language, or common understanding of languages, which will join all the people of the earth into one brotherhood," gushed John J. Carty, AT&T chief engineer, in 1907.

---

[3]pundit—an expert who shares opinions with the public

(70)　　　These utopian[4] views, of course, were wildly optimistic. But the gloomy views of pessimists, as [author, Claude] Fischer notes, didn't come true either. Even Emily Post, the etiquette expert, came around to the telephone. By the 1920s, she'd accepted "Hello" as a suitable greeting, and even thought it was acceptable to invite someone to dinner with a call. "Custom which has

(75) altered many ways and manners has taken away all opprobrium[5] from the message," she shrugged.

　　　Nowadays, the telephone call seems like a quaint throwback to a gentler era. When Jenna Birch, the journalist, started dating a man who insisted on calling her on the phone, she found it warm and delightful—though her

(80) friends thought the behavior odd. Phone calls now seem retro.[6]

　　　Academics have observed this shift, too. "My students just do not think of the phone as a mechanism of vocal interaction—they think of that as very rare," says John Durham Peters, a communication professor at the University of Iowa, and author of *Speaking Into the Air*. He doesn't

(85) think the shift to texting has degraded our interactions, though. By the middle of the 20th century, studies found that the telephone appeared not to have eroded social contact—indeed, some research found those with phones wrote more old-fashioned letters than those without. Similarly, modern surveys by the Pew Research Center have found that teenagers

(90) who text the most are also those who spend the most time face to face with friends. Communication, it seems, begets more communication, and— as Peters argues—just because talk happens in text doesn't mean it's not meaningful.

　　　"Media scholars," he notes, "have this long romance with 'conversation'

(95) as the cure to the disease of media."

　　　Still, it's not hard to be dispirited[7] by the divided attention so many of Turkle's subjects bemoaned in their lives. Indeed, Michéle Martin, of Carleton, thinks we're living through a replay of the telephone, where the things that made it valuable—instant communications—are the same that

(100) made it annoying. "People believe they are liberated because they can bring the mobile phone everywhere," Martin says. "But at the same time they are slaves to it."

　　　The poet Carl Sandburg captured that dissonance in a 1916 poem about the telephone. He imagined a telephone wire being aware of the disparate[8]

---

[4]utopian—idealistic
[5]opprobrium—disgrace
[6]retro—dated
[7]dispirited—discouraged
[8]disparate—varying

(105) uses to which it was being put—coursing with conversations both deep and frivolous. "It is love and war and money; it is the fighting and the tears, the work and want/Death and laughter of men and women passing through me, carrier of your speech."

—Clive Thompson
excerpted and adapted from "OMG! We've Been Here B4"
Smithsonian, March 2016

15 The first paragraph of the text serves to

    (1) highlight the prevalence of texting
    (2) stress the benefits of texting
    (3) explain the origins of texting
    (4) support the abolition of texting   15 _____

16 As used in line 9, the word "surreptitiously" most nearly means

    (1) politely
    (2) boldly
    (3) secretively
    (4) earnestly   16 _____

17 The details in lines 19 through 23 reveal that the telephone was initially

    (1) associated with the supernatural
    (2) not considered very useful
    (3) often blamed for worker illness
    (4) not used for social purposes   17 _____

18 The use of the word "cooed" (line 28) implies that telephone advertisers were

    (1) helpful and patient
    (2) strategic and persuasive
    (3) childish and inconsiderate
    (4) sarcastic and relentless   18 _____

19 Lines 35 to 46 illustrate society's

    (1) enthusiasm about using new technology
    (2) dependence on those proficient in new technology
    (3) grasp of the significance of new technology
    (4) concern about the impact of new technology   19 _____

20 The figurative language in 47 and 48 implies that telephone use would cause people to

(1) lose self-confidence and motivation
(2) lack substance and individuality
(3) attract danger and adversity
(4) become narrow-minded and uninformed   20 _____

21 The statements from a Bell ad (lines 59 and 60) and the AT&T chief engineer (lines 65 through 69) offer

(1) contrasting perspectives on the potential effects of the telephone
(2) strong support for the growing popularity of the telephone
(3) alternative options for communicating with family members
(4) insightful evaluation of the importance of long-distance conversations   21 _____

22 The "utopian views" of the early 1900s (line 70) suggested that telephone use could

(1) improve local commerce
(2) encourage language studies
(3) promote global unity
(4) influence community values   22 _____

23 The information about Emily Post (lines 72 through 76) contributes to a central idea that

(1) rules of proper behavior can be confusing
(2) norms of good conduct are universal
(3) concepts of politeness can evolve over time
(4) conventions of salutation depend on status   23 _____

24 The quotations in lines 100 through 102 reflect a sense of

(1) bias
(2) irony
(3) suspense
(4) resolution   24 _____

PART 2—Argument Response

Directions: Closely read each of the *four* texts provided on pages 328 through 337 and write a source-based argument on the topic below. You may use the margins to take notes as you read and scrap paper to plan your response. Write your argument on a separate sheet of paper.

Topic: Should pets be allowed in the workplace?

Your Task: Carefully read each of the *four* texts provided. Then, using evidence from at least *three* of the texts, write a well-developed argument regarding whether or not pets should be allowed in the workplace. Clearly establish your claim, distinguish your claim from alternate or opposing claims, and use specific, relevant, and sufficient evidence from at least *three* of the texts to develop your argument. Do *not* simply summarize each text.

Guidelines:

Be sure to:
- Establish your claim regarding whether or not pets should be allowed in the workplace.
- Distinguish your claim from alternate or opposing claims.
- Use specific, relevant, and sufficient evidence from at least *three* of the texts to develop your argument.
- Identify each source that you reference by text number and line number(s) or graphic (for example: Text 1, line 4 or Text 2, graphic).
- Organize your ideas in a cohesive and coherent manner.
- Maintain a formal style of writing.
- Follow the conventions of standard written English.

Texts:

Text 1—Do Pets in the Workplace Improve Morale?

Text 2—Why Pets in the Workplace May Not Be As Great As You Thought

Text 3—Why a Pet-Friendly Office May Be the Key to Employee Satisfaction

Text 4—Don't Bring Your Dog to Work

Text 1

Do Pets in the Workplace Improve Morale?

Human resource managers are always looking for ways to improve morale and create a more appealing workplace culture. The popularity of the recent film release "The Secret Life of Pets" [2016] underscores the love we Americans have for our pets. In fact, around 65 percent of U.S.
(5) households are home to at least one pet. The majority of these are dogs and cats. . . .

The benefits of being around animals have inspired human resource personnel and other business decision makers to allow pets in the workplace. The top motive for making this allowance is the stress-reducing effect that
(10) animals bring. Employees who are less stressed at work are more productive and miss fewer days due to being sick.

Pet-friendly businesses usually focus mainly on allowing dogs in the workplace. However, some allow cats, birds and reptiles. A retail business might have "shop cats" that live on the premises, or smaller animals kept in
(15) cages that can become company mascots and offer a source of stress relief for workers.

An Internet giant paves the way with pets in the workplace.
. . .These days, about 2,000 dogs accompany their owners to Amazon each day. Workers and management have embraced the culture, and the pet-friendly policy benefits both owners and those who don't own pets. No
(20) matter what the workday brings, Amazon staff members are never far away from a coworker's terrier or spaniel poking its head around a corner. Any stress they were feeling melts away. . . .

Pet-friendly workplaces rate higher.
Banfield Pet Hospital recently surveyed over 1,000 employees and 200 human resource decision makers for its Pets At Work barometer called
(25) "Pet-Friendly Workplace PAWrometer." The goal was to measure worker opinions about pets in the workplace. Those who worked in pet-friendly offices were found to believe it improves the atmosphere in the workplace significantly.

The majority of workers in pet-friendly workplaces consider the policy
(30) to be positive. A full 91 percent of managers and 82 percent of employees felt workers become more loyal to the company with this policy. A large majority felt it made the workplace more productive, and 86 percent of workers and 92 percent of management reported decreased worker stress

levels. Not only do pets in the workplace make the environment less
(35) stressful, workers are also less burdened with guilt about leaving a pet at
home alone while they are at work. They are then more likely to work
longer hours if required.

While pet-friendly businesses improve existing employees' lives, they
are also appealing to new applicants. It's a benefit that millennials[1] find
(40) appealing and offers a way to draw in a larger talent pool.

So, how do pet-friendly workplaces stack up in terms of pros and cons?
Let's take a look:

The benefits of pets in the workplace.

- **Happier, more productive workers.** Both pet owners and non-pet
  owning employees report lowered stress levels and a higher level of job
(45)   satisfaction with pets on the premises. This naturally leads to increased
  productivity.
- **Healthier workers.** In addition to reduced stress levels, being around
  animals has documented positive effects on blood pressure, cholesterol
  levels and the immune system.
(50) - **Increased loyalty.** Over half of employees in non-pet-friendly workplaces report they'd be more likely to continue working for a company if
  they could bring their pet to work.

**Potential problems you may encounter by allowing pets in the
workplace.**

- **Not everyone is an animal lover.** There are people who dislike animals for one reason or another. Allergies, phobias, or a general dislike of
(55)   animals could cause pets in the workplace to encroach[2] upon productivity and quality of life for these individuals.
- **Hygiene and cleanliness issues.** Even potty-trained pets can have an
  accident now and then. There is no guarantee this won't happen in the
  workplace, especially with a high volume of animals brought to work.
(60) - **Interoffice squabbles.** Not all animals get along, so there is the potential for fights between dogs and cats brought to work.

While worker distraction is a concern for some human resource
managers considering a pet-friendly policy, the vast majority report that

---

[1]millennials—the generation born in the 1980s or 1990s, especially in the U.S.
[2]encroach—intrude

the benefits to morale and overall productivity far outweigh time spent
(65) "distracted" by pets in the workplace.

Advocates of allowing pets in the workplace insist that there are ways
around the "cons" or risks of pet-friendly workplaces. The key to a successful
pet policy is a clear structure. . . .

—excerpted and adapted from "Do Pets in the
Workplace Improve Morale?"
https://online.arbor.edu, August 8, 2016

Text 2

Why Pets in the Workplace May Not Be As Great As You Thought

    . . . Study after study has proven how pets have a calming effect on our bodies and minds, how they help children with A.D.D. [Attention Deficit Disorder] focus better, how they reduce blood pressure and lower stress, how pets at the workplace make employees more creative, productive, and
(5) cordial to each other, and how they're such awesome additions to our lives overall.

    So it would seem that if we spend the best parts of our waking hours at work, there's no better way to carry forward these wonderful benefits that pets bring into our work lives too, right? Well, unfortunately there are no
(10) simple answers here.

    While there is a growing wave of companies led by the usual suspects— Google, Zynga, Ben & Jerry's, and others—that allow employees to take their pets along to the workplace, there's also a growing debate about the practicality of the whole idea. And these voices of concern are not just
(15) coming from the minority of pet-haters or pet-neutral folks around. Even pet owners have reservations about bringing their beloved pooch to the office with them on a daily basis. Here's why:

Not in the Pink of Health

    . . . Spare a thought for the millions of your fellow Americans who suffer from pet related allergies. The Asthma and Allergy Foundation of America
(20) pegs the figure of Americans with one form of pet allergy or another at 15% to 30% of the total population. Some of these allergies are so severe that they cause rashes, temporary breathlessness, panic attacks, and even severe respiratory disorders.

    In addition to a physical reaction to the presence of pets around them,
(25) you could have coworkers who are genuinely scared of animals and feel stressed out around them. For such individuals a pet in their workplace is not a calming presence, but rather a constant threat to their wellbeing and safety.

Safety First

    . . . Many industries by their very nature are not conducive[1] to having
(30) pets sauntering around. Medical facilities, pharmaceutical companies,

---

[1]conducive—favorable

chemical laboratories, and food businesses are all sectors where a pet can be a serious threat to the quality of the final product or service. In such environments, pets pose a genuine contamination hazard and are best kept out, no questions asked.

(35)   In some cases, it's in your pet's best interest to chill out at home and skip the trip to the workplace. Industries like construction, mining, refineries, and more can be dangerous for your pet's health and well-being. You wouldn't want to put your pet at risk just so you can be happy at work, would you? . . .

Real Costs to the Company

As any pet owner will tell you, owning their bundle of joy is not cheap.
(40) From $1570 for a large dog to $575 for a parakeet per year, pet ownership comes at an ever-increasing price tag. When you turn your office into a pet friendly zone, you are in turn taking on some of the expenses of owning a pet upon yourself. Be prepared to stock your workplace with at least basic pet supplies like snacks, water bowls, kitty litter, and chew toys.

(45)   If you think your costs end there (or are tangible), you are mistaken. Pets at the workplace also bring with them a built-in deterrent[2] for employees seeking career opportunities at your organization. With the market for talented and qualified workers already so scarce, adding an extra filter to your recruitment process may not be the smartest idea from a competitive
(50) perspective. . . .

While the benefits that pets bring with them are numerous and the pro-pet lobby gets louder with every passing day, organizations need to also give credence[3] to the real issues that four-legged and feathered guests at work bring along with them. . . .

—Rohan Ayyar
excerpted and adapted from "Why Pets in the Workplace
May Not Be As Great As You Thought"
www.fastcompany.com, November 14, 2014

---

[2]deterrent—obstacle
[3]credence—support

Text 3

Why a Pet-Friendly Office May Be the Key to Employee Satisfaction

. . . The pet-friendly office is transforming our current idea of the typical nine-to-five workspace. Although the primary allure appears to be 24/7 cuddles with man's best friend, the actual benefits of a pet-friendly office go much deeper.

(5) Some of the world's biggest companies have proudly joined the ranks of pet-friendly businesses, from Googleplex,[1] to Build-A-Bear Workshop, to hospitals in New Jersey. This shift in office culture has shown that pet-friendly offices can provide unexpected (and positive) results to all varieties of businesses. . . .

Employee Satisfaction and Stress

(10) Employee satisfaction is a constant concern for an engaging and exciting place. Studies have shown that unhappy workers can cause businesses to lose thousands of dollars over time due to sick leave, mediocre work, and destructive behavior. Keeping the office engaging and exciting can be a struggle, and combating organizational stress may be key to improving a

(15) company's profits. . . .

Giving employees the option to bring their pet to work could also save them the worry associated with leaving a pet at home. Instead of scrambling through the end of the day to go home and let the dog out, they have the dog with them and can continue to work without rushing. Instead of spending

(20) money on a pet daycare on a regular basis, workers can watch their furry friend while in the office.

Pets are also known to be great stress-relievers in general. It's no wonder that Animal-Assisted Therapy is recognized as one of the leading treatments for post-war PTSD [Post-Traumatic Stress Disorder] and is gaining ground

(25) as a popular solution for social workers. Multiple studies have shown that simply petting cats or dogs can be extremely beneficial for our health; from lowering blood pressure to increasing bone density.

Attract Millennials

As a millennial, I can assure you: I would choose a pet-friendly office over the majority of other job offers out there. The benefit of bringing my

(30) pup to work is a much stronger pull than a larger paycheck or fancy corner office.

---

[1]Googleplex—Google headquarters

Millennials love their pets, and millennials love pet-friendly offices. In fact, you could even argue that millennials are the reason pet-friendly offices are taking the business world by storm. Being the largest demographic to (35) enter the workforce, they have already brought with them a demand for a new form of workplace flexibility and a break from the traditional office culture of our predecessors. . . .

Improve Communication

If you've ever walked your dog through a park or downtown area, there's a significant chance that you've received more waves, 'hellos', and (40) acknowledgements than if you had been walking by yourself. Walking or even being near a dog is an excellent ice-breaker.

Shifting to a pet-friendly workspace can bring that same level of open and enthusiastic communication into the office. Water cooler conversations[2] will lose some of their awkward chatter, and employees (45) will have the added encouragement of meeting new people in the building through their pets. This can lead to some inspiring brainstorm conversations as well as an increase in camaraderie[3] and trust among workers.

A 2012 study by the Virginia Commonwealth University found that (50) employees that brought their dogs to work were not only less stressed than their pet-free predecessors, but those employees believed they were 50 percent more productive with the presence of their pets. The public relations manager of the company that participated, Lisa Conklin of Replacements Dinnerware, stated after the conclusion of the study:

(55)   "The study proved what we always thought: having dogs around leads to a more productive work environment, and people get to know each other through the pets. If you are in a position where something is stressful, seeing that wagging tail and puppy smile brightens the day—it can turn around the whole environment."

Promote Employee Activity

(60)   On top of all these benefits, pets can also improve employee activity. Dog owners in the office will most likely have to walk their dog at least once a day, allowing them the opportunity to get away from their computer and into the open air. Workplace wellness has received considerable attention lately and more companies are making this a

---

[2]water cooler conversations—informal conversation
[3]camaraderie—fellowship

(65) priority. Pet-friendly offices can inspire a smooth transition to a more 'mobile' office. . . .

—Katie McBeth
excerpted and adapted from "Why a Pet-Friendly Office May Be the
Key to Employee Satisfaction"
https://thebossmagazine.com, September 28, 2016

Text 4

Don't Bring Your Dog to Work

If there's a dog in the cubicle next to you, you're hardly alone: About 7 percent of employers now allow pets in the workplace, reports NPR [National Public Radio]. Five years ago, that figure stood at 5 percent. That might not seem like a big jump, but once you remove jobs that
(5) don't have offices from the equation—manufacturing and agriculture, for instance—that's about a 50 percent increase. That rise is a victory for people who tout the benefits of inviting dogs and other furry friends into the office: It lowers the stress of employees, increases morale, produces tangible health benefits, and reduces turnover, all at no cost to
(10) the company.

But how do the dogs feel about it?

"Most people do not understand dog body language," said E'Lise Christensen, a board-certified veterinary behaviorist in Colorado. One major concern she has with the rise of pet-friendly work environments is the
(15) corresponding increased risk for behavioral problems, especially dog bites. Since almost no one, not even many dog trainers, knows how to properly interpret dog body language, co-workers might interpret the panting of a dog in the office as a friendly smile, rather than a sign of nervousness. And in dogs, nervousness can lead to bites. "[People] can identify abject[1] fear,
(20) and they can identify extreme aggression, but they cannot reliably identify things in between," said Christensen. It's in that wide middle area where we may not recognize pet discomfort.

Bonnie Beaver, executive director of the American College of Veterinary Behaviorists and a professor at Texas A&M University, said in
(25) an email that dog bites are not the only behavioral issues that might present problems. Generally, dogs are expected to sit still in an office setting, which can be difficult for active dogs, leading to boredom (which, in turn, leads to problem behaviors like chewing up desk legs). These policies are also particularly hard on dogs if they're taken to the office only occasionally,
(30) instead of regularly; dogs are big on routines, and uncertainty adds to their fear and stress.

Once you expand the conversation beyond our most domesticated companion, the prospects get even iffier. "Not all animals are comfortable with a very social setting," said Christensen. Each new animal, like cats

---

[1]abject—severe

(35) or pot-bellied pigs, brings its own social complexities, not to mention the possibility of contagious disease (it's rare that employers require proof of vaccination). Rabies, ringworm, and parasitic infections like scabies are all potential health risks for humans that come into contact with pets that haven't been properly vetted.[2]

(40)   Of course there's obvious appeal. Many people love dogs. They write whole articles gushing about a furrier workplace. (Dog skeptics, at least vocal ones, are harder to find.) When an employer is on board, the policy is often as informal as a person in charge saying, "Yeah, sure, whatever. Bring your dogs. It'll be great." Little or no oversight is applied to a matter that

(45) needs it in order to ensure the environment is conducive[3] to pets in the workplace.

       Christensen said companies should ideally hire an in-house behavioral expert to oversee a pet-at-work policy, especially in the initial stages, "but unless you're Google, I don't see that happening." More realistically, she

(50) said, better awareness will go a long way. Employers should take care to craft a policy that works for dogs' well-being as well as humans'. This can include requiring proof of vaccinations, as well as providing training for offices on dog behavior (which can be as basic as watching videos).

       "It's critical that people with dogs get special education, in at least

(55) body language, even if they think they know normal body language," said Christensen. Given that most people can't even tell the difference between a relaxed and anxious dog, this advice seems prudent. Before more offices throw open their doors to dogs willy-nilly[4] and more pets start tagging along on the morning commute, we should learn how better to listen to them.

(60) They might be asking to stay at home.

—Matt Miller

excerpted and adapted from "Don't Bring Your Dog to Work"
www.slate.com, August 15, 2016

---

[2]vetted—examined
[3]conducive—favorable
[4]willy-nilly—in an unplanned manner

PART 3—Analysis Response

Your Task: Closely read the text provided on pages 339 and 340 and write a well-developed, text-based response of two to three paragraphs. In your response, identify a central idea in the text and analyze how the author's use of *one* writing strategy (literary element or literary technique or rhetorical device) develops this central idea. Use strong and thorough evidence from the text to support your analysis. Do *not* simply summarize the text. You may use the margins to take notes as you read and scrap paper to plan your response. Write your response on a separate sheet of paper.

Guidelines:

Be sure to:
- Identify a central idea in the text.
- Analyze how the author's use of *one* writing strategy (literary element or literary technique or rhetorical device) develops this central idea. Examples include: characterization, conflict, denotation/connotation, metaphor, simile, irony, language use, point-of-view, setting, structure, symbolism, theme, tone, etc.
- Use strong and thorough evidence from the text to support your analysis.
- Organize your ideas in a cohesive and coherent manner.
- Maintain a formal style of writing.
- Follow the conventions of standard written English.

Text

. . . There were a number of people out this afternoon, far more than last Sunday. And the band sounded louder and gayer. That was because the Season had begun. For although the band played all the year round on Sundays, out of season it was never the same. It was like some one playing
(5) with only the family to listen; it didn't care how it played if there weren't any strangers present. Wasn't the conductor wearing a new coat, too? She was sure it was new. He scraped with his foot and flapped his arms like a rooster about to crow, and the bandsmen sitting in the green rotunda blew out their cheeks and glared at the music. Now there came a little "flutey" bit—very
(10) pretty!—a little chain of bright drops. She was sure it would be repeated. It was; she lifted her head and smiled.

Only two people shared her "special" seat: a fine old man in a velvet coat, his hands clasped over a huge carved walking-stick, and a big old woman, sitting upright, with a roll of knitting on her embroidered apron. They did
(15) not speak. This was disappointing, for Miss Brill always looked forward to the conversation. She had become really quite expert, she thought, at listening as though she didn't listen, at sitting in other people's lives just for a minute while they talked round her.

She glanced, sideways, at the old couple. Perhaps they would go soon.
(20) Last Sunday, too, hadn't been as interesting as usual. An Englishman and his wife, he wearing a dreadful Panama hat and she button boots. And she'd gone on the whole time about how she ought to wear spectacles;[1] she knew she needed them; but that it was no good getting any; they'd be sure to break and they'd never keep on. And he'd been so patient. He'd suggested
(25) everything—gold rims, the kind that curved round your ears, little pads inside the bridge. No, nothing would please her. "They'll always be sliding down my nose!" Miss Brill had wanted to shake her.

The old people sat on the bench, still as statues. Never mind, there was always the crowd to watch. To and fro, in front of the flower-beds and the
(30) band rotunda, the couples and groups paraded, stopped to talk, to greet, to buy a handful of flowers from the old beggar who had his tray fixed to the railings. Little children ran among them, swooping and laughing; little boys with big white silk bows under their chins, little girls, little French dolls, dressed up in velvet and lace. And sometimes a tiny staggerer came
(35) suddenly rocking into the open from under the trees, stopped, stared, as suddenly sat down "flop," until its small high-stepping mother, like a young

---

[1]spectacles—glasses

hen, rushed scolding to its rescue. Other people sat on the benches and green chairs, but they were nearly always the same, Sunday after Sunday, and—Miss Brill had often noticed—there was something funny about (40) nearly all of them. They were odd, silent, nearly all old, and from the way they stared they looked as though they'd just come from dark little rooms or even—even cupboards!

Behind the rotunda the slender trees with yellow leaves down drooping, and through them just a line of sea, and beyond the blue sky with gold-(45) veined clouds.

Tum-tum-tum tiddle-um! tiddle-um! tum tiddley-um tum ta! blew the band. . . .

Oh, how fascinating it was! How she enjoyed it! How she loved sitting here, watching it all! It was like a play. It was exactly like a play. Who could (50) believe the sky at the back wasn't painted? But it wasn't till a little brown dog trotted on solemn and then slowly trotted off, like a little "theatre" dog, a little dog that had been drugged, that Miss Brill discovered what it was that made it so exciting. They were all on the stage. They weren't only the audience, not only looking on; they were acting. Even she had a part and (55) came every Sunday. No doubt somebody would have noticed if she hadn't been there; she was part of the performance after all. How strange she'd never thought of it like that before! And yet it explained why she made such a point of starting from home at just the same time each week—so as not to be late for the performance—and it also explained why she had (60) quite a queer, shy feeling at telling her English pupils how she spent her Sunday afternoons. No wonder! Miss Brill nearly laughed out loud. She was on the stage. She thought of the old invalid gentleman to whom she read the newspaper four afternoons a week while he slept in the garden. She had got quite used to the frail head on the cotton pillow, the hollowed (65) eyes, the open mouth and the high pinched nose. If he'd been dead she mightn't have noticed for weeks; she wouldn't have minded. But suddenly he knew he was having the paper read to him by an actress! "An actress!" The old head lifted; two points of light quivered in the old eyes. "An actress—are ye?" And Miss Brill smoothed the newspaper as though it (70) were the manuscript of her part and said gently; "Yes, I have been an actress for a long time." . . .

—Katherine Mansfield
excerpted from "Miss Brill"
The Garden Party and Other Stories, 1922
Alfred A. Knopf, Inc.

Regents ELA Answers June 2019

English Language Arts

Answer Key

PART 1

1. 3	9. 4	17. 4
2. 2	10. 4	18. 2
3. 1	11. 3	19. 4
4. 2	12. 3	20. 2
5. 1	13. 2	21. 1
6. 1	14. 3	22. 3
7. 3	15. 1	23. 3
8. 2	16. 3	24. 2

PART 2 *See Answers and Explanations*

PART 3 *See Answers and Explanations*

Regents Examination in English Language Arts—June 2019
Chart for Converting Total Weighted Raw Scores to Final Exam Scores (Scale Scores)

Weighted Raw Score*	Scale Score	Performance Level	Weighted Raw Score*	Scale Score	Performance Level
56	100	5	27	55	2
55	99	5	26	52	1
54	99	5	25	50	1
53	99	5	24	47	1
52	98	5	23	45	1
51	97	5	22	42	1
50	96	5	21	40	1
49	95	5	20	37	1
48	93	5	19	34	1
47	92	5	18	31	1
46	90	5	17	28	1
45	89	5	16	25	1
44	88	5	15	22	1
43	86	5	14	19	1
42	85	5	13	16	1
41	84	4	12	13	1
40	82	4	11	10	1
39	80	4	10	9	1
38	79	4	9	8	1
37	77	3	8	6	1
36	75	3	7	5	1
35	72	3	6	4	1
34	70	3	5	3	1
33	68	3	4	3	1
32	66	3	3	2	1
31	65	3	2	1	1
30	61	2	1	1	1
29	59	2	0	0	1
28	57	2			

The conversion table is determined independently for each administration of the exam.

Answers Explained

PART 1—Reading Comprehension

Multiple-Choice Questions

Passage A

1. **3** "create a feeling of anticipation." The images in this paragraph describe the narrator being led through levels of what we gradually understand to be a created environment, a Colony on the moon perhaps, where humans now live after life on Earth has been destroyed by nuclear Armageddon. The narrator, a ten-year-old child, wants to linger at various levels. However, the Father rushes ahead insistently, and the boy experiences "a sense of rising excitement." Note that the questions are best understood and answered after you read the entire story.

2. **2** "the inhospitable conditions of Outside." The description of vehicles with pressurized cabins exiting through airlocks establishes that the environment outside the Colony does not support human life. This question is also an example of how, on the ELA Regents, knowledge of vocabulary is assessed in context. None of the other choices is supported by the text.

3. **1** "a change in Marvin's understanding." At this point, the boy only senses something "strange" in his father's behavior. At the end of the story, though, Marvin reveals how he finally "understood the purpose of this pilgrimage."

4. **2** "desolation of the Outside." The grim barrenness (desolation) of the landscape further reveals the inhospitable conditions of the Outside. (See also question 2.)

5. **1** "romantic vision of the Earth." Once Marvin could see Earth through the brilliant glare, "It was beautiful, and it called to his heart across the abyss of space." (line 77) *Romantic* here refers to a view that is characterized by intense emotion and an idealized appreciation of nature. Marvin dreams that one day, succeeding generations of humans may return to the beautiful, "lost and legendary world" of Earth.

6. **1** "sense of deprivation." Marvin feels that life on a beautiful Earth "should have been his rightful heritage." Marvin feels denied (deprived) of that possibility because he will know the beauties of Earth only through books and ancient records.

7. **3** "human actions." Images of "evil phosphorescence . . . radioactive aftermath . . . [and] glow of dying atoms" establish that in this story, life on Earth was destroyed by human actions—nuclear war. This was often a theme in 20th-century literature, especially after the use of atom bombs at end of the World War II.

8. **2** "cleansing and renewal." These lines offer images of winds and rains that would "scour [scrub clean] the poisons" and where the seas would "waste their [the poisons'] venom," making possible the return (renewal) of human life on Earth. The feelings offered in the other choices are not suggested in lines 98 through 100.

9. **4** "He [his father] would never walk beside the rivers of that lost and legendary world, or listen to the thunder raging above its softly rounded hills" (lines 93 through 95). These lines best capture Marvin's understanding of his father's profound feelings of loss and of his father's knowledge that he will never return to Earth. None of the other choices reflects details of the father's understanding.

Passage B

10. **4** "optimistic outlook." The images of "good days/to counter the dark ones" and of "blue skies in the heart" are expressions of the grandmother's confidence that life offers positive and hopeful things to balance pain or discouragement. Optimism best characterizes the tone in these lines.

11. **3** "strategy to impart wisdom." The images in the previous lines and the metaphor of baking a cake to measure a life represent the grandmother's use of language as a tactical way (strategy) to give valuable advice and guidance (wisdom) to her grandchild. Lines 9 and 10 include no significant expression of conflict, secrets, or humor.

12. **3** "measure his life in deeds" (line 28). Just as words "carried their treasures/like a grape clusters around its own juice," a person whose life is measured in how well he or she has acted can be seen as a cluster of meaningful deeds. None of the other choices expresses what the grandmother would admire in the life of her grandchild.

13. **2** "commanding presence." *Commanding* denotes something or someone who is impressive, strong, and demands obedience. The image of "even the books" coming "to attention" vividly expresses the powerful influence the grandmother had on those around her.

14. **3** "respectful." This is the best answer among the choices, even if it somewhat understates the admiration and appreciation the poet has for the grandmother.

Passage C

15. **1** "highlight the prevalence of texting." These lines report on the frequency, popularity, and widespread use (*prevalence*) of texting. The paragraph cites "six billion text messages a day in the United States, . . . and a few billion more on" worldwide services. These details do not directly stress the benefits, explain the origins, or support the abolition of texting.

16. **3** "secretively." This is the familiar image of an individual hanging out with friends in a café while also holding his or her phone under the table to check messages and pretending to be fully engaged with the friends who are present.

17. **4** "not used for social purposes." This brief paragraph offers examples of how at first the telephone was seen "as a tool for business." Lines 19 through 23 offer no examples of telephones being used for social purposes.

18. **2** "strategic and persuasive." The word *cooed* is used here to identify the gentle, quiet manner in which one—a mother soothing a baby, for example—speaks calmly and reassuringly to persuade another to do something. Choice (1), "helpful and patient," seems at first to be a good answer because it expresses the tone and feeling of cooing. However, the telephone advertisers are actually using this as a strategy to persuade customers that frequent phone calls are the most meaningful way to stay in touch with family and friends. Choice (2) is the best answer.

19. **4** "concern about the impact of new technology." These two paragraphs offer several examples of concern expressed in the 1920s by critics, scientists, and social groups, who began to wonder, "Was all this phone chatter good for us?"

20. **2** "lack substance and individuality." Among the choices, this phrase best describes the image of telephone users as "transparent heaps of jelly." Each of the other choices describes strong and specific feelings, which do not suggest "heaps of jelly."

21. **1** "contrasting perspectives on the potential effects of the telephone." The Bell ad from 1910 warned that phone use might create "new forms of rude behavior." In contrast, in 1907 the chief engineer at AT&T had proclaimed that the advent of the telephone could promote a "common understanding of languages" and a universal brotherhood, thereby preventing misunderstandings and even war.

22. **3** "promote global unity." The idealistic vision of the AT&T engineer cited in question 21 is an example of the "utopian views" of the 1900s. These views suggested that misunderstanding and distrust among nations could be overcome when people could speak directly to one another through telephone communication. This passage does not consider the benefits to local commerce, language studies, or the influence on community values.

23. **3** "concepts of politeness can evolve over time." Even though choices (1) and (4) offer statements that could be true, the reference to Emily Post and *etiquette*—standards of correct (polite) behavior in social situations—makes this the best answer. In Emily Post's time, she offered guidelines for good manners and acceptable behavior. As the world changed, Emily Post's "rules" changed as well.

24. **2** "irony." The mobile phone is convenient and annoying at the same time. The ironic contradiction expressed here is that people feel liberated in being able to take a phone with them everywhere, but "at the same time they are slaves to it." None of the other choices expresses the intended irony in the quotations.

PART 2—Argument Response

Sample Essay Response

The modern workplace is the center of many debates. Sexual harassment, racism, and the encroachment of technology on jobs are all topics that have come up in the working world. Compared to these, the discussion over whether or not pets should be allowed in the workplace might be noncontroversial to the point of being dull. However, many people have clashing opinions over whether and how the growing practice of bringing one's pets to work should continue. Although there should be some adjustments or limits to the current practice, I believe it would be beneficial if some workplaces allowed their employees to bring pets to work.

A key reason for bringing pets to work is in the psychological benefits. Having a parakeet to chat with or a fluffy friend to hug creates a more positive atmosphere, which in turn increases loyalty to and productivity for the company. One study showed that "86 percent of workers and 92 percent of management reported decreased worker stress levels" following the implementation of the policy. (Text 1, lines 32–34) Having pets around also improves worker communication by giving people topics of discussion and shared interest since "walking or even being near a dog is an excellent ice-breaker." (Text 3, lines 40–41) The presence of pets in the workplace can lead to closer emotional bonds or even valuable brainstorms among workers.

Having pets around can leave workers and, by extension, their employers much more satisfied and stress-free. Besides the pleasant psychological effects, having pets around can also have a positive impact on one's physical well-being. Petting a cat or a dog can have healthy side effects, which can range from "lowering blood pressure to increasing bone density." (Text 3, line 27) Pets can also increase employee activity since walking dogs or feeding cats requires workers to move around more than they would when just sitting at their computers. Younger workers, who represent a large percentage of the workforce, are especially attracted to workplaces that permit pets. For employers, this can be a way to attract millennials as new workers. (Text 3, lines 32–37) Finally, workers of all ages are less likely to rush through work or request shorter hours when they don't need to worry about caring for house-bound pets.

Of course, having pets in a workplace is not all cuddles and birdsong. There are legitimate concerns about workers who have harmful physical or psychological reactions to having animals around. For example, 15% to 30% of the total American population has some kind of pet allergy (Text 2, lines 19–21), and there are people who are genuinely uneasy in the presence of animals. Contact between humans and pets may even pose the risk of spreading parasitic infections such as ringworm. (Text 4, lines 37–39)

Moreover, pets themselves may fare badly in a workplace setting. Restrictive spaces or erratic schedules may lead dogs, a favorite American pet, to suffer psychologically and display bad behavior in the workplace. One writer argues that there is a general human illiteracy in the intricacies of dog body language, leading people to interpret "the panting of a dog in the office as a friendly smile, rather than a sign of nervousness." (Text 4, lines 17–19) These are all valid concerns and need to be taken seriously. However, many difficulties can be addressed by educating pet owners about how to identify physical or psychological discomfort in fellow workers

I believe that a policy that welcomes pets would be beneficial to many workplaces. Pets have positive psychological and physical effects on the humans around them. They can even support hiring and worker productivity. Pets need to be protected from dangerous environments, and only well-trained and healthy pets should be permitted in the workplace. These measures would not make the office pets movement welcome everywhere, but they would help smooth the way.

Analysis

Unlike many of the topics presented in Part 2 of the Regents ELA exam, this topic leaves room for a qualified position. This essay meets the requirement to present an argument in support of a particular position, allowing pets in the workplace, but accepts the need for exceptions as well. This writer presents a precise and thoughtful argument, which is balanced with both claims and counterclaims.

The essay is well organized. It opens with an introductory paragraph to outline the issue and establish the writer's position. The information is then developed, with clear exposition of relevant ideas and with specific evidence from the texts to represent alternative points of view. The conclusion appropriately restates the writer's position, which is strengthened by including guidelines to meet many of the concerns of those who may not agree. The use of language is fluent and often sophisticated. "Of course, having pets in a workplace is not all cuddles and birdsong" is a particularly pleasant way to recognize the concerns of those who are not comfortable with pets in the workplace. There are no significant errors in usage or conventions. This essay would merit a high score.

(See pages 79–80 for the scoring guidelines.)

PART 3—Text-Analysis Response

Sample Essay Response

Through the use of characterization, the author expertly crafts the idea that life is like one big play and that everyone is merely acting out their own parts while simultaneously observing as the audience. The author recounts all of the little details Miss Brill notices about those around her, while the other characters' quirks, mannerisms, or actions create the image of life in this town as action in a play.

Miss Brill is characterized as an actor playing a role in her own life. As a member of the audience, "she had become really quite expert, she thought, at listening as though she didn't listen, at sitting in on other people's lives . . . while they talked round her." (lines 16–18) As a listener or watcher, Miss Brill always observes the people around her. On this afternoon, though, they are less interesting. The people sitting on the benches appear "nearly always the same." (line 38) Each Sunday, she is at the performance of the band: "How she loved . . . watching it all. It was like a play!" (lines 48–49) She is both listening to the music and taking part in the performance herself. Someone would notice if she was absent from her role. Although she never thought about it that way before, "it explained why she made such a point of starting from home at just the same time each week—so as not be late for the performance." (lines 57–59) The author shows how Miss Brill now understands that she is acting out her own part in the play of life by attending the little band concerts each week. To those around her, she is a character in the play and they are her audience. The events—the drama—of this particular day in Miss Brill's life lead her to the realization that she is "an actress!" (line 67) Miss Brill is no longer just an observer but an actress on the stage of the life around her.

Analysis

This response clearly introduces a central theme from the text: life is a play in which people are both actors/players and audience. The discussion effectively shows how the author's characterization of Miss Brill dramatizes how that life is lived. With specific references to the text and appropriate quotations, the essay shows how the author's strategy is to recount "all of the little details Miss Brill notices" and to reveal the pleasure Miss Brill takes in both listening to and seeing herself as part of the performance.

This response is logically organized. The opening paragraph establishes the central idea and the writing strategy for analysis. The second paragraph contains details from the story that are presented sequentially to reveal the character's own growing understanding of herself and her life. The language and style are appropriately formal and demonstrate control of the conventions. This response would merit a high score.

(See pages 81–82 for the scoring guidelines.)

Regents ELA Examination August 2019
English Language Arts

PART 1—Reading Comprehension

Directions (1–24): Closely read each of the three passages below. After each passage, there are several multiple-choice questions. Select the best suggested answer to each question and write its number in the space provided. You may use the margins to take notes as you read.

Reading Comprehension Passage A

Brooklyn

    Eilis Lacey, sitting at the window of the upstairs living room in the house on Friary Street, noticed her sister walking briskly from work. She watched Rose crossing the street from sunlight into shade, carrying the new leather handbag that she had bought in Clerys in Dublin [Ireland] in the
(5) sale. Rose was wearing a cream-coloured cardigan over her shoulders. Her golf clubs were in the hall; in a few minutes, Eilis knew, someone would call for her and her sister would not return until the summer evening had faded.
    Eilis's bookkeeping classes were almost ended now; she had a manual on her lap about systems of accounting, and on the table behind her was a
(10) ledger where she had entered, as her homework, on the debit and credit sides, the daily business of a company whose details she had taken down in notes in the Vocational School the week before.
    As soon as she heard the front door open, Eilis went downstairs. Rose, in the hall, was holding her pocket mirror in front of her face. She was
(15) studying herself closely as she applied lipstick and eye make-up before glancing at her overall appearance in the large hall mirror, settling her hair. Eilis looked on silently as her sister moistened her lips and then checked herself one more time in the pocket mirror before putting it away.

Their mother came from the kitchen to the hall. . . .

(20)   Rose reached into her handbag and took out her purse. She placed a one-shilling piece on the hallstand. "That's in case you want to go to the pictures," she said to Eilis.

"And what about me?" her mother asked.

"She'll tell you the story when she gets home," Rose replied. . . .

(25)   All three laughed as they heard a car stop outside the door and beep its horn. Rose picked up her golf clubs and was gone.

Later, as her mother washed the dishes and Eilis dried them, another knock came to the door. When Eilis answered it, she found a girl whom she recognized from Kelly's grocery shop beside the cathedral.

(30)   "Miss Kelly sent me with a message for you," the girl said. "She wants to see you."

"Does she?" Eilis asked. "And did she say what it was about?"

"No. You're just to call up there tonight.". . . .

Miss Kelly slowly came down the stairs into the hallway and turned on
(35) a light.

"Now," she said, and repeated it as though it were a greeting. She did not smile. . . .

"I hear you have no job at all but a great head for figures."

"Is that right?"

(40)   "Oh, the whole town, anyone who is anyone, comes into the shop and I hear everything.". . . .

"And we are worked off our feet every Sunday here. Sure, there's nothing else open.

And we get all sorts, good, bad and indifferent. And, as a rule, I open
(45) after seven mass,[1] and between the end of nine o'clock mass until eleven mass is well over, there isn't room to move in this shop. I have Mary here to help, but she's slow enough at the best of times, so I was on the lookout for someone sharp, someone who would know people and give the right change. But only on Sundays, mind. The rest of the week we can manage
(50) ourselves. And you were recommended. I made inquiries about you and it would be seven and six a week, it might help your mother a bit." . . .

"Well?" Miss Kelly asked.

Eilis realized that she could not turn down the offer. It would be better than nothing and, at the moment, she had nothing. . . .

---

[1] seven mass—church service at 7 A.M.

(55) Rose, at thirty, Eilis thought, was more glamorous every year, and, while she had had several boyfriends, she remained single; she often remarked that she had a much better life than many of her former schoolmates who were to be seen pushing prams[2] through the streets. Eilis was proud of her sister, of how much care she took with her appearance and how much care she put
(60) into whom she mixed with in the town and the golf club. She knew that Rose had tried to find her work in an office, and Rose was paying for her books now that she was studying bookkeeping and rudimentary accountancy, but she knew also that there was, at least for the moment, no work for anyone in Enniscorthy, no matter what their qualifications.
(65) Eilis did not tell Rose about her offer of work from Miss Kelly; instead, as she went through her training, she saved up every detail to recount to her mother, who laughed and made her tell some parts of the story again.

"That Miss Kelly," her mother said, "is as bad as her mother and I heard from someone who worked there that that woman was evil incarnate.[3] And
(70) she was just a maid in Roche's before she married. And Kelly's used to be a boarding house as well as a shop, and if you worked for her, or even if you stayed there, or dealt in the shop, she was evil incarnate. Unless, of course, you had plenty of money or were one of the clergy."

"I'm just there until something turns up," Eilis said.
(75) "That's what I said to Rose when I was telling her," her mother replied. "And don't listen to her if she says anything to you." . . .

One day at dinnertime Rose, who walked home from the office at one and returned at a quarter to two, mentioned that she had played golf the previous evening with a priest, a Father Flood, who had known their father
(80) years before and their mother when she was a young girl. He was home from America on holidays, his first visit since before the war. . . .

"Anyway," Rose said, "I invited him in for his tea when he said that he'd like to call on you [the mother] and he's coming tomorrow." . . .

Father Flood was tall; his accent was a mixture of Irish and American.
(85) Nothing he said could convince Eilis's mother that she had known him or his family. His mother, he said, had been a Rochford.

"I don't think I knew her," her mother said. "The only Rochford we knew was old Hatchethead."

Father Flood looked at her solemnly. "Hatchethead was my uncle," he
(90) said. "Was he?" her mother asked. Eilis saw how close she was to nervous laughter. . . . Rose poured more tea as Eilis quietly left the room, afraid that if she stayed she would be unable to disguise an urge to begin laughing.

---

[2] prams—baby carriages
[3] incarnate—in bodily form

When she returned she realized that Father Flood had heard about her job at Miss Kelly's, had found out about her pay and had expressed shock at (95) how low it was. He inquired about her qualifications.

"In the United States," he said, "there would be plenty of work for someone like you and with good pay." . . .

"In Brooklyn, where my parish is, there would be office work for someone who was hard-working and educated and honest."

(100)   "It's very far away, though," her mother said. "That's the only thing." . . .

"It would be a great opportunity, especially if you were young," Father Flood said

finally. . . .

Eilis felt like a child when the doctor would come to the house, her (105) mother listening with cowed respect. It was Rose's silence that was new to her; she looked at her now, wanting her sister to ask a question or make a comment, but Rose appeared to be in a sort of dream. As Eilis watched her, it struck her that she had never seen Rose look so beautiful. And then it occurred to her that she was already feeling that she would need to (110) remember this room, her sister, this scene, as though from a distance. In the silence that had lingered, she realized, it had somehow been tacitly arranged that Eilis would go to America. Father Flood, she believed, had been invited to the house because Rose knew that he could arrange it. . . .

—Colm Tóibín
excerpted and adapted from *Brooklyn*, 2009
Scribner

1 The first three paragraphs serve to introduce

    (1) a contrast between the sisters
    (2) Rose's condescension toward her sister
    (3) the competition between the sisters
    (4) Eilis's concern about her sister   1 _____

2 Lines 20 through 24 show Rose's

    (1) impatience with her mother
    (2) restlessness in her home
    (3) satisfaction with her work
    (4) thoughtfulness toward her sister   2 _____

3 The dialogue in lines 36 through 41 depicts Miss Kelly as

    (1) indecisive   (3) jealous
    (2) abrupt   (4) bitter   3 _____

4 The statement "And we are worked off our feet" (line 42) illustrates that Miss Kelly's shop is

    (1) disorderly   (3) bankrupt
    (2) bustling   (4) treasured   4 _____

5 Eilis's attitude toward Rose in lines 55 through 60 can best be described as

    (1) protective   (3) admiring
    (2) critical   (4) indifferent   5 _____

6 The phrase "no work for anyone in Enniscorthy, no matter what their qualifications" (lines 63 and 64) supports a central idea about Eilis's

    (1) respect for Miss Kelly's successful business
    (2) incentive to accept any employment
    (3) pressure to pursue further education
    (4) envy of Rose's comfortable situation   6 _____

7 The author's choice of the word "mentioned" (line 78) as well as Father Flood's comments (lines 98 and 99) most likely indicate that Rose is

(1) afraid that her mother will object to Father Flood's visit
(2) anticipating that Eilis will help her with the meal
(3) careful about ensuring that Father Flood feels welcomed
(4) subtle about putting her plan for Eilis in motion

7 _____

8 The recognition that a job "had somehow been tacitly arranged" (line 111) suggests that

(1) an agreement was made without Rose's permission
(2) actions were taken to deceive Eilis's family
(3) an agreement was made without Eilis's knowledge
(4) actions were taken to limit Father Flood's influence

8 _____

9 Which quotation best reflects a central idea in the passage?

(1) "All three laughed as they heard a car stop outside the door and beep its horn" (line 25)
(2) " 'Miss Kelly sent me with a message for you,' the girl said. 'She wants to see you' " (lines 30 and 31)
(3) "Rose, at thirty, Eilis thought, was more glamorous every year, and, while she had had several boyfriends, she remained single" (lines 55 and 56)
(4) " 'In the United States,' he said, 'there would be plenty of work for someone like you and with good pay' " (lines 96 and 97)

9 _____

Reading Comprehension Passage B

Slam, Dunk, & Hook

Fast breaks. Lay ups. With Mercury's[1]
Insignia on our sneakers,
We outmaneuvered to footwork
Of bad angels. Nothing but a hot
(5)   Swish of strings like silk
Ten feet out. In the roundhouse
Labyrinth our bodies
Created, we could almost
Last forever, poised in midair
(10) Like storybook sea monsters.
A high note hung there
A long second. Off
The rim. We'd corkscrew
Up & dunk balls that exploded
(15) The skullcap of hope & good
Intention. Lanky, all hands
& feet. . .sprung rhythm.
We were metaphysical[2] when girls
Cheered on the sidelines.
(20) Tangled up in a falling,
Muscles were a bright motor
Double-flashing to the metal hoop
Nailed to our oak.
When Sonny Boy's mama died
(25) He played nonstop all day, so hard
Our backboard splintered.
Glistening with sweat,
We rolled the ball off
Our fingertips. Trouble
(30) Was there slapping a blackjack
Against an open palm.
Dribble, drive to the inside,
& glide like a sparrow hawk.
Lay ups. Fast breaks.
(35) We had moves we didn't know

---

[1] Mercury—Roman god who acted as a messenger to the gods
[2] metaphysical—superhuman

We had. Our bodies spun
On swivels of bone & faith,
Through a lyric slipknot
Of joy, & we knew we were
(40) Beautiful & dangerous.

—Yusef Komunyakaa
"Slam, Dunk, & Hook"
from *Pleasure Dome: New and Collected Poems*, 2004
Wesleyan University Press

10 The images in lines 6 through 12 create a sense of

    (1) youth ending
    (2) anxious movement
    (3) time stopping
    (4) imaginative strategy   10 _____

11 In the context of the poem as a whole, lines 24 through 26 present

    (1) an example of the players' excitement with the game
    (2) a shift in the players' expectations
    (3) a contrast to the players' feelings of invincibility
    (4) an illustration of the players' skill   11 _____

12 Lines 32 through 36 most clearly reflect the players'

    (1) competition   (3) insecurity
    (2) agility   (4) devotion   12 _____

13 In the context of the poem as a whole, the mythological allusions best reflect the players' sense of being

(1) popular   (3) competent

(2) extraordinary   (4) successful   13 _____

14 Which quotation best reflects a central idea of the poem?

(1) "We'd corkscrew/Up & dunk balls that exploded" (lines 13 and 14)

(2) "We were metaphysical when girls/Cheered on the sidelines" (lines 18 and 19)

(3) "Glistening with sweat/We rolled the ball off/Our fingertips" (lines 27 through 29)

(4) "Of joy, & we knew we were/Beautiful & dangerous" (lines 39 and 40)   14 _____

Reading Comprehension Passage C

How We Make Sense of Time

"What is the difference between yesterday and tomorrow?" The Yupno man we were interviewing, Danda, paused to consider his answer. A group of us sat on a hillside in the Yupno Valley, a remote nook high in the mountains of Papua New Guinea.[1] Only days earlier we had arrived on a single-engine

(5) plane. After a steep hike from the grass airstrip, we found ourselves in the village of Gua, one of about 20 Yupno villages dotting the rugged terrain. We came all the way here because we are interested in *time*—in how Yupno people understand concepts such as past, present and future. Are these ideas universal, or are they products of our language, our culture and our

(10) environment?

As we interviewed Danda and others in the village, we listened to what they said about time, but we paid even closer attention to what they did with their hands as they spoke. Gestures can be revealing. Ask English speakers about the difference between yesterday and tomorrow, and they

(15) might thrust a hand over the shoulder when referring to the past and then forward when referring to the future. Such unreflective movements reveal a fundamental way of thinking in which the past is at our backs, something that we "leave behind," and the future is in front of us, something to "look forward" to. Would a Yupno speaker do the same?

(20) Danda was making just the kinds of gestures we were hoping for. As he explained the Yupno word for "yesterday," his hand swept backward; as he mentioned "tomorrow," it leaped forward. We all sat looking up a steep slope toward a jagged ridge, but as the light faded, we changed the camera angle, spinning around so that we and Danda faced in the opposite direction,

(25) downhill. With our backs now to the ridge, we looked over the Yupno River meandering[2] toward the Bismarck Sea. "Let's go over that one more time," we suggested.

Danda obliged, again using his hands to enliven his explanation. But as we expected, his gestures had changed. As he referred to "yesterday," he now

(30) gestured, not backward, but forward. As he explained "tomorrow," he gestured back over his shoulder, up toward the ridge. Inconsistent as these movements may seem, Danda was not confused. His gestures expressed the Yupno way of understanding time, one in which the future is not something in front of you—it is uphill. By having interviewees change sitting positions, we were able to

(35) show that it does not matter whether the slope is in front of you, behind you, to

---

[1] Papua New Guinea—an oceanic country, north of Australia

[2] meandering—winding

your left or to your right. The Yupno conception of time is not anchored to the body, as the Western one is, but to the world and its contours. By investigating cases such as these, we and other researchers are starting to piece together an answer to a question that has puzzled thinkers for centuries: How are human
(40) beings able to make sense of time?

Humans, like creatures ranging from amoebas and bees to mockingbirds and elephants, come with built-in equipment for perceiving some aspects of time, such as the rhythms of night and day, the waxing and waning of the moon, and the turning of the seasons. What separates humans from other
(45) animals is that we do not stop at merely sensing time's passage. We tackle time head-on—or at least we try. We dice it into units, even ones that go beyond what is perceivable, such as milliseconds, or that transcend our life span, such as millennia. We depict time graphically, talk about it ceaselessly and even make gestural models of it in the air as we talk. In short, humans
(50) everywhere create and rely on time concepts—ideas about the nature of time that allow us to make plans, follow recipes, share memories and discuss possible futures.

But what are our time concepts made of? What is going on in the mind of a speaker of Yupno, or English for that matter, when answering our
(55) question about the difference between yesterday and tomorrow? Recent research in cognitive science[3] is uncovering a surprising answer. Across cultures, human time concepts depend, in large part, on metaphor—in particular, on what cognitive scientists call conceptual metaphor, in which we think about something, in this case time, in terms of something else,
(60) in this case space. Thus, we build our understanding of duration, of time's passage and of sequences of events out of familiar spatial ideas such as size, movement and location. The latest findings reveal that this basic "time is like space" metaphor appears to be universal around the world—yet it also takes strikingly different forms from one culture to the next. . . .
(65) We sometimes imagine ourselves inside the sequence of events, with past, present and future conceptualized as locations where we once were, currently are and will be. This internal perspective on time motivates English expressions such as "the week ahead of us." When we take the external perspective, however, we view the succession of events from the
(70) outside, much like watching a lineup of people all moving in one direction. This external perspective motivates phrases such as "a reception follows the ceremony."

---

[3] cognitive science—the study of the mind and its processes

These basic ideas about time are expressed spatially[4] in a dazzling variety of unrelated languages, across cultures that differ in every way imaginable.
(75) The idea that temporal[5] sequences are like queues[6] of people is found, for example, in Tamil (India), Maori (New Zealand), Greenlandic (Greenland) and Sesotho (South Africa), where the idea that "spring follows winter" can be expressed as "spring is in the footprints left by winter."

But now we come to a wrinkle. Even as people of all cultures lean on
(80) spatial concepts for understanding time, exactly *which* spatial metaphors they use can vary. Take the internal perspective, future-in-front metaphor mentioned earlier, found in English and many other languages. This metaphor was long thought to be universal, but in 2006 members of our team investigated a striking counterexample in South America. In Aymara,
(85) a language spoken high in the Andes, many phrases suggest the opposite metaphor is at work. For example, the expression "a long time ago" could be loosely rendered in Aymara as "a lot of time in front." Analysis of video-recorded interviews with 30 speakers showed conclusively that Aymara speakers gesture according to this future-behind, past-in-front metaphor.
(90) The pattern is especially strong among older speakers who do not speak Spanish, which has the future-in-front metaphor common to English and most European languages. . . .

The human reliance on spatial metaphors for abstract thinking may have deep evolutionary roots and is not likely to change any time soon. The
(95) particular metaphors we lean on, however, are a product of culture—not of biological evolution—and are much more malleable.[7] Literacy is a recent and rapid achievement in the scope of the human saga, but it already has had profound consequences for how people conceptualize[8] time. New spatial metaphors for our dearest abstract concepts will almost certainly
(100) enter the picture as our culture evolves. E-mail in-boxes show the most recent items at the top, but text messages go the other way, with the newest at the bottom. And so we must wonder: Which way will time flow next?

—Kensy Cooperrider and Rafael Núñez
excerpted from "How We Make Sense of Time"
Scientific American Mind, November/December 2016

---

[4] spatially—with gestures
[5] temporal—relating to time
[6] queues—lines of people
[7] malleable—adaptable
[8] conceptualize—form ideas about

15 A primary function of the first paragraph is to introduce

(1) a challenge to the author's research
(2) the goals of the author's research
(3) an ease of accessing the Yupno villages
(4) the hardness of life in the Yupno villages   15 _____

16 As used in line 16, the word "unreflective" most nearly means

(1) unreliable   (3) unconscious
(2) unnatural   (4) uncertain   16 _____

17 The details in lines 25 through 29 show that the author

(1) wanted to influence the way Danda would react
(2) had a theory about how Danda would respond
(3) needed to complete the interview with Danda before dark
(4) had difficulty in communicating instructions to Danda   17 _____

18 Lines 36 and 37 support a central idea by demonstrating

(1) a contrast between small and large societies
(2) the difference in interpretation between cultures
(3) the relationship between language and customs
(4) a change in behavior adapted over time   18 _____

19 Which statement best summarizes the information in lines 41 through 44?

(1) Nature interferes with creatures' awareness of time.
(2) All creatures align their behavior to lunar cycles.
(3) Physical size inhibits creatures' adaptations to seasonal change.
(4) All creatures have some awareness of time.   19 _____

20 The statements "We tackle time head-on" and "We dice it into units" (lines 45 and 46) emphasize human attempts to

(1) enjoy the passage of time
(2) structure the concept of time
(3) control the speed of time
(4) make efficient use of time   20 _____

21 Which word helps clarify the meaning of "transcend" (line 47)?

   (1) "beyond" (line 47)
   (2) "milliseconds" (line 47)
   (3) "span" (line 48)
   (4) "depict" (line 48)   21 _____

22 Researchers found that humans can best understand time (lines 48 through 64) through

   (1) examination of philosophical explanations of change
   (2) observation of the regularity in daily schedules
   (3) using figurative language to express complex ideas
   (4) recording the beginning, ending, and duration of events   22 _____

23 The text is developed primarily through the use of

   (1) point counterpoint
   (2) detailed examples
   (3) parallel structure
   (4) chronological sequence   23 _____

24 Which quotation reflects a central idea of the text?

   (1) "By having interviewees change sitting positions, we were able to show that it does not matter whether the slope is in front of you, behind you, to your left or to your right" (lines 34 through 36)
   (2) "Recent research in cognitive science is uncovering a surprising answer" (lines 55 and 56)
   (3) "The latest findings reveal that this basic 'time is like space' metaphor appears to be universal around the world—yet it also takes strikingly different forms from one culture to the next" (lines 62 through 64)
   (4) "New spatial metaphors for our dearest abstract concepts will almost certainly enter the picture as our culture evolves" (lines 98 through 100)   24 _____

PART 2—Argument Response

Directions: Closely read each of the *four* texts provided on pages 367 through 374 and write a source-based argument on the topic below. You may use the margins to take notes as you read and scrap paper to plan your response. Write your argument on a separate sheet of paper.

Topic: Should plastic shopping bags be banned?

Your Task: Carefully read each of the *four* texts provided. Then, using evidence from at least *three* of the texts, write a well-developed argument regarding whether or not plastic shopping bags should be banned. Clearly establish your claim, distinguish your claim from alternate or opposing claims, and use specific, relevant, and sufficient evidence from at least *three* of the texts to develop your argument. Do *not* simply summarize each text.

Guidelines:

Be sure to:
- Establish your claim regarding whether or not plastic shopping bags should be banned.
- Distinguish your claim from alternate or opposing claims.
- Use specific, relevant, and sufficient evidence from at least *three* of the texts to develop your argument.
- Identify each source that you reference by text number and line number(s) or graphic (for example: Text 1, line 4 or Text 2, graphic).
- Organize your ideas in a cohesive and coherent manner.
- Maintain a formal style of writing.
- Follow the conventions of standard written English.

Texts:

Text 1 – The Right Chemistry: Ban Plastic Bags? It's Not So Simple

Text 2 – The Effects of Plastic Bags on Environment

Text 3 – Should Cities Ban Plastic Bags?

Text 4 – The Economic Effect of Plastic Bag Bans

Text 1

The Right Chemistry: Ban Plastic Bags? It's Not So Simple

...There's no question that plastic bags are a symbol of our throw-away culture and are an inviting target for scorn, because they are a visible sign of pollution. They can be seen fluttering from trees, floating in that much publicized patch of plastic detritus[1] in the middle of the Pacific Ocean and
(5) clogging sewers in parts of Asia. But the bags don't dive into the ocean, jump into sewers or take flight without help. Human help. We are the real problem. With proper recycling, reuse or disposal, benefits can outweigh risks.

What then are the perceived risks? Arguments usually revolve around
(10) the bags being made from oil, a non-renewable resource, the plastic being non-biodegradable,[2] the bags taking up space in landfills, the bags being unnecessary because of ready replacement by paper or reusable bags, and the bags leaving a large carbon footprint.[3] Disposable bags are made of high-density polyethylene, which is manufactured from ethylene derived either
(15) from petroleum or natural gas. In Canada, the source is usually ethylene made from ethane, a component of natural gas that otherwise is commonly burned off.

Plastic bags do not biodegrade in a landfill, as we are often told. This is true, but modern landfills are designed to have a low oxygen environment
(20) to prevent biodegradation that would result in the formation of methane, a greenhouse gas. The purpose of a landfill is to seal in the contents and prevent substances from leaching[4] out. Since plastic bags are highly compressible, they take up very little volume in landfills. In any case, plastic shopping bags are estimated to make up less than 1 percent of litter.

(25) Paper shopping bags do not biodegrade in a landfill either and because of their greater mass they are a greater burden on the waste stream. Paper manufacture is an energy intensive process and requires the use of many chemicals. Cradle to grave calculations generally show that plastic bags have a lower carbon footprint than paper bags. "Biodegradable" bags are a
(30) marketing scheme; they don't degrade under normal conditions.

But why should we make an issue of plastic versus paper? Why not rely on reusable bags? Here too, the issue is not as simple as it seems.

---

[1] detritus—debris
[2] non-biodegradable—unable to break down
[3] carbon footprint—the amount of greenhouse gas associated with a product
[4] leaching—leaking

A cotton bag would have to be used about 130 times in order to have a carbon footprint that is less than that of a plastic bag. Growing cotton requires more (35) pesticides than most crops and processing and transport require a great deal of energy. If the plastic bag is reused to line your garbage can, a cotton bag would have to be used over 300 times to have a lower global warming potential.

Reusable plastic bags are often made of laminated plastics and are (40) not recyclable. Depending on the type of plastic, whether low density polyethylene, or non-woven polypropylene, a reusable bag would have to be used at least 10–20 times before it becomes more environmentally friendly than a disposable bag. There is also the issue of contamination if reusable bags are not cleaned properly. A warm trunk is an excellent incubator for (45) bacteria originating from that trace of meat juice left in the bag.

If not reused for that next trip to the grocery store, or for lining garbage bins, or for collecting garbage in a car, or for picking up after pets, or for covering food in the fridge, disposable plastic bags are eminently recyclable into plastic lumber, trash cans, containers and new plastic bags.

(50)   Many municipalities[5] and even countries have banned the giveaway of plastic bags or have introduced fees for them. That has resulted in the use of more paper bags, not an environmental plus, and an increase in the sales of plastic bags for garbage bins. . . .

—Joe Schwarcz
excerpted from "The Right Chemistry: Ban Plastic Bags? It's Not So Simple"
http://montrealgazette.com, March 25, 2016

---

[5] municipalities—communities

Text 2

The Effects of Plastic Bags on Environment

   . . .There is no way to strictly limit the effects of plastic bags on the environment because there is no disposal method that will really help eliminate the problem. While reusing them is the first step, most people either don't or can't based on store policies. They are not durable enough to
(5) stand up to numerous trips to the store so often the best that citizens can do is reuse them when following pooper scooper laws.

   The biggest problem with this is that once they have been soiled, they end up in the trash which then ends up in the landfill or burned. Either solution is very poor for the environment. Burning emits toxic gases that
(10) harm the atmosphere and increase the level of VOCs[1] [Volatile Organic Compounds] in the air while landfills hold them indefinitely as part of the plastic waste problem throughout the globe.

   Even when citizens try to manage their plastic bag disposal, wind plays a role in carrying them away as litter. This litter is not biodegradable and
(15) thus where it lands it tends to stay for a long period of time. A bag that is eventually ripped to shreds from high winds or other factors doesn't disappear but instead is spread in smaller amounts throughout the area. This can cause more problems as these smaller pieces are carried away through storm drains and often end up in the waterways. . . .

(20)   One of the greatest problems is that an estimated 300 million plastic bags end up in the Atlantic Ocean alone. These bags are very dangerous for sea life, especially those of the mammal variety. Any hunting mammal can easily mistake the size, shape, and texture of the plastic bag for a meal and find its airway is cut off. Needless deaths from plastic bags are increasing every year. . . .

(25)   The environmental balance of the waterways is being thrown off by the rate of plastic bags finding their way into the mouths and intestinal tracts of sea mammals. As one species begins to die off at an abnormal rate, every other living organism in the waterway is impacted. There are either too many or too few and changes within the environment continue to kill off yet
(30) more organisms.

   The indefinite period of time that it takes for the average plastic bag to break down can be literally hundreds of years. Every bag that ends up in the woodlands of the country threatens the natural progression of wildlife. Because the breakdown rate is so slow the chances that the bag

---

[1] VOCs—carbon-based chemicals that easily become a vapor or gas at room temperature

(35) will harmlessly go away are extremely slim. Throughout the world plastic bags are responsible for suffocation deaths of woodland animals as well as inhibiting soil nutrients.

    The land litter that is made up of plastic bags has the potential to kill over and over again. It has been estimated that one bag has the potential to (40) unintentionally kill one animal per every three months due to unintentional digestion or inhalation. If you consider the number of littered plastic bags ranges from 1.5 million to 3 million depending on location, this equals a lot of ecosystem-sustaining lives lost. . . .

    While it's a noble thought to place the plastic bags in the recycling bin (45) every week, studies have proven that there are very few plants that actually recycle them. Most municipalities either burn them or send them off to the landfill after sorting. This is because it can be expensive to recycle this type of plastic. It doesn't melt down easily and is often not realistically able to be reused from its original form without considerable overhaul to the (50) facility.

    The premise of recycling these bags is nice. Yet funding for the upgrades just has not happened and thus less than 1% of all bags sent to recycling plants worldwide end up in the recycling project. Most are left to become a pollution problem in one way or another. . . .

—Jamey Wagner
excerpted and adapted from
"The Effects of Plastic Bags on Environment"
www.healthguidance.org, 2017

Text 3

Should Cities Ban Plastic Bags?

This excerpt from a Wall Street Journal article includes a journalist's introduction to the plastic bag ban issue and the viewpoints of an environmental expert, Todd Myers, against the ban.

Plastic bags are one of the most common items in everyday life. And they are at the heart of a fight raging in municipalities world-wide.

Many cities around the globe have already banned the ubiquitous[1] bags from stores, and activists are pushing for bans elsewhere. They argue that
(5) cities must spend vast sums to clean up the bags and the damages caused by them, money that's better spent elsewhere. Not to mention that plastic bags are a blight on the environment, polluting waterways and other natural areas and killing off animals. Banning plastic bags, the activists say, will redirect funds to infrastructure[2] and spur entrepreneurial[3] efforts to come up with
(10) alternatives to plastic. . . .

But there's no evidence that banning bags helps the environment—and plenty of evidence that it may actually hurt. Bans yield little benefit to wildlife while increasing carbon emissions[4] and other unhealthy environmental effects.

Little Harm to Wildlife

(15)   Let's go through the arguments for banning bags. Ban backers cite impacts on marine life, but they consistently sidestep the actual data. The National Oceanic and Atmospheric Administration, for one, says there are currently no published studies about how many marine mammals die because of marine debris. Meanwhile, other sources of marine debris, such
(20) as discarded fishing gear, are recognized as a danger to sea life. Why the frenzy over *one* source—plastic bags—in the absence of evidence?

As for the pollution caused by plastic bags, consider a study by Ospar, the European organization working to protect the marine environment. The study found plastic shopping bags represented less than 3% of marine litter
(25) on European beaches, a figure that includes scraps of plastic from shredded bags.

---

[1] ubiquitous—found everywhere
[2] infrastructure—fundamental facilities and structures, such as roads, bridges, and power supplies
[3] entrepreneurial—business leadership
[4] carbon emissions—greenhouse gases released into the atmosphere

Meanwhile, the claim that municipalities spend a substantial amount of their trash budget, let alone millions of dollars, on picking up plastic bags is hard to believe. In many cases, these claims are guesses by advocates instead
(30) of data based on actual studies, and cost is often thrown in as a justification after bans are enacted for political reasons. . . .

Some ban supporters claim plastics harm human health, even when studies from organizations like the Environmental Protection Agency, the Centers for Disease Control and Prevention, and Pacific Northwest
(35) National Labs show these claims are false or exaggerated.

Consider a study from the U.K. Environment Agency that found plastic grocery bags have the lowest environmental impact in "human toxicity" and "marine aquatic toxicity" as well as "global-warming potential" even after paper bags are used four times and reusable cotton bags are used 173 times.
(40) Why? Largely because paper and cotton bags come from crops that require fertilizer, pesticides, herbicides and the like.

Environmental Effects

Critics also say that ban opponents ignore the environmental impact of bags over the course of their lifetime. But many studies do just that. The U.K. Environment Agency's study, for instance, compared the energy expended
(45) in creating, using and disposing of plastic, paper and reusable bags to arrive at its figures. Consumers would have to use a cotton bag 173 times before they match the energy savings of one plastic bag, assuming 40% of bags are reused—a percentage that's actually *lower* than the rate in some cities.

Some critics say we need to ban bags because voluntary take-back
(50) programs don't work. But the point of the programs is simply to reuse bags, and consumers *already* reuse bags to hold garbage or pick up after pets.

As for the idea that plastic bags cost consumers more, the reason grocery stores use plastic instead of paper or other bags is that they cost less and hold more. Reusable bags are even more expensive.

Let's Be Honest

(55)   . . .Weighing the costs and benefits makes it clear that banning plastic bags yields little benefit at very high cost. Unfortunately, the political symbolism of banning the bags is powerful. It is often easier to ignore the science that indicates such bans may actually harm the environment than to make an honest effort to weigh these issues. All of this is why plastic-bag
(60) bans are more about environmental image than environmental benefit.

—excerpted from "Should Cities Ban Plastic Bags?"
www.wsj.com, October 8, 2012

Text 4

The Economic Effect of Plastic Bag Bans

A study from the National Center for Policy Analysis [NCPA] claims that a ban on plastic bags used by grocers and retailers can negatively impact sales in the ban area and increase sales among stores just outside the bag ban region. . . .

(5)   During a one-year period, before and after the ban, the majority of stores surveyed in areas with a ban reported an overall average sales decline of nearly 6%. While the majority of respondents surveyed in areas without a ban reported an overall average sales growth of 9%. . . .

The NCPA survey said that stores under the bag ban also experienced
(10) a 10% reduction in employment, while employment in stores outside of the ban slightly increased. [NCPA senior fellow, Pamela] Villarreal said that was particularly "alarming."

"We often hear about the environmental effects of plastic bags, but the economic effects are generally ignored," she said. "When you think about
(15) the unemployment rate in this country, any negative impact on employment is something to take notice of."

The U.S. plastic bag manufacturing and recycling sector employs more than 30,000 workers in 349 communities across the nation, according to the American Progressive Bag Alliance, an organization representing the plastic
(20) bag manufacturing and recycling sector. . . .

Leila Monroe, staff attorney for the oceans program at the Natural Resources Defense Council (NRDC), looks at the impact on jobs in a different way. She said bag bans provide an opportunity for the industry to innovate.

"They can pull together and look at how they can design better products that are
(25) truly durable and easily recyclable," Monroe said. "I have no doubt that if the industry put in the time and investment to retool operations, they can ensure there aren't job losses, but instead work on ways to move the industry forward."

Plastic bag alternatives

As paper bags are starting to also get listed on the ban list, more attention is now focused on reusable bags. Reusable shopping bags can be
(30) made from fabric, woven synthetic fibers, or even polypropylene.

Vincent Cobb, founder of Reuseit.com, first launched the site in 2003 to offer alternatives to single-use plastic shopping bags. The site then expanded to include all types of reusable products. . . .

Brad Nihls, VP [Vice President] of operations for Reuseit.com, said the
(35) company is all too aware that the reusable bag market is flooded with cheap

quality, green-washing[1] products. He said the company warns customers about looking out for cheaply made reusable shopping bags.

"One item of concern with reusable shopping bags are the very cheap reusables that are often given away during promotions or selling at grocery (40) stores for 99 cents," he said. "The concern here is that while they are marketed as reusable shopping bags, they really are just a glorified disposable bag, which we feel is even more damaging than the single-use plastic shopping bags." . . .

When it comes to plastic shopping bag bans, Nihls said the company doesn't view bans as a big "windfall" for the company. . . .

(45)   Some reports state that plastic bags are responsible for less than 1% of all litter. For instance, litter audit data from major Canadian municipalities show that plastic shopping bags are less than 1% of litter. In San Francisco, surveyors found that plastic bags consisted of 0.6% of the city's litter before a local ban was enacted.

(50)   What can be lost in the debate between bans, taxes and consumer choice at the checkout, is the fact that plastic shopping bags are fully recyclable, when disposed of properly.

Still, a study conducted by Boustead Associates found that only 5.2% of plastic bags are recycled. . . .

(55)   However, plastic bag recycling requires a different type of infrastructure than plastic bottles and containers. It's been reported that when people put plastic bags in their curbside bin, it has the potential to clog machines at the recycling facilities.

"The problem with plastic bags is that they are extremely difficult, if (60) not almost impossible, to recycle," Monroe said. "At municipality recycling facilities, plastic bags have to be removed because the lightweight thin film can impact the recycling process." . . .

Recycling plastic bags can be turned into raw materials for fencing, decking, building and construction products, shopping carts and new bags, (65) according to the American Chemistry Council.

Monroe points out that the 5% recycling of bags is still the current and, potentially, future reality.

"There's just a large number of bags available where there is no incentive really to recycle them," she said. "In contrast when bag bans and fees are put (70) in place, they show it's working to reduce waste." . . .

—Heather Caliendo
excerpted and adapted from "The Economic Effect of Plastic Bag Bans"
www.npr.com, February 6, 2013

---

[1] green-washing—falsely claiming that a product is environmentally friendly

PART 3—Text-Analysis Response

Your Task: Closely read the text provided on pages 376 through 378 and write a well-developed, text-based response of two to three paragraphs. In your response, identify a central idea in the text and analyze how the author's use of *one* writing strategy (literary element or literary technique or rhetorical device) develops this central idea. Use strong and thorough evidence from the text to support your analysis. Do *not* simply summarize the text. You may use the margins to take notes as you read and scrap paper to plan your response. Write your response on a separate sheet of paper.

Guidelines:

Be sure to:
- Identify a central idea in the text.
- Analyze how the author's use of *one* writing strategy (literary element or literary technique or rhetorical device) develops this central idea. Examples include: characterization, conflict, denotation/connotation, metaphor, simile, irony, language use, point-of-view, setting, structure, symbolism, theme, tone, etc.
- Use strong and thorough evidence from the text to support your analysis.
- Organize your ideas in a cohesive and coherent manner.
- Maintain a formal style of writing.
- Follow the conventions of standard written English.

Text

The Edge of the Sea

The edge of the sea is a strange and beautiful place. All through the long history of Earth it has been an area of unrest where waves have broken heavily against the land, where the tides have pressed forward over the continents, receded, and then returned. For no two successive days is the shore line
(5) precisely the same. Not only do the tides advance and retreat in their eternal rhythms, but the level of the sea itself is never at rest. It rises or falls as the glaciers melt or grow, as the floor of the deep ocean basins shifts under its increasing load of sediments, or as the earth's crust along the continental margins warps up or down in adjustment to strain and tension. Today a little
(10) more land may belong to the sea, tomorrow a little less. Always the edge of the sea remains an elusive and indefinable boundary.

The shore has a dual nature, changing with the swing of the tides, belonging now to the land, now to the sea. On the ebb tide it knows the harsh extremes of the land world, being exposed to heat and cold, to wind,
(15) to rain and drying sun. On the flood tide it is a water world, returning briefly to the relative stability of the open sea.

Only the most hardy and adaptable can survive in a region so mutable, yet the area between the tide lines is crowded with plants and animals. In this difficult world of the shore, life displays its enormous toughness and
(20) vitality by occupying almost every conceivable niche. Visibly, it carpets the intertidal rocks; or half hidden, it descends into fissures and crevices, or hides under boulders, or lurks in the wet gloom of sea caves. Invisibly, where the casual observer would say there is no life, it lies deep in the sand, in burrows and tubes and passageways. It tunnels into solid rock and bores
(25) into peat and clay. It encrusts weeds or drifting spars[1] or the hard, chitinous[2] shell of a lobster. It exists minutely, as the film of bacteria that spreads over a rock surface or a wharf piling; as spheres of protozoa, small as pinpricks, sparkling at the surface of the sea; and as Lilliputian[3] beings swimming through dark pools that lie between the grains of sand.
(30) The shore is an ancient world, for as long as there has been an earth and sea there has been this place of the meeting of land and water. Yet it is a world that keeps alive the sense of continuing creation and of relentless

---

[1] spars—pieces of wood
[2] chitinous—tough, protective
[3] Lilliputian—tiny

drive of life. Each time that I enter it, I gain some new awareness of its
beauty and its deeper meanings, sensing that intricate fabric of life by which
(35) one creature is linked with another, and each with its surroundings. . . .

The flats took on a mysterious quality as dusk approached and the last
evening light was reflected from the scattered pools and creeks. Then birds
became only dark shadows, with no color discernible. Sanderlings scurried
across the beach like little ghosts, and here and there the darker forms of the
(40) willets stood out. Often I could come very close to them before they would
start up in alarm—the sanderlings running, the willets flying up, crying.
Black skimmers flew along the ocean's edge silhouetted against the dull,
metallic gleam, or they went flitting above the sand like large, dimly seen
moths. Sometimes they "skimmed" the winding creeks of tidal water, where
(45) little spreading surface ripples marked the presence of small fish.

The shore at night is a different world, in which the very darkness that
hides the distractions of daylight brings into sharper focus the elemental
realities. Once, exploring the night beach, I surprised a small ghost crab
in the searching beam of my torch. He was lying in a pit he had dug just
(50) above the surf, as though watching the sea and waiting. The blackness of the
night possessed water, air, and beach. It was the darkness of an older world,
before Man. There was no sound but the all-enveloping, primeval sounds
of wind blowing over water and sand, and of waves crashing on the beach.
There was no other visible life—just one small crab near the sea. I have seen
(55) hundreds of ghost crabs in other settings, but suddenly I was filled with the
odd sensation that for the first time I knew the creature in its own world—
that I understood, as never before, the essence of its being. In that moment
time was suspended; the world to which I belonged did not exist and I might
have been an onlooker from outer space. The little crab alone with the sea
(60) became a symbol that stood for life itself—for the delicate, destructible, yet
incredibly vital force that somehow holds its place amid the harsh realities
of the inorganic world. . . .

Looking out over the cove I felt a strong sense of the interchangeability
of land and sea in this marginal world of the shore, and of the links between
(65) the life of the two. There was also an awareness of the past and of the
continuing flow of time, obliterating much that had gone before, as the sea
had that morning washed away the tracks of the bird. . . .

There is a common thread that links these scenes and memories—the
spectacle of life in all its varied manifestations as it has appeared, evolved,
(70) and sometimes died out. Underlying the beauty of the spectacle there is
meaning and significance. It is the elusiveness of that meaning that haunts
us, that sends us again and again into the natural world where the key to the

riddle is hidden. It sends us back to the edge of the sea, where the drama of life played its first scene on earth and perhaps even its prelude; where the (75) forces of evolution are at work today, as they have been since the appearance of what we know as life; and where the spectacle of living creatures faced by the cosmic realities of their world is crystal clear.

—Rachel Carson
excerpted from *The Edge of the Sea*, 1955
Houghton Mifflin Company

Regents ELA Answers August 2019

English Language Arts

Answer Key

PART 1

1. 1	9. 4	17. 2
2. 4	10. 3	18. 2
3. 2	11. 3	19. 4
4. 2	12. 2	20. 2
5. 3	13. 2	21. 1
6. 2	14. 4	22. 3
7. 4	15. 2	23. 2
8. 3	16. 3	24. 3

PART 2 *See Answers and Explanations*

PART 3 *See Answers and Explanations*

Regents Examination in English Language Arts—August 2019
Chart for Converting Total Weighted Raw Scores to Final Exam Scores
(Scale Scores)

56	100	5		27	55	2
55	98	5		26	53	1
54	97	5		25	50	1
53	96	5		24	47	1
52	95	5		23	45	1
51	94	5		22	42	1
50	93	5		21	39	1
49	91	5		20	36	1
48	90	5		19	33	1
47	89	5		18	31	1
46	88	5		17	28	1
45	87	5		16	24	1
44	86	5		15	21	1
43	85	5		14	18	1
42	84	5		13	15	1
41	83	5		12	12	1
40	82	5		11	10	1
39	81	4		10	9	1
38	79	4		9	8	1
37	77	4		8	6	1
36	76	4		7	5	1
35	74	3		6	4	1
34	72	3		5	4	1
33	69	3		4	3	1
32	67	3		3	2	1
31	65	3		2	1	1
30	63	3		1	1	1
29	60	2		0	0	1
28	58	2				

Answers Explained

PART 1—Reading Comprehension

Multiple-Choice Questions

Passage A

1. **1** "a contrast between the sisters." These first paragraphs introduce the sisters and reveal how different their daily lives are. We learn that Rose is popular, outgoing, and attentive to her overall appearance. Eilis, on the other hand, is at home, silently observing her lively sister. Eilis, we learn, is going to vocational school, studying to become a bookkeeper. The attitudes offered in the other choices are not suggested in the first three paragraphs.

2. **4** "thoughtfulness toward her sister." Rose, who is picking up her golf clubs and about to go out again for the rest of the day, makes a point of leaving money for Eilis to "go to the pictures [movies]." This passage reveals that Eilis has no money for herself, nor does she have a social life like her sister's.

3. **2** "abrupt." In this brief interview, Miss Kelly doesn't even greet Eilis. Instead, Miss Kelly immediately and unexpectedly announces what she knows about Eilis and lists all the reasons she has decided Eilis will be the best person for a job helping in her store. Nothing in lines 36 through 41 suggests Miss Kelly is indecisive, jealous, or bitter; she is simply "all business." This question is an example of how knowledge of vocabulary is assessed indirectly.

4. **2** "bustling." This term best describes a store that is crowded and hurriedly busy. At certain times on Sunday mornings, Miss Kelly and her employees are "worked off our feet." (This question is an example of how knowledge of vocabulary is assessed indirectly)

5. **3** "admiring." In the opening paragraphs (question 1), we have little sense of how Eilis feels about her sister. In lines 55 through 60, however, we learn that Eilis is proud of her sister in the way Rose takes care of her appearance, chooses friends wisely, and values her independence. Eilis also appreciates the way her sister is supporting Eilis's own efforts to gain employment and have a life for herself.

6. **2** "incentive to accept any employment." This is clearly the best answer to the question. Where Eilis lives, there simply is no work, even for people with qualifications. Eilis accepts the job at Miss Kelly's because it is a rare opportunity to earn a bit of money to help her mother.

7. **4** "subtle about putting her plan for Eilis in motion." These lines reveals Rose's clever and indirect (subtle) way of arranging, through Father Flood, a plan for Eilis to go to America, to Brooklyn, in fact, where, "there is plenty of work for someone like you with good pay." Rose is careful about ensuring that her mother will welcome Father Flood, choice (3) but the significance of these lines is in what it reveals about Rose's plan.

8. **3** "an agreement was made without Eilis's knowledge." This paragraph describes Eilis's feelings as she gradually realizes, especially in observing Rose's silence, that a tacit (unspoken) arrangement had been made without her knowledge. She also realizes that, unknown to her, Father Flood had made inquiries about her job and pay at Miss Kelly's.

9. **4** "'In the United States,' he said, 'there would be plenty of work for someone like you and with good pay'" (lines 96 and 97). Each incident in the passage leads to the final scene, which in turn reflects this reality for many in the Ireland of the early 1950s. (Note that Colm Tóibín's lovely and much-celebrated novel *Brooklyn* tells the story of how Eilis makes a new life for herself in America.)

Passage B

10. **3** "time stopping." The images of players ". . . poised in midair . . . hung there / A long second" capture those instants, within the "fast breaks and lay ups" of the game, when players seem suspended in air and time.

11. **3** "a contrast to the players' feelings of invincibility." This sudden insertion of the image of Sonny Boy's grief and anger over the death of his mother is a reminder of the boys' world just beyond the sidelines of their game.

12. **2** "agility." These images of the boys' swift and nimble (agile) moves on the court are a further reflection of the energy in the opening lines and of the poem's title, "Slam, Dunk, & Hook."

13. **2** "extraordinary." The boys believed ". . . we could almost / Last forever . . . Like storybook sea monsters. . . . We were metaphysical . . . We had moves we didn't know / We had." The word "extraordinary" best expresses the boys' feelings.

14. **4** "Of joy, & we knew we were / Beautiful & dangerous" (lines 39 and 40). These lines complete the theme expressed in the lines cited in Question 13 and conclude the poem with a declaration of the central idea. The other choices are examples of the vivid details that develop this theme in the body of the poem.

Passage C

15. **2** "the goals of the author's research." The last three lines of the first paragraph state clearly that the researchers are "interested in time—in how the Yupno people understand concepts [of time]," and whether concepts of time are universal or are products of language, culture, and environment.

16. **3** "unconscious." We are meant to understand in context here that "unreflective movements" are spontaneous and natural, done without the need for serious thought or contemplation (reflection).

17. **2** "had a theory about how Danda would respond" In lines 28 and 29, the author reveals that after Danda is facing in the opposite direction, "his gestures had changed" and that this was "as we expected." This passage reveals how the researchers carefully planned their experiment to confirm their theory. By only suggesting casually that Danda change position, the researchers seek to avoid influencing his behavior in any way. None of the other choices are supported by these lines.

18. **2** "the difference in interpretation between cultures." Lines 36 and 37 assert a clear difference between the Yupno conception of time, which is "anchored to the . . . world," and the Western concept of time, which is "anchored to the body." This is the most precise answer among the choices.

19. **4** "all creatures have some awareness of time." This is the best answer among the choices. The range of creatures mentioned, from amoebas to elephants, implies that the researchers believe all creatures have some awareness of time. The article continues by illustrating how humans go beyond awareness to ". . . tackle time head-on." (See question 20.)

20. **2** "structure the concept of time." This point is developed further when, in lines 45 and 46, the authors outline how human ideas about time ". . . allow us to make plans, follow recipes, share memories and discuss possible futures." The emphasis here is on how humans *attempt to structure* ideas about time.

21. **1** "beyond." Millennia are periods of thousands of years. They represent periods of time far beyond the human life span. In other words, humans have concepts of time that far exceed our ability to experience those lengths of time.

22. **3** "using figurative language to express complex ideas." Lines 48 through 64 develop the researchers' observation that in nearly all cultures, understanding of time is expressed in metaphor—thinking about something in terms of something else by using in figurative language.

23. **2** "detailed examples." This article is developed through a series of examples of how time is understood, in concept and metaphor, in different cultures. None of the other choices accurately describes the structure of this article.

24. **3** "The latest findings reveal that this basic 'time is like space' metaphor appears to be universal around the world—yet it also takes strikingly different form from one culture to the next" (lines 62 through 64). This is the most comprehensive statement of the central idea here. Choices (1) and (2) offer specific details, and choice (4) states a conclusion.

PART 2—Argument Response

Sample Essay Response

The argument over whether or not to ban plastic shopping bags from use in stores is a very heated issue. Those who have not researched the other options, or actually looked at the harm they create, may say that banning plastic shopping bags is a good step in the right direction for saving our planet. However, the damage that banning plastic bags can create may be greater than the current damage caused by using plastic bags. There is convincing evidence that plastic bags should not be banned, because the alternative options often create an even bigger problem.

Plastic shopping bags are both economical and good for the economy. They are often reused by customers, which saves them money by not having to buy bags for other purposes. One recent article lists the many secondary uses for plastic bags, showing that they can be "reused for that next trip to the grocery store, or for lining garbage bins, or for collecting garbage in a car, or for picking up after pets, or for covering food in the fridge." (Text 1, lines 46–48) This list shows some of the many other uses of plastic bags that cannot simply be replaced by paper or reusable bags. Besides customers saving money by reusing them, plastic bags are also good for both business owners and employees. They are cheap and easy for store owners to buy, and when stores were surveyed *before and after a ban, most of the stores with the ban lost up to 6% of sales while those "in areas without a ban reported an overall average sales growth of 9%." (Text 4, lines 5–8) The use of plastic bags supports employment as well: "The U.S. plastic bag manufacturing and recycling sector employs more than 30,000 workers in 349 communities across the nation." (Text 4, lines 17–18)*

On the other hand, many activists argue that overuse of plastic bags causes serious harm to the environment; they demand a ban on plastic bags and insist on the exclusive use of reusable or paper bags. As persuasive as this may seem, these alternatives are not better for the environment and may create more harm to the ecosystem than plastic bags do. One report indicates that "paper shopping bags do not biodegrade in a landfill either and because of their greater mass they are a greater burden on the waste stream." (Text 1, lines 25–26) Reusable bags are not a realistic fix either: "Consumers would have to use a cotton bag 173 times before they match the energy saving of one plastic bag." (Text 3, lines 46–47) Since reusable bags need to be cleaned often and may rip, it is unreasonable to expect that every customer uses their reusable bag almost 200 times before losing it, breaking it, or getting a new one. Overall, plastic bags generally have the same or less of an impact than some of the alternatives.

Despite the evidence presented by those opposed to banning plastic bags, some may still believe that plastic bags are harmful to animals and people. A study from a U.K. Environment Agency found, however, that "plastic grocery bags have the lowest environmental impact in 'human toxicity' and 'marine aquatic toxicity' as well as 'global warming potential.'" (Text 3, lines 36–38) This same study also disputes the argument that plastic bags are harmful to animals when it reports that the U.S. National Oceanic and Atmospheric Administration says, "There are currently no published studies about how many marine mammals die because of marine debris." (Text 3, lines 17–19). As for plastic bags being harmful to people, "the U.S. Environmental Protection Agency, the Centers for Disease Control and Prevention, and Pacific Northwest National Labs show these claims are false or exaggerated." (Text 3, lines 34–35)

Overall, plastic shopping bags should not be banned, because the cost of the ban is greater than the reward. Plastic bags have many uses besides holding groceries, many of which cannot be replaced by paper or cotton bags. In addition, recent evidence suggests that plastic bags are less harmful to wildlife and humans than we thought.

Analysis

This is an excellent response to the task. In the first paragraph, the writer identifies the topic and opposing positions and then establishes a clear and forceful claim: "There is convincing evidence that plastic bags should not be banned, because the alternative options often create an even bigger problem." The argument is well developed, with several supporting examples from the texts, relying most heavily on the one that supports the writer's position. The argument is coherent in its focus on the claim, restated in the conclusion: "Overall, plastic shopping bags should not be banned, because the cost of the ban is greater than the reward." The essay does not consistently identify the issue as plastic *shopping* bags, but the context makes this sufficiently clear.

The argument might be even more effective if it were balanced in acknowledging some additional details from the opposing view; however this is not required in the task. The writing is clear and appropriately formal, with no significant errors in the conventions. This essay would merit a high score.

(See pages 79–80 for the scoring guidelines.)

Part 3—Text-Analysis Response

Sample Essay Response

   A *central idea of this passage focuses on the recognition of the sea and its shoreline as an ever-changing and vital force. The author effectively uses diction in the observations of this "spectacle" of the meeting of these two natural elements. Through the use of selective and vivid word choice, the author relates both the variations and the energy created in this meeting.*

   The author's effective use of diction to portray this scene is evident in the various descriptions that focus on its vitality. The shore is described as being a "relentless drive of life," (lines 32–33) whose inhabitants display "enormous toughness and vitality." (line 19–20) One of these creatures, a little crab, is viewed as a "delicate, destructible, yet incredibly vital force that somehow holds its place." (lines 60–61) Words like "relentless" and "toughness" are not ones that would ordinarily be associated with a shoreline and its creatures. As used here, however, they make the reader aware of the true energy and drive that exist within them.

   Diction also plays an important role in helping the reader to understand that this "meeting place" between land and sea is ever changing. The word "mutable" (line 17) to describe this region immediately allows the reader to recognize that nothing stays the same here. When speaking of the shore's dual nature, the author describes it as "changing with the swing of the tides, belonging now to the land, now to the sea." (lines 12–13) Using an expression like "the swing of" emphasizes the constant ebb and flow of the water as it alters the landscape of the shoreline, helping the reader to not only visualize, but also feel, the rhythm of the phenomenon. The author goes on further to describe this "meeting of land and water" (line 31) as "a world that keeps alive the sense of continuing creation," (line 32) and the link of land and sea as "an awareness of the past and of the continuing flow of time." (lines 65–66) The repetition of the word "continuing," when coupled with the word "flow" in the latter example, serves to complete an image of an ongoing progression of life, over time and space, and its ever changing nature.

Analysis

The richness of language and imagery in this passage makes "diction" a good choice of writing strategy for this task. This passage also presents a significant challenge to the student writer: how to find appropriate language of one's own to discuss how good prose is achieved. This writer succeeds in appreciating not only the beauty of the passage but also the power of language itself to convey a complex natural phenomenon.

This response is brief but coherent. The first paragraph establishes the central idea of the text and the writer's choice of diction for analysis. The second paragraph discusses the power of the language to portray the scene "in the various descriptions that focus on its vitality." The third paragraph demonstrates how the language helps the reader understand ". . . this meeting place between land and sea." The discussion is well developed, with a variety of relevant examples to illustrate how diction supports the central idea. This writer demonstrates command of the conventions and notable skill in quoting phrases within sentences. This response to the task would merit a high score.

(See pages 81–82 for the scoring guidelines.)